# MILLION DOLLAR
# BASH

BOB DYLAN, THE BAND, AND THE BASEMENT TAPES

# MILLION DOLLAR BASH

## BOB DYLAN, THE BAND, AND THE BASEMENT TAPES

## Sid Griffin

**A JAWBONE BOOK**
First edition 2007
Published in the UK and the USA by Jawbone Press
2A Union Court,
20-22 Union Road,
London SW4 6JP,
England
www.jawbonepress.com

ISBN: 978-1-906002-05-3

● ● ● ● ● ● ● ● ● ● ● ● ● ● ● ● ● ● ● ● ● ●

Editor: **Tony Bacon**
Design: **Adam Yeldham**

Origination and print by Colorprint (Hong Kong)

07 08 09 10 11  5 4 3 2 1

# CONTENTS

**BEFORE THE BASEMENT TAPES:** Dylan in Paris, 1966 (top); Ron Hawkins Quartet, 1958 (bottom right), with Levon Helm (left); Levon & The Hawks, 1964 (left), with Robbie Robertson (far right) then Garth Hudson, Richard Manuel, Levon Helm, Rick Danko, and one other.

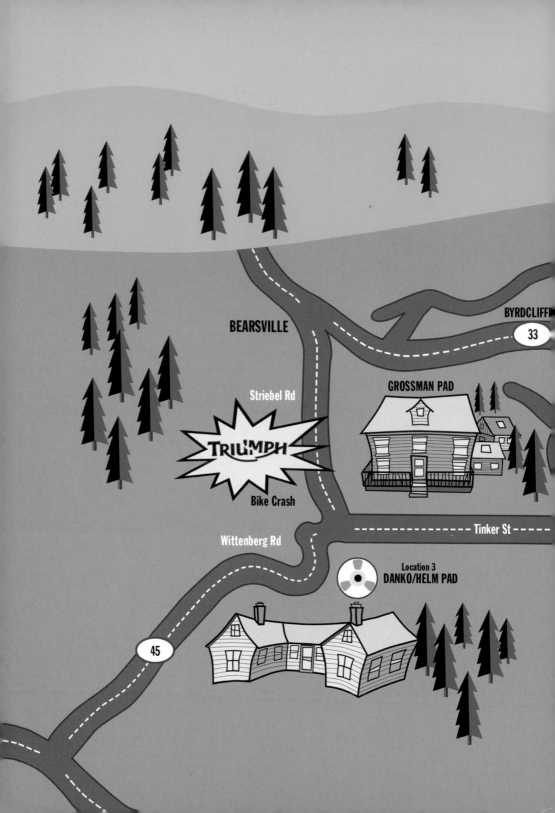

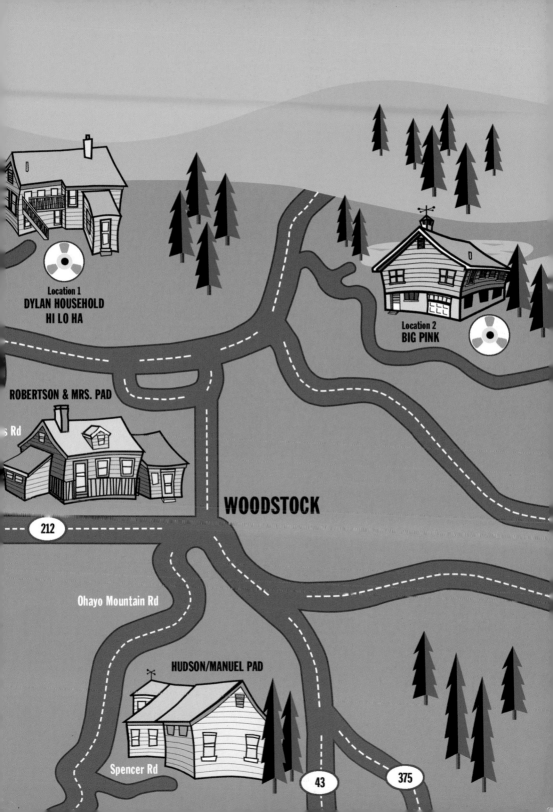

AFTER THE BASEMENT TAPES: The Band on the Ed Sullivan Show, 1969 (top left); Dylan at Isle Of Wight press conference, 1969 (bottom left); Dylan at Columbia Studios in Nashville, 1969 (right).

 # INTRODUCTION

*"No man gains immortality thru public acclaim."*
Bob Dylan [1]

This book is about a specific chapter in the life of a wonderfully talented, wonderfully frustrating singer and songwriter from America's Midwest, born Robert Allen Zimmerman but known to his public as Bob Dylan.

It's about an era in the life of the still young Dylan when he and some dear friends decided to stop the clock moving forward and to stop the music being quite so deafening. Just the year before, he had been strenuously booed for using those same musical companions and was advised by some professionals in the music business not to re-hire them.

These five (later six) men turned their backs on the worldwide fame that their leader had worked so very hard to win during the previous five years and decided to make music for themselves and by themselves.

They stopped the studio clock. They turned down their amps (and in some musical instances turned them off). They ignored or failed to return phone calls from the industry. Deadlines came and went, spring went into summer, summer turned into fall, and as organically as they started, they stopped.

The year was 1967. The place was Woodstock, then a humble and pretty much unheralded village about a hundred miles north of New York City. In the book, we'll back up a bit before 1967 for the necessary back-story and then cruise a little past 1967 to tell the entire tale, but at its heart this is the story of what must be rock's strangest, most unusual, least illuminated, and yet most famous unreleased recording sessions of all time. Longtime Dylan biographer and expert Clinton Heylin echoed the feelings of millions of Bob's supporters when he wrote that the original material on the 37 reels of Basement Tapes "may well be Dylan's greatest collection of songs." [2]

Some of you will already be saying to yourselves that Dylan didn't officially release anything in 1967 and that the public didn't hear anything but the first bootleg LP until the 1975 two-LP set of Basement Tapes, which wasn't the complete or even n accurate story. True on each count. While Dylan did not release anything in 1967, save a very well received Greatest Hits package with no unreleased material, 1967 was nonetheless his – brace yourselves – most prolific year both as a songwriter and a recording artist.

In no other calendar year would Bob Dylan write more songs. In no other calendar year would he record as much or be in the studio longer (if we allow such places as a recreation room in one house and a basement in another to be referred to as studios). And in no other calendar year would Dylan's pen turn out more classics, more undeniably great music.

At the time, 1967 seemed a very quiet year for Bob Dylan. Yet it was anything but. Like the suburban dad he was threatening to morph into that year, he was down in the basement away from the wife and kids. He was down in the basement hanging out with old friends, having a few beers and a smoke and a chat and a few laughs. Some of this – frankly, a good deal of this – was recorded by his pals. They were down in the basement getting away from it all by making a racket.

One of Dylan's very favorite books clearly states "… and make a joyful noise unto the Lord." They did. They made a joyful noise, Bob Dylan and his dear friends, back there some 40 years ago.

And you notice that in the Good Lord's request for joyous and sincere music, He doesn't say a damn thing about being on key.

Sid Griffin
Hampstead, London,
England, summer 2007

# MILLION DOLLAR BASH

## Alphabetical list of Basement Tapes songs

● ● ● ● ● ● ● ● ● ● ● ● ● ● ● ● ● ● ● ● ● ●

● *RR = Red Room*
● *BP = Big Pink*
● *WR = Wittenberg Road*
● *BA = Band-alone recordings*
Titles in bold are included on 1975 two-LP set
Composed by Bob Dylan unless stated
(or unless obvious jams etc)

A Fool Such As I (Bill Trader) *RR*
All You Have To Do Is Dream take one *WR*
All You Have To Do Is Dream take two *WR*
The All American Boy (Bobby Bare,
  Orville Lunsford) *BP*
Apple Suckling Tree take one *BP*
**Apple Suckling Tree** take two *BP*
Baby, Ain't That Fine (Dallas Frazier) *RR*
Baby, Won't You Be My Baby *RR*
The Banks Of The Royal Canal (The Auld
  Triangle) (Brendan Behan) *BP*
Be Careful Of Stones That You Throw
  (Bonnie Dodd) *RR*
Beautiful Thing (Richard Manuel) *BA*
The Bells Of Rhymney (Idris Davies,
  Pete Seeger) *BP*
Belshazzar (Johnny Cash) *BP*
Big River (Johnny Cash) take one *BP*
Big River (Johnny Cash) take two *BP*
Blue Moon (Richard Rodgers, Lorenz Hart) *BA*
Blues Instrumental *BA*
Bonnie Ship The Diamond (Traditional) *RR*
Bourbon Street *BP*
Bring It On Home *RR*
Caledonia Mission (Robbie Robertson) *BA*
**Clothes Line Saga (Answer To Ode)** *BP*
Come All Ye Fair And Tender Ladies *BP*
Comin' Round The Mountain (Traditional) *WR*
Confidential (Dorinda Morgan) *BP*
Cool Water (Bob Nolan) *BP*
Crash On The Levee (Down In The Flood)
  take one *BP*
**Crash On The Levee (Down In The Flood)**
  take two *BP*
Don't Ya Tell Henry *BP*
Don't You Try Me Now *RR*
Down On Me (Traditional) *RR*
Even If It's A Pig, Part Two (Rick Danko,
  Garth Hudson, Richard Manuel) *BA*
Ferdinand The Imposter (Robbie Robertson) *BA*
Flight Of The Bumble Bee *BP*
Folsom Prison Blues (Johnny Cash) *BP*
Four Strong Winds (Ian Tyson) *BP*
The French Girl (Ian Tyson, Sylvia Fricker)
  take one *BP*
The French Girl (Ian Tyson, Sylvia Fricker)
  take two *BP*
Garth Hudson Piano Solo (Garth Hudson) *BA*
Get Your Rocks Off *BP*

Gloria In Excelsis Deo / Banana Boat (Day-O)
  (Traditional / William Attaway, Irving Burgie) *BA*
Goin' Down The Road Feelin' Bad (Woody
  Guthrie, Lee Hays) *BP*
**Goin' To Acapulco** *BP*
Gonna Get You Now *BP*
The Hills Of Mexico (Traditional) *RR*
I Can't Come In With a Broken Heart *RR*
I Can't Make It Alone *RR*
I Don't Hurt Anymore (Don Robertson,
  Jack Rollins) *RR*
I Forgot To Remember To Forget (Stan Kesler,
  Charlie Feathers) *BP*
I Shall Be Released *BP*
I'm A Fool For You *BP*
I'm Alright *RR*
I'm Guilty Of Loving You *BP*
I'm In The Mood (John Lee Hooker) *BP*
I'm Not There (1956) *BP*
I'm Your Teenage Prayer *BP*
If I Lose (Charlie Poole, Norman Woodlieff,
  arr. Ralph Stanley) *BA*
Instrumental *BA*
Instrumental *BA*
Instrumental *BA*
Instrumental Blues *BA*
Instrumental Jam *WR*
Johnny Todd (Traditional) *BP*
Joshua Gone Barbados (Eric von Schmidt) *BP*
Katie's Been Gone (Robbie Robertson,
  Richard Manuel) *BA*
The King Of France *RR*
Lo And Behold! take one *BP*
**Lo And Behold!** take two *BP*
Lock Your Door *RR*
Long Distance Operator *BA*
Million Dollar Bash take one *BP*
**Million Dollar Bash** take two *BP*
Next Time On The Highway *BP*
Nine Hundred Miles (Traditional) *BP*
**Nothing Was Delivered** take one *BP*
Nothing Was Delivered take two *BP*
Nothing Was Delivered take three *WR*
Odds And Ends take one *BP*
**Odds And Ends** take two *BP*
Ol' Roisin The Beau (Traditional) *BP*
On A Rainy Afternoon *BP*
One For The Road *RR*
One Man's Loss *RR*
**Open The Door, Homer** take one *BP*
Open The Door, Homer take two *BP*
Open The Door, Homer take three *BP*
Orange Juice Blues (Blues For Breakfast)
  (Richard Manuel) version one *BA*
Orange Juice Blues (Blues For Breakfast)
  (Richard Manuel) version two *BA*
Organ Riffs *BA*
People Get Ready (Curtis Mayfield) *RR*

**Please Mrs. Henry** *BP*
Po' Lazarus (Traditional) *BP*
Quinn The Eskimo (The Mighty Quinn)
  take one *BP*
Quinn The Eskimo (The Mighty Quinn)
  take two *BP*
Rock, Salt & Nails (Bruce Phillips) *RR*
Ruben Remus (Robbie Robertson,
  Richard Manuel) *BA*
Santa Fe *BP*
See That My Grave Is Kept Clean (Blind
  Lemon Jefferson) *WR*
See You Later, Alligator (Robert Charles
  Guidry) *BP*
Sign On The Cross *BP*
Silent Weekend *WR*
Silhouettes (Frank C. Slay Jr., Bob Crewe) *RR*
Song For Canada (Ian Tyson, Sylvia Fricker) *RR*
Spanish Is The Loving Tongue (Charles
  Badger Clark, Billy Simon) *BP*
The Spanish Song take one *BP*
The Spanish Song take two *BP*
Spoken Word / Instrumental *BA*
Still In Town (Johnny Cash) *BP*
Tears Of Rage (Bob Dylan, Richard Manuel)
  take one *BP*
Tears Of Rage (Bob Dylan, Richard Manuel)
  take two *BP*
**Tears Of Rage** (Bob Dylan, Richard Manuel)
  take three *BP*
They Gotta Quit Kickin' My Dawg Aroun'
  (Webb M. Oungst, Cy Perkins) *BP*
**This Wheel's On Fire** (Bob Dylan,
  Rick Danko) *BP*
**Tiny Montgomery** *BP*
**Too Much Of Nothing** take one *BP*
Too Much Of Nothing take two *BP*
Try Me, Little Girl *RR*
Tupelo (John Lee Hooker) *BP*
Under Control *BP*
Waltzing With Sin (Red Hayes,
  Sonny Burns) *BP*
Wildwood Flower (A.P. Carter) *WR*
Will The Circle Be Unbroken (A.P. Carter) *BA*
Words And Numbers (Richard Manuel) *BA*
Yazoo Street Scandal (Robbie Robertson)
  version one *BA*
Yazoo Street Scandal (Robbie Robertson)
  version two *BA*
Yea! Heavy And A Bottle Of Bread take one *BP*
**Yea! Heavy And A Bottle Of Bread**
  take two *BP*
You Ain't Goin' Nowhere take one *BP*
**You Ain't Goin' Nowhere** take two *BP*
You Don't Come Through (Robbie Robertson) *BP*
You Say You Love Me (Robbie Robertson) *BA*
You Win Again (Hank Williams) *BP*
Young But Daily Growing (Traditional) *RR*

**AMPEX 602:** It was probably on this type of tape machine that Garth Hudson recorded the Basement Tapes.

# MILLION DOLLAR BASH

## 1. The Beginning Of The Beginning

*Background to the Woodstock area*

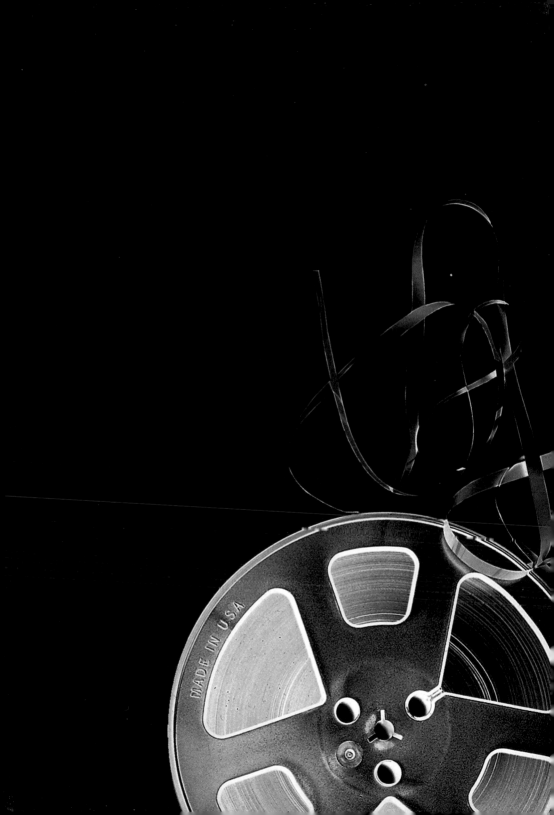

Nothing can grow in a vacuum. The quality of a planting season is dependent upon outside influences such as soil quality, the amount of sunshine, the frequency of rain. Art too does not grow in a vacuum.

In 1967 Bob Dylan created some of his greatest music, wrote some of his most dynamic songs, and ably captured much of it on tape. In great part this was due to his situation, with his family nearby in a small-town atmosphere. It enabled Dylan and his musical brothers to stop the clock and allow themselves and the songs the time to breathe peacefully. But how did he end up in Woodstock, and how did it influence him?

*In early September 1609 a small, clumsy, high-pooped craft manned by a score of Dutch and English veteran seamen, adventurers, and grim explorers came to the mouth of a grand, lonely river flowing silently out of the heart of an unknown continent. The Half Moon had been restlessly darting along the eastern coast of North America in a futile search for a water route leading to India.*

*The boat was commanded by an Englishman and his search was paid for by the Dutch, who called him Hendrik Hudson. It was a typical arrangement of the time. Hardy seamen and their captains were frequently British and Dutch: those nations had two of the strongest navies and two of the strongest sailing traditions. It was a period when the bravest – and those with the least to lose – would eagerly sail under any flag that promised glory and profit, when the greatest nautical statements were made by rough sons of the cutlass and brave students of the compass.*

Right there. Stop. Doesn't this sound like the scenario of one of those old folk songs that so inspired the adolescent Bob Dylan? All we need to know is that Henry Hudson anchored in what today is New York harbor and soon discovered he was by the mouth of a river. He spent the next three weeks exploring and eventually started his homeward journey in October. Back in Holland, merchants were keen to hear and learn more about the furs that Hudson and his men had seen on the natives and in their encampments along the river. Furs were as valuable to Europeans as silks or ivory, and soon companies were sending more ships to the newly

discovered river, sailing northward again and again to further document the country. That area today consists of the counties of Green, Orange, Ulster, Delaware, and Sullivan.

Woodstock, New York, was formed on April 11, 1787, its name inspired by the town of Woodstock in England, although it was first settled – if the descendants of the Native Americans there can forgive us for using that term – by the Dutch and then other Europeans. The Delaware & Hudson Canal was finished in 1828 and this waterway led to a leap in communication within the county. Late in the 19th century the area was becoming known for its proximity to New York City, which could be reached relatively quickly on the train that headed north to the state capital of Albany, but it was rural enough to remain a semi-sophisticated pleasure.

By 1900, Woodstock was a fully-formed small rural village, as unlike Albany or New York City as a Dordogne farm is to Paris. Yet its reputation as an artist's haven was already established. In fact America's first home-grown, coherent, and noted group of landscape artists of any prominence began in the area some 50 years before the start of the 20th century, when a group now known as the Hudson River painters put the Woodstock area on the artistic map.

At exactly the point when this school of landscape portraiture reached the height of its influence, an Englishman began a search across the United States for a location for a colony of artists to live and work together in rural splendor. Ralph Radcliffe Whitehead, a wealthy English entrepreneur, knew he had found his idyllic spot, the home for his artisans and craftsmen. On the side of Mt. Guardian that overlooks Woodstock, this proud Englishman began to build his experimental home for independent artists, which he called Byrdcliffe.

Byrdcliffe is now a famous arts colony, located just outside Woodstock, on Upper Byrdcliffe Road. It is America's oldest continuing Arts & Crafts colony. Bohemians had begun to use the Woodstock area in small but noticeable numbers, many of them members of that Hudson River painting school. Construction of the Byrdcliffe Arts Colony was completed in 1903 on approximately 1,500 acres of land that had contained seven farms, all purchased specifically by Whitehead. The new utopian arts community consisted of 40 artists cottages and studios.

A parallel arts movement, now called Arts & Crafts, had begun around 1875 in Whitehead's native England as a reaction against urbanization and industrialization and the strait-laced Victorian sensibility of the day. Most of the participants shared a utopian ideal based on artistic collaboration and a love and respect for rustic rural life. They believed modern people could regain control of their life and soul if their daily work reflected the grace and dignity thought lost when industrialization brought soulless machinery to the dark satanic mills where so many worked. Whitehead and his associates prized hand craftsmanship above all else and they sought a brotherhood of artisans and craftsmen working together creatively. They thought this brotherhood was the ideal society, the utopian promise they'd witnessed in their dreams.

Whitehead's Byrdcliffe School of Art was the first permanent art school in the Hudson Valley. It brought students, teachers, craftsmen, and their ilk in some numbers to Woodstock, providing an economic boost that continues today. And the influx of such artists would help to transform the vicinity into the proud, socially aware community it is now – whether the forgotten names of the pre-World War I era or the rock'n'rollers who followed in Bob Dylan's wake. The sleepy town of Woodstock may still rest peacefully in the darkness of the night that falls upon it, but during the day there is some heavy duty thinkin' goin' on in these parts.

Of course, the rural working man of Ulster County was as busy staying alive as his humble contemporaries elsewhere. He seldom had the time to stop and ponder the creation of an artistic utopia anywhere, much less in his own back yard. He needed to work to live. And work hard to live. Out of that came one of the great ironies of Byrdcliffe, and indeed of Woodstock. Whitehead was the son of a wealthy mill owner from Yorkshire and started on his utopian rural society while studying at Oxford under the famous art critic John Ruskin. Had Whitehead not been wealthy and had he not come to America in 1892, he might have pursued his vision elsewhere – and Bob Dylan, Van Morrison, Tim Hardin, The

Band, Peter Yarrow of Peter Paul & Mary, and so many others would have resided elsewhere.

In the years before World War I, the Byrdcliffe colony grew as a home to actors, authors, painters, and poets – but no guitar pickers and no singers of popular song. Not yet, anyway. The roll call of Byrdcliffe's resident artists reads like a list that high school students memorize for Humanities class, but even the culturally challenged would notice the names of former residents Aaron Copeland, Edward G. Robinson, John Cage, and Lee Marvin.

An early visitor to the town was the young Ramblin' Jack Elliott, then still Elliot Adnopoz. He remembers: "I must've have been in Woodstock about 20 years before Albert [Grossman] or Bob [Dylan] were, 'cause my parents had some friends who moved up there, and we visited those people. So we'd visit those folks in Woodstock. Then I found out about Sam Eskine, a folk singer and retired postal employee from Baltimore, who had bought a very expensive tape recorder and a jeep and had been to Mexico and down there, traveling all around recording folk music in the wild. He was a nice man and played the guitar, one of the earlier Woodstock musicians.

"So there was that type of person up there then, a folk singer if you will, but no famous ones as there were later on, when Bob lived there and other musicians moved there. Now that I think about it, I later even got married in Woodstock.

"I remember Bob used to ride over to us in Woodstock on his Triumph. It was such a pretty place then, early 1960s or so. I later learned to dislike Woodstock, and after several visits to Bob I grew less and less enamored of the place and have avoided it in recent years, hardly ever going near it, 'cause it's full of New Yorkers and a lot of weird people up there. I'm not too fond of going around large crowds of city people. But it got to be real New Yorky up there, though in fact there is a mountain there with a claim that there are more rattlesnakes on it than any other land in the world. This is right behind Sam Eskine's farm. You'd think that would keep some of the New York City folks away. Maybe we should publicize those rattlesnakes more; might be a good idea." True Dylanologists and folk music lovers everywhere will know that Ramblin' Jack Elliott is called Ramblin' not for his hard-travelin' hobo ways but for his verbal ramblin' when telling a tale. The singer Odetta claimed her mother gave Elliott his affectionate nickname by remarking one day: "That Jack – he sure can ramble on!" Bear this in mind when reading Ramblin' Jack's reply when I ask him about the presence of graphic artists in the town of Woodstock, pre-Dylan residency.

"Yeah, there were artists there, but there wasn't a colony feel to the town," says Elliott. "There was probably not more than one art gallery in town at the time and it wasn't so cute then. I was more enamored of the west, the real west, further west, and I always wanted to be a cowboy. That's how I got into music in the first place. I ran away from home when I was 15 and joined a traveling rodeo, grooming horses for two dollars a day on a J.E. Ranch Rodeo, and I lasted three months.

"I had to return home as I was losing weight: didn't get much to eat. There was an old rodeo clown called Braemer Rodgers who performed with his trick mule. He played guitar and banjo and sang a lot of cowboy songs and hillbilly songs. When I got home I played a lot of guitar. I never practiced anything or devoted more time to anything like I did the guitar then. Five hours a day for the first six months. And after three years I met Woody Guthrie, and that's how I got groovin' right there." [1]

Compare the above answer to the biographical tales about the young Bob Dylan found on the back of the *Freewheelin'* LP and a pattern begins to emerge.

Although America had only one Woody Guthrie, one Jack Elliott, and one Bob Dylan, it nevertheless had several artists' colonies operating around and about the continental United States. Then as now, communities and their civic fathers were keen to seize on anything that set the community apart from other localities, to promote anything that made the town unique. Even early on, as Ramblin' Jack explains, Byrdcliffe and its residents brought new prominence to Woodstock and Ulster County, and the proximity of Byrdcliffe to New York City gave it an advantage that other utopian attempts didn't have: you could conduct the artistic side of your business with the owners of the dark satanic mills over lunch in Manhattan yet still be home in plenty of time for a supper whose soundtrack was the mooing of cattle and the gurgle of a running brook.

If the 25-year-old Bob Dylan wasn't already overly familiar with the Manhattan business lunch he was certainly quite familiar with those who were. And he was already growing tired of the city, although he still loved New York for embracing him and showing him the various wide open, greater possibilities life could offer. Dylan's manager Albert Grossman was also the manager of Peter Paul & Mary, a folk act he assembled from three Greenwich Village soloists.

Dylan first visited Woodstock when Peter Yarrow of Peter Paul & Mary invited him to get away from New York City's clang and clatter and stay in a summer cabin that Yarrow's mother owned up on Broadview Road. Yarrow had been going there since he was a young boy. He remembers bringing Dylan to Woodstock the first time.

"Let me put it this way. It was 1963, we [Peter Paul & Mary] had 'Blowin' In The Wind,' it was a really hot summer, it was really miserable in the city, and I was going up to my mother's cabin in Woodstock. I told Bobby [Dylan], 'Come on up with Suze Rotolo,' his sweetheart. And they did. Suze was an amazing, terribly kind person. Suze and I would go paint in the morning and Bob would write songs. And we'd come home from our art student scene and Bobby would have written 'Masters Of War' or 'Only A Pawn In Their Game.' He would type them out and then sit down at the piano and play. And then ask for his breakfast! And so it went."

Word got around, says Yarrow. "The fatal mistake, if you want to call it that, was that a once charming full-out art colony that had been there for decades and decades with a real bohemian tradition turned into a place to which people would make pilgrimages in order to catch a sight of Bobby Dylan."

Yarrow says he became uncomfortable as people looked at him and others as though they were walking album covers. "Bob has written or spoken extensively about his uncomfortableness when forced into that persona. Woodstock was a strange mixture of the bohemian existence – which had gone on for decades with opera and theatre, which I remember so well from when I was seven or eight. But by the time I was 24 years old it was partly a reflection of what was new and exciting and fantastic and convention defying – and yet, like most of these transformations, it reiterated the very things it presumably poised to challenge." [2]

Dylan loved the town. Years later he confided to his friend and road manager Victor Maymudes that he felt comfortable in the small-town atmosphere, that no one bothered him – even though some tangible fame was already his, following the noteworthy second LP, *The Freewheelin' Bob Dylan,* and the remarkable popularity that summer of 'Blowin' In The Wind' from the same album.

Dylan was already becoming leader of the pack to the denizens around Bleecker and MacDougal in New York City, and as 'Blowin' In The Wind' first became a hit single for Peter Paul & Mary and was then covered by everyone from Percy Faith to Sam Cooke, his fame grew further. The song became something of the new unofficial anthem of the civil rights movement and seemingly replaced the veteran 'We Shall Overcome' in the hearts of many of the young Freedom Riders who so valiantly railed against the Jim Crow laws of segregation.

Already, the young Bob Dylan needed some space and some time away. Maymudes later said that Dylan thought the Woodstock of the mid 1960s was "a hip Hibbing," containing many of the better points of small-town life shared by his hometown of Hibbing, Minnesota. Yet clearly Woodstock was a more forward looking, more free thinking town. And the Dylan of '63 to '66 was doing some seriously free thinking. He would soon need a hip Hibbing.

The painters, writers, and poets who went to Woodstock, who moved to the Byrdcliffe arts colony in Dylan's day, had the same desires as their artistic antecedents in Ralph Radcliffe Whitehead's era, 60 years before. They sought a place to work, they sought privacy, they sought comfort in beautiful natural surroundings. They wanted inspiration, they wanted a peer group of like minds to bounce ideas off, and they wanted a broad-minded town. A volunteer for the Woodstock Byrdcliffe Guild noted, off the record, that the community at large contained many perfectly normal working families of 2.4 children, the official average for a U.S. family then. But there is little doubt the artisans flocking to Byrdcliffe were more liberal in their mores and less concerned about the formal rituals of heterosexual courtship than most Americans were back then, 40, 50, 60, or 70 years ago. Which made the area even more cozy for the young bohemian musicians soon to flee the *Billboard*-chart pressures of their professional lives.

Albert Grossman and his wife, the ever tolerant Sally, purchased an estate in nearby Bearsville in 1964. They bought it from an artist, John Striebel, who drew the comic strip *Dixie Dugan*. There were several cabins on the estate where Grossman planned to plant various members of his artistic stable so they could woodshed, so he could keep an eye on them, and, in two particularly sad cases, so one of his artists could sober up and the other could attempt to kick drugs. Dylan stayed in one of the cabins in 1964 and, still impressed and inspired by the area, he bought one of the Byrdcliffe homes, approximately one mile from Grossman's sprawling property.

Dylan had visited John and Cynthia Lennon at their suburban home in Weybridge, south-west of London in the stockbroker belt, and was taken by the idea of Lennon having a proper home for his wife and young Julian. Dylan also liked the accoutrements chez Lennon, such as Beatle John's big stuffed gorilla in the hallway and his seemingly authentic suit of armor from the Middle Ages.

In July 1965, Dylan and his wife Sara purchased a sprawling 11-room Byrdcliffe Arts & Crafts home on Camelot Road named *Hi Lo Ha*. (The name was not due to any Native American influence, as has been stated, but derived from the first two letters of the forenames of the mother and two daughters who originally resided there.) The house was rough-hewn but modern and had a commanding view. The Dylans probably moved in during August. The home the Dylans purchased was built by an early. Byrdcliffe family named Stoehr and was on the part of Byrdcliffe that

Ralph Radcliffe Whitehead named the East Riding. The Byrdcliffe Arts Colony owned the houses in the West Riding, which remains the heart of the colony. Yet Whitehead sold land to like-minded folks and so the properties in the East Riding have largely been in private hands since they were built. Dylan's new home *Hi Lo Ha* was one of these properties as the Stoehr family had bought the land from Whitehead.

*Hi Lo Ha* had deep forest all around, meaning privacy, and the necessary babbling brook gurgling through the property. There was a charming sign out front, donated by Grossman, which read: IF YOU HAVE NOT TELEPHONED YOU'RE TRESPASSING. It had a driveway big enough for basketball games – Dylan was and remains a fan of the sport and played, later taking up boxing as well – and a large heated garage, which the singer partially converted into a private pool hall for himself and his cronies. The house cost just $12,000. (Today that figure would be closer to the property tax.) Friends noted that it was the first time Dylan had visibly treated himself to any major fruits from his many toils, and they were pleased for him.

Like any wife seeking the best possible home for her man and her daughter (by a previous marriage), Sara found the original style of the house, in its Byrdcliffe artisan simplicity, a tad Spartan. The Dylans made several necessary renovations over the years, brought on by their growing family.

Today the house still stands and is still called *Hi Lo Ha*, although the only connection the property maintains to Byrdcliffe is that it resides on acreage first purchased from a forgotten farmer by Whitehead shortly after the beginning of the 20th century. Suffice to say the property remains Byrdcliffe's most famous building.

The Woodstock of today has stood fast through some windy days since Byrdcliffe was founded. Still a refuge for artists and still a shopping stop for local farmers, Ulster County's artistic centre is an easy drive from the gray grim of New York City's concrete canyons. Take the George Washington Bridge to the Palisades Parkway and you are soon driving alongside and indeed above the mighty Hudson River: take the exit for the New York State Thruway and head upstate, exit the Thruway at a sign for

Kingston, and follow the signs west until you start seeing signs for Woodstock. The sleepy and not-so-sleepy town of Woodstock will greet you soon enough, carrying on its business as it always did, but with the added attraction of answering the odd visitor who asks where Dylan or Van Morrison or Tim Hardin resided and the even more frequent question from the sadly confused tourist who wants to know where the famous rock festival was held. The festival was called Woodstock but of course it was not held in Woodstock. It was held miles away, near Bethel, New York, on the farm of the late Max Yasgur.

Dylan was in negotiations to perform at Yasgur's farm but, understandably, was afraid of the hippies who were already turning up on his property (hence Grossman's trespassing sign). He decided to have nothing to do with the festival. Despite this decision, for years afterward one of the great Woodstock rumors insisted Dylan was there for all three days, Our Hero allegedly in disguise and traversing the now hallowed and then quite muddy grounds.

And there have been other Woodstocks since – none of them held in the town that gave refuge to Dylan, that provided the vibe for the entire Basement Tapes saga, and that helped prompt The Band to define not just their music but themselves with *Music From Big Pink*.

Dylan resides primarily in Los Angeles these days. Whether or not he is aware of some of the above isn't known, and he isn't saying. Remember, this man once acted in a movie playing a character called Alias. According to longtime friends, he didn't do much small-talk 40 years ago, either, but all those queried agree he had a lot to say. Dylan didn't communicate then or now as others would or when others would. He doesn't communicate as social guidelines or musical trends dictate, yet his deeds have said so much. Alias rather fits him.

MILLION DOLLAR
**BASH**

## 2. Backbeat

*Bob Dylan, 1941–1966*

Bob Dylan was born in Duluth, Minnesota, in May 1941 but was raised about 55 miles to the north-west in the Iron Range town of Hibbing, where he grew up in a loving family.

Two other locals who found fame outside the bleak Iron Range are Boston Celtic great Kevin McHale and New York Yankees legend Roger Maris, whom Dylan cites in his *Chronicles*. R.E.M.'s original drummer Bill Berry has claimed he was born in Hibbing out of his respect for Dylan, but the truth is he first saw daylight in Duluth.

In August of the year of Dylan's birth, Pete Seeger and Woody Guthrie played a Democratic Party fundraiser in Seattle, which the organizers called a hootenanny, the first use of the word. Back in Hibbing, future hootenanny enthusiast Bob Dylan fell in love with music at an early age listening late at night to powerful clear-channel radio stations such as Chicago's rockin' WLS, Nashville's country WSM, Memphis's R&B WDIA, and Louisville's eclectic WHAS.

His uncle owned several movie theatres in Hibbing, and the young Robert Allen Zimmerman was a frequent visitor, not merely to escape the cold, not only because cinema allowed him to escape the grayness of a town that had been built near to the world's largest mining pit, not only because he was seemingly a loner (though conversely he was blessed with a few boyhood friends), but because the movies fired his imagination. It was the dialog, the drama, the ideas displayed so freely; the whole wide world was opening up before him, coming to him, beckoning him forward.

The young Bobby Zimmerman loved the scriptwriting so deftly displayed by Mississippi's William Faulkner, humorist S.J. Perelman, and the blacklisted Dalton Trumbo, the latter perhaps most famous as a non-recanting member of the Hollywood Ten, a group of screenwriters cited by Congress for contempt, most of whom served prison sentences as a result. Later, Dylan also expressed an admiration for the work of film writers Marguerite Duras and Joseph L. Mankiewicz.

Of the several hundred books and dissertations published on Dylan's art, some of the more recent say that he has in the later stages of his career occasionally transposed or borrowed passages of silver-screen dialog, snatches of cinematic chat, or offhand remarks tossed out by some struggling protagonist, and adapted them for his own lyrics. Even earlier in his career, this form of writing would take center stage in such cinematic Basement Tapes songs as 'Clothes Line Saga' and 'Don't Ya Tell Henry.'

Dylan is more noted for his love of poetry, be it the French symbolism of Arthur Rimbaud, the American Civil War verse of Henry Timrod, or the Beat howls of Allen Ginsberg. Yet it appears that Dylan – the man who with some accuracy said, "I live like a poet and I will die like a poet" [1] – may well be more akin to a member of the Screen Writer's Guild than a poet, or at least the popular perception of a poet. And after all, the Screen Writer's Guild in West Hollywood is less than an hour's drive from his Malibu home. Where do you go to find a poet?

One of the grand themes of 20th century art, appearing in everything from novels to movies to country & western songs, is the young country boy or girl, oh so green and wet behind the ears, who nonetheless has the courage to pull up stakes and go traipsing off to the Big City to experience the big bad world. Robert Allen Zimmerman did exactly that.

Anyone reading that sentence will know enough about Dylan, about his life and his art, to find it impossible to think of him in any other way than his admittedly chameleon-like series of public images: young Dylan as folk balladeer; Dylan as wild-eyed rock'n'roll hit maker; mature Dylan as country squire and family man; Dylan as God's faithful spokesperson; and so on.

The idea of Bob Dylan still back in Hibbing, having never left, preparing for his retirement party (as he would be now, for he is over 65), preparing for another day at the pharmacy or perhaps another day of teaching English at the Hibbing High School, is an image that appears only via the strongest imagination available to man.

No, young Master Zimmerman did what he had to do, and Mr. Zimmerman senior reacted as any concerned, loving parent would have when his music-obsessed elder son expressed no interest in the family business. He worried. A counselor at Hibbing High told Abram Zimmerman that his son displayed all the sensibilities of an artist; the boy would later recall dad's reply as: "Isn't an artist a fellow who paints?"

In the dreary, disheartening summer that followed this conversation, the U.S. House of Representatives voted 373 to 9 to cite Peter Seeger for contempt of Congress for refusing to answer House Un-American Activities questions. This banjo pickin' artist, no painter he, began to appear not only as a popular folk singer but also as a popular folk hero, just like Woody was to Dylan and to so many others. Hibbing's Robert Zimmerman liked rock'n'roll singers and folk singers and loved those who he perceived as earthly representatives of truth and justice. His first heroes were Robin Hood and St. George the Dragon Slayer. Now they were Guthrie and Little Richard.

### 1961: from Minnesota to Albert Grossman

The young Dylan arrives in New York City in February accompanied by his friend Fred Underhill. They head straight for the Café Wha?, where Dylan performs two songs. The owner asks the crowd if anyone has space for them to stay the night. • The same month, the University of Chicago presents the first of their legendary and groundbreaking Folk Festivals, the debut line-up featuring Roscoe Holcomb, Elizabeth Cotten, and Frank Proffitt. • The fresh-faced young Dylan has the good fortune to be reviewed by Robert Shelton in *The New York Times* while opening up the show for The Greenbriar Boys bluegrass group at Gerde's Folk City. Dylan is soon thrilled by the *Times* of Friday September 29 where he sees his photo next to Shelton's favorable report. • The 20-year-old has been turned down by several labels already, including Elektra, Vanguard, and Folkways, and is considering asking Clancy Brothers & Tommy Makem manager Marty Erlichman if he can record for their Tradition record company when the legendary John Hammond offers him a deal. • After signing to Columbia (and not before, as has been written) Bob Dylan starts to attract the interest of a certain Chicago businessman looking to manage folk-music acts. Albert Grossman opened and ran The Gate of Horn back in Chicago, where he occasionally escorted an under-age Roger McGuinn out the door. By 1961, Grossman already represented Odetta. He also represented Bob Gibson, setting him up with Hamilton Camp as, logically, Gibson & Camp. He thought these two strong talents would be even stronger with a female singer but couldn't find one to fill his Joan

Baez-styled role. He also tried Gibson with Carolyn Hester and Ray Boguslav, finally getting the kind of trio he wanted when he placed Peter Yarrow with Noel Stookey, told Stookey he was now Paul, and brought in golden-haired Kentucky girl Mary Travers for the Baez role.

## 1962: from acoustic debut LP to full-band single

History and now this book both record the cherubic Dylan releasing a self-titled LP this year. • A few weeks later the White House confirms that U.S. pilots are flying combat missions in Vietnam and that American ground troops, previously thought only to be military advisors, are exchanging fire with Viet Cong guerrillas. A clock is ticking. • *Broadside* magazine number one, launched by Sis Cunningham of The Almanac Singers along with Pete Seeger and Gil Turner, is published and contains 'Talking John Birch Society Blues' by Bob Dylan. His songwriting has particularly caught the ear and imagination of Seeger, who envisions Woody's torch of social protest through singing passing to another generation, another Woody figure even. • In May, *Broadside* number six features the lyrics and chords to a new Dylan song, 'Blowin' In The Wind.' • The Students For A Democratic Society complete The Port Huron Statement, a manifesto for their activist movement. • Dylan signs with Witmark Music publishers in July. • The last French Foreign Legion soldiers leave Algeria after the bloodshed of the rebellion there. A referendum is held in the country on independence, overwhelmingly voted for, with some districts voting 99 percent to end France's role in their affairs. • Dylan cancels his planned second LP, *Bob Dylan Blues*. Heavily under the influence of English folk melodies he heard on a visit to London when he was filmed in the BBC TV play *The Madhouse On Castle Street*, he begins to record his second album, the major breakthrough and self-penned *The Freewheelin' Bob Dylan*. • A group called The Rollin' Stones make their debut, opening at London's Marquee for Long John Baldry on July 12. • A U2 spy-plane flight over Cuba in October reveals the presence of Soviet nuclear weapons. • The year ends with a Dylan single, 'Mixed Up Confusion,' released by Columbia and then quickly withdrawn. The song has a full band bashing out a rockabilly backing behind the young singer. It is deemed by the label as the wrong direction for their youthful troubadour.

## 1963: from 'Masters Of War' to a Woodstock visit

The new year gives topical songwriters much to write about. On January 11 the Whisky A Go Go nightclub opens in Los Angeles, the first disco in the U.S.A. • Three days later Governor George Wallace of Alabama declares "segregation now, segregation tomorrow, and segregation forever!" • Dylan's 'Masters Of War' appears in *Broadside* number 20 with an accompanying illustration by his girlfriend Suze Rotolo. • Poetically enough, the second Peter Paul & Mary album, *Moving*, reaches Number 2. • French President Charles De Gaulle vetoes the United Kingdom's entry to the EEC. • Joan Baez starts performing Dylan songs live. • ABC TV broadcasts a new folk music show called *Hootenanny*, but Pete Seeger is blacklisted from appearing, so Baez, Dylan, Ramblin' Jack Elliott, Phil Ochs, Tom Paxton, Carolyn Hester, The Kingston Trio, and Peter Paul & Mary all refuse to appear on the show, leaving it to second-raters and wannabe talents. These folkies even picket the ABC offices, protesting the non-appearance of Seeger, who popularized the term hootenanny two decades earlier. • Yoko Ono's on-again off-again marriage to film-maker and later Christian fundamentalist adherent Anthony Cox is annulled.

In April in Birmingham, Alabama, Sheriff Bull Connor instructs his police to unleash attack dogs on peaceful anti-segregation protestors, some of them children. Footage of the events is viewed worldwide. • In a national radio and television address in June, President Kennedy tells the nation that segregation is morally wrong. The next day, civil rights worker Medgar Evers is shot and killed by a bullet in the back while leaving his car at his home in Jackson, Mississippi. • *The Freewheelin' Bob Dylan* further cements his public image as a protest singer and, even worse for Dylan, confirms his media image as Spokesperson For A Generation. Those twin images of protest singer and S.F.A.G. prove to be mere snapshots of a forever changing artist whose life would be a continual series of restless farewells to various artistic styles. • 'Blowin' In The Wind' proves to be a breakthrough song for Dylan and it will eventually be covered by some 200 artists. Peter Paul & Mary have a huge hit with it – and so in the Freedom Summer of 1963 the U.S.A. is singing along to a song about segregation and inhumanity. • Dylan is invited up to Woodstock by Peter Yarrow, whose mother owns a home there, and he appreciates the tenor of the town and its contrast to New York City.

On August 6 Dylan begins to record *The Times They Are A-Changin'*, an LP full of black-and-white vignettes of social breakdown and injustice. • August 28 sees Dylan singing at the climax of the civil rights march on Washington, DC, and he is standing nearby Dr. Martin Luther King as some quarter of a million Americans listen peacefully out in front of the Lincoln Memorial as Dr. King delivers his "I have a dream" speech. • The next month, four African-American schoolgirls are killed when a bomb goes off one Sunday morning in the Sixteenth Street Baptist Church in Birmingham, Alabama. Twenty-two others are injured. • *Sing Out!* magazine's circulation rises to 20,000 readers, who are told enthusiastically that "there are now 87 albums with the word hootenanny in their title!" • November 22: the Kennedy assassination. Dylan reluctantly keeps a concert commitment for the next day. The entire U.S.A. is sleepwalking through these hours. Jack Ruby kills Lee Harvey Oswald. • Even Chubby Checker and Guy Lombardo are currently recording folk music. The year's biggest-selling album is the soundtrack to *West Side Story* but the second and third are the first two releases by Peter Paul & Mary. The battle is on!

## 1964: from electric covers to electric wordplay

It gets better for the world at large as it gets worse for the protest fans. The Beatles, already heroes in the U.K., appear on *The Ed Sullivan Show* on CBS TV on consecutive Sundays in February 1964 and wow some 90 million Americans. • Dylan's career is rolling relentlessly forward, a clock ticking ever louder though its coil never lessens. As his life and lifestyle change he struggles to adapt to his new importance. Manager Albert Grossman is concerned about moving too fast with Dylan and limits his gigging to approximately 50 concerts during the year. • U.S. Defense Secretary Robert McNamara delivers an address that reiterates American determination to give South Vietnam increased military and economic aid in its war against the Communist insurgency. • In June, The Animals hit Number 1 in Britain with 'The House Of The Rising Sun' and the following month the record starts to rise to the same spot in the United States. The Newcastle band first heard the song on Dylan's eponymous debut album. Producer Tom Wilson attempts to dub a rock band onto Dylan's version of the song in July but he's too late. • Acoustic guitars and banjos are starting to appear in pawn shops in the States as electric guitar sales rise, yet this doesn't slow the search for real, authentic music by the white middle class. • This year sees young blues lovers Dick Waterman, Nick Perls, and Phil Spiro find Son House, thought dead, working in Rochester, New York, and John Fahey, Henry Vestine (later of Canned Heat), and Bill Barth find Skip James living in Tunica, Mississippi.

Dylan, recoiling under the cultural weight and demand of being a Spokesperson For A Generation, makes his first well known leap away from S.F.A.G. hell with *Another Side Of Bob Dylan*, released this year. It puzzles his denim'd and work-booted folk festival followers, who unsuccessfully seek high and low for a glimpse of the "finger-pointin' songs" on which he has risen to fame. Now he appears to be self-absorbed, or at least his writing appears to be self-absorbed to *Sing Out!* and *Broadside* magazines. • And in the interest of artistic equity and setting the record straight, Sony Music's *Bootleg Series* of Dylan recordings will show that the S.F.A.G. is by summer 1963 already writing so prolifically and so bang on target that he is recording yet discarding songs on which other artists would have based a successful career, including 'Eternal Circle,' 'Only A Hobo,' 'Percy's Song,' and 'Lay Down Your Weary Tune.' • This very summer of 1964, Dylan's producer Tom Wilson reunites and records songwriter Paul Simon with his old schoolmate and former doo-wop partner Art Garfunkel for a failed album that nonetheless features the first version of 'The Sounds Of Silence.'

In August, the slain bodies of three civil rights workers missing for two months are found buried near Philadelphia, Mississippi. • That same month, The Beatles play Forest Hills in New York City and invite Dylan to their suite at the Hotel Delmonica on Park Avenue. There the Fab Four smoke pot for the first time, Lennon passing the initial joint to a curious

Ringo as if the drummer were His Sovereign's Royal Taster. The former Richard Starkey of 10 Admiral Grove in Dingle, Liverpool, smokes the entire jazz cigarette by his lonesome as if it was a Marlboro, marijuana etiquette being completely unknown to the surprisingly green Liverpudlians. • The Warren Commission Report, the first official investigation of the assassination of President Kennedy, is published. • As 1964 rolls to a close, Joan Baez is one of 796 arrested for leading a Free Speech Movement march that attempted to occupy the administration building at the University of California at Berkeley.

## 1965: from spring U.K. acoustic tour to fall U.S. electric tour

*Sing Out!* publishes some of Dylan's prose excerpted from his *Walk Down Crooked Highway* book, which eventually mutates into *Tarantula*. • Recording sessions for *Bringing It All Back Home* start this month and, when released March 22, the album creates more consternation within the traditional folk community. The first side features all-out electric rock'n'roll with more than one homage to Chuck Berry – Mr. Berry not being a particular hero to the folkies of the Café Wha? and The Gaslight. Side two is acoustic, but the symbolist/Beat/psychedelic wordplay found there bears little resemblance to the undeniable message of humanity of 'Blowin' In The Wind' or its sweet, barebones simplicity. Few crowds will ever sing along to 'Gates Of Eden.' So while easier on folk ears, the flip offers very little respite for the folk audience after hearing Chuck Berry rhythms crossed with Ferlinghetti on the top side. Dylan aims and shoots. Bang. Gotcha! • Allen Ginsberg remarks that the album is a continuation of Jack Kerouac's "chains of flashing images" writing style and claims Dylan is unconsciously or perhaps even consciously presenting himself as the natural heir to the Beat poetry tradition. • In Washington DC the head of the FBI, J. Edgar Hoover, repeats his claim that "beatniks are one of the three greatest threats to America." He would worry even more if informed *Bringing It All Back Home* is Dylan's biggest selling album yet.

Donovan hits the U.K. pop charts with his debut single 'Catch The Wind' and is sold as Britain's answer to Dylan. • *Variety,* the American entertainment bible, runs a June headline stating "The Folk Boom Is

Dead" as folk-rock replaces folk music, something perhaps best symbolized by the release of 'Mr. Tambourine Man' by The Byrds the month before. This cover version, soon to be Number 1 in two dozen countries, encourages Dylan and seemingly confirms he is headed in the right direction. • Albert Grossman owns property west of Woodstock at his Bearsville estate and he and his wife Sally invite Dylan to stay with them for weekend breaks and working retreats. The artistic atmosphere of the Ulster County small town makes it feel more and more like a hip Hibbing to the bard. • John Hammond, Jr., son of the famous CBS executive, releases *So Many Roads* in May. The lethal backing band is Levon Helm, Robbie Robertson, Garth Hudson, and Michael Bloomfield. So hot is Robertson's guitar work that Bloomfield appears as pianist. Robertson: "[Bloomfield] wasn't so hot yet. In the early days I had that youthful exuberance: I am at the starting gate, chomping on the bit, saying: 'Go ahead and ring that bell, start this race now!' I went through that whole soldier-of-fortune period of guitar playing in The Hawks while others were just learning it." [2] • Dylan plays Britain with road manager Bob Neuwirth and cinematographer D.A. Pennebaker in tow; the result of his final solo acoustic tour will be the *Dont Look Back* film.

In June, Dylan records 'Like A Rolling Stone' with Michael Bloomfield on guitar and guitarist Al Kooper sneaking over to the organ, turning it on, and remaining on the track. Six minutes long, twice the length of most singles, it proves a huge hit, rising to Number 2 in the U.S.A. • The song is debuted at the chaos of the Newport Folk Festival, where Dylan performs three songs with an ad hoc backup band of Kooper and members of The Paul Butterfield Blues Band. The sound coming off the stage at Newport is loud, unbalanced, and revolutionary. It is electric rock'n'roll with lyrics unlike any previously heard in pop music. Audio evidence reveals cheers and jeers among the 70,000 festival attendees, some of whom loudly boo Dylan's first live performance as a rocker. • Kooper: "I played Newport with him and I didn't hear one boo. This situation at Newport was we only had three songs rehearsed. So you have an act, Dylan, headlining a four-day festival, and he gets up and plays for 15 minutes where everyone else on the show got up and played for 45

minutes to an hour. The audience were extremely upset but they were yelling for 'more,' they were not yelling 'booooo.' I would say probably ten percent of the audience were upset he played electric music."[3]
• President Lyndon Johnson announces his order to increase the number of U.S. troops in South Vietnam from 75,000 to 125,000 and to double the number of men drafted per month from 17,000 to 35,000. • Dylan buys property in Woodstock in July, an 11-room home called *Hi Lo Ha* on Camelot Road off Upper Byrdcliffe Way in the Byrdcliffe Arts Colony, for his soon-to-be-growing family.

Albert Grossman ups the ante as Dylan performs approximately 67 concerts this year, but there is a sea change. Early in the year, his concerts are solo acoustic, but after his challenging appearance at the Newport Folk Festival, this is only half the story. Dylan enters Columbia Studios in New York four days after Newport to begin recording his next album, *Highway 61 Revisited*. It is released August 30. • There is one acoustic track on the LP, the apocalyptic 'Desolation Row' (later the improvised name of a muddy avenue of stalls and too few public conveniences at the original Woodstock Festival in 1969). To his old denim-and-work-boots audience, Dylan is seemingly turning to commercial rock'n'roll in the wake of the Beatles/Animals/Manfred Mann/Kinks wave of British acts dominating the American airwaves • Dylan wants Johnny Rivers' backing band to be his backing band. Most of them moonlight as Shindogs on the ABC TV show *Shindig!*, a rock'n'roll equivalent of ABC's now axed *Hootenanny*. Guitarist James Burton tells Dylan's office they will stay put, though drummer Mickey Jones will defect in early April next year.

On August 11, the Watts Riots break out in south central Los Angeles. o The Lovin' Spoonful, a New York City act with two ex-Dylan *Bringing It All Back Home* sidemen, John Sebastian and bassist Steve Boone, release their debut single, 'Do You Believe In Magic?' • Jonathan Myrick Daniels, an Episcopal seminarian from New Hampshire, is murdered in Hayneville, Alabama, while working for the civil rights movement. • Dylan singles continue to hit the charts: 'Positively Fourth Street' is a hit in September; 'Can You Please Crawl Out Your Window?' stalls halfway up the Hot 100 in December. • Dylan plays Forest Hills in New York and the Hollywood

Bowl in L.A., but Al Kooper and bassist Harvey Brooks find the booing hard going, while guitarist Robbie Robertson and drummer Levon Helm keep lobbying Dylan hard for the rest of The Hawks to be hired. By the Carnegie Hall show on October 1, 1965 they are. Every Hawk is now onstage behind Dylan: Rick Danko now on bass, Richard Manuel on piano, and Garth Hudson in Al Kooper's organ chair, as well as Robertson and Helm.

The same month, producer Tom Wilson exhumes 'The Sounds Of Silence' from the now disbanded Simon & Garfunkel and tacks on a Byrds-styled folk-rock backing band. In November, the song starts its climb to the top spot. Garfunkel calls Simon back from England, where he has been living and touring, to re-start their singing career. Wise move. • In the pages of *Sing Out!*, Israel Young, an early Dylan supporter and lynchpin of the Greenwich Village folk scene, questions the validity of the electric Dylan music and his inner-directed lyrics, accusing Bob of openly courting commercial success. • November: in New York City, Roger Allen LaPorte, a 22-year-old member of the Catholic Worker Movement, sets himself on fire in front of the United Nations building in protest at the war in Vietnam. This is the second such incident this month; on November 2, a 32-year-old Quaker, Norman Morrison, did the same thing at The Pentagon. • November 22 is the wedding day of Bob Dylan and Sara Lownds at a judge's office on Long Island. Two guests were present: a maid of honor and Albert Grossman. o On December 3 in San Francisco a Dylan press conference is broadcast live on KQED TV. Questions come from local media as well as figures such as Allen Ginsberg, Ralph J. Gleason, comedian Larry Hankin, and Bill Graham. Beat poet Michael McClure appears on camera but holds his tongue. Dylan on Newport: "They certainly booed, I'll tell you that. You could hear it all over the place." • In Palo Alto, south of San Francisco, Ken Kesey and his Merry Pranksters hold the first public acid test, with the guests invited to sample LSD.

**1966: a loud world tour, a motorcycle ride, a deafening silence**
A full-page advertisement in *The New York Times* is headlined STOP THE WAR IN VIETNAM NOW and is signed by almost every respected name

from the contemporary folk music world. Except Bob Dylan. • Already a stepfather, Dylan celebrates the birth of his first son, Jesse. Rumors spread among music fans that singer Bob Dylan is actually married. • Jac Holzman decides to open an Elektra office in London, and Joe Boyd, a veteran of last summer's Newport Folk Festival chaos and musical revolution, is sent to run it. • *Reflections In A Crystal Wind* by Richard & Mimi Fariña is released on Vanguard. • In Louisville, Kentucky, on February 4, Dylan with The Hawks in tow opens up what proves to be a world tour of 48 gigs. Grossman is already organizing a Shea Stadium concert in New York City and more tour dates starting in August, believing his charge can catch and surpass The Beatles in popularity. The booing reaches a crescendo when the European dates commence May 1 in Copenhagen. • President Lyndon Johnson states that the United States should stay in South Vietnam until Communist aggression there is ended. Eight-thousand more U.S. soldiers land in South Vietnam. American troops there now total over 190,000. A B-52 Stratofortress bomber collides with a KC-135 Stratotanker over Spain, dropping three 70-kiloton hydrogen bombs near the town of Palomares and one into the sea.

The first book on Bob Dylan is published when Dell market Sy & Barbara Ribakove's *Folk Rock: The Bob Dylan Story*. Robert Shelton, who kickstarted Dylan's professional career with his *New York Times* rave less than five years earlier, is signed by Viking Press to write a Dylan biography. It is published in 1986, almost two decades late. • Folk-rock bands keep coming out of the woodwork with covers of Bob Dylan songs or Dylanesque originals, but this doesn't stop U.S. Army Staff Sergeant Barry Sadler hitting the top of the charts with 'The Ballad Of The Green Berets,' a pro-Vietnam war song sung to the tune of the traditional Irish ballad 'The Butcher Boy.' • In March, an Irish Republican Army bomb destroys Nelson's Pillar in Dublin. • The Mamas & The Papas' debut album *If You Can Believe Your Eyes And Ears* is Number 1 in America. • Pro-war protesters who seek to protest the protesters demonstrate outside Pete Seeger gigs, calling him anti-American and a Communist. They are right about the latter, but Seeger sings on. Go, Pete, *go!* • Arlo Guthrie, the teenage son of Woody, signs a management contract with Harold

Leventhal, who managed his father. • Buffalo Springfield play their first gigs ever at the Whisky A Go Go in Hollywood. • 'Eight Miles High' by The Byrds and Dylan's 'Rainy Day Women #12 & 35' are named by radio tipsters The Gavin Report as songs with drug references. A great debate begins and many radio stations ban these recordings as an evil influence on the ears and indeed minds of young America.

In May, Richard Fariña is killed near Carmel, California, while riding home on the back of a friend's Harley-Davidson motorcycle. He had been attending a book-signing party celebrating his first novel, *Been Down So Long It Looks Up To Me*. He was 29 years old. • *Blonde On Blonde* is released May 16 and is the first rock'n'roll two-disc set. It soon resides in the Top 10. Dylan is the first artist in pop music to have one song take up the entire side of an LP: 'Sad Eyed Lady Of The Lowlands' is the sole track on side four. • At the Manchester Free Trade Hall performance of Dylan and The Hawks, 22-year-old John Cordwell stands up in the balcony and yells "Judas!" right before the final song, 'Like A Rolling Stone.' • Dylan's world tour ends with a pair of shows at the Royal Albert Hall in London on May 26 and 27. He returns exhausted to Camelot Road and his wife Sara and family. His body clock is at odds with the real world due to the jumbled, hectic schedule of the world tour. • Grossman's planned second leg of the tour starts Saturday August 5 in New Haven, Connecticut, with 63 more concerts in the U.S.A., and rumor has it that following a break there will be more concerts abroad. Dylan now has two children, a wife, and a new home beckoning him.

June sees U.S. planes bomb Hanoi and Haiphong in North Vietnam for the first time. • Columbia releases 'I Want You' as a single, which grazes the Top 20. • On June 11, American poet Delmore Schwartz dies. • In a landmark obscenity case, the United States Supreme Court rules that the banned novel *John Cleland's Memoirs Of A Woman Of Pleasure* (a.k.a. *Fanny Hill*) did not meet the Roth standard for obscenity. The good news is too late for author Cleland, who died in 1789. • Dylan has signed a deal with ABC TV for an hour-long special filmed during the European tour dates. Much footage has been shot, so Dylan asks D.A. Pennebaker and Bob Neuwirth to make a rough cut. Dylan eventually feels their effort looks too much like *Dont Look Back* so he re-cuts it using equipment Pennebaker has sent up to Woodstock. Howard Alk is drafted in to be his assistant. ABC TV will reject the Dylan–Alk cut as incomprehensible. • Dylan and his publisher Macmillan both agree his 'novel,' now called *Tarantula*, requires some changes, as suggested by the author in May. They give Dylan two weeks to complete a new, perfected manuscript as their promotional campaign is ready to launch. Two weeks.

Dylan's contract with Columbia Records would be up for renewal in late October 1966, and manager Grossman was keen to negotiate with Columbia sooner rather than later. Bob Dylan was a hot property, and in the ever-changing world of popular music neither the artist nor the manager were certain that he would remain that way.

In terms of business, it was time to strike before the iron could have a chance to chill. In terms of one man's personal welfare, in terms of a true artist's soul and spirit, the internal clock was not only ticking without its spring losing any tension, this particular clock was now ticking faster. And ticking louder, much louder. The noise it made with its repetitive tick-tock tick-tock tapping inside Dylan's head must have been deafening.

His Triumph motorcycle would have been every bit as loud a racket – had it been running properly. But it was over at the Grossmans' Bearsville property, sitting in the garage there, as it needed some minor repairs.

This break from touring had brought some peace and quiet to hand. So it seemed to Dylan like a good time to go get the Triumph motorbike and ride it easterly over to the repair shop off Mill Hill Road in Woodstock and get it fixed. He could even visit Barry Feinstein at home while the powerful bike was being repaired. Early on the morning of July 29, 1966 he decided to do exactly that.

**MILLION DOLLAR BASH**

# 3. Rolling Down The Road
*Bob Dylan's motercycle crash*

*Bob Dylan is dead. The CIA killed him. The Mafia killed him. His motorcycle accident killed him or at least left him a disfigured cripple for life. He can walk but he cannot move without great pain. The real Bob Dylan is alive, barely, but he cannot play the guitar any more and has lost any muse he ever knew. No more songs. Have you heard? This is all being hushed up.*

*A short-haired conservatively dressed imposter is taking his place and has been seen playing chess in Woodstock, New York, a small town about 100 miles north of New York City. But that guy ain't the real Dylan, he is some jokerman who buys groceries and walks his daughter to the bus stop every morning and waits patiently for the school bus to come pick her up.*

*That person ain't Dylan, no way.*

*A clever ruse has been pulled. Dylan is still out there, man, underground, he's gone underground as it got too heavy for him. No, the CIA killed him, he had to be shut up. Or maybe the Mafia killed him and the CIA had paid them to do it like they did with the Kennedy assassination.*

These rumors and others even more outlandish are familiar to many Baby Boomers now reaching retirement age. The stories grew at least in part because it was in Dylan's interest to let them. Albert Grossman could have staged a photo call or a press conference and displayed Dylan in whatever shape he was in post-motorcycle accident, be it in rude health, recovering nicely if slowly, or bent, bruised, and broken. Yet Grossman did not call the press to Woodstock in the aftermath of the motorcycle accident as rumors grew.

As Dylan's manager, he could easily have called one reporter, one mere lonely but respected reporter from a quality publication, to interview Dylan and see how the Spokesperson For A Generation was getting on. He did not. Grossman could have informed a TV news or arts program that they could have a worldwide exclusive on Bob's situation – and television executives would have sent a camera crew up to Woodstock before the phone line went dead. He did not. It is not known if Grossman made this decision or if his most famous client did. Perhaps Dylan did

instruct his manager to keep shtum. But word was out about Dylan's motorcycle accident later the very same day.

Dylan's first interview after the accident was some nine months later, on May 7, 1967, with Michael Iachetta of *The New York Daily News,* and this was granted only after it became apparent that the intrepid Iachetta, who had been digging on Dylan for some time by speaking to Robbie Robertson and others, was not going away. By the time of this May interview, Dylan's legend had grown further and more out of focus. The lack of media contact led most to believe Dylan was incapable of work, incapable of public presentations, and that in fact he had been seriously hurt and perhaps was still.

Dylan has in almost every media conversation preposterously protested his myths and simultaneously helped them grow by referring interviewers to these very myths (and then frequently denying them). In 1966, he and Grossman would have known Bob Dylan could have told the media anything post-accident, could have put any spin on his accident that he wanted, and they would have run with that story. Grossman would at first have been thrown wildly off course by the cancellation of concert dates and TV commitments, but it would have taken little time for a manager so extremely savvy to spot the advantages of letting Dylan lay low. He would have spotted the advantages of Dylan not talking to the press, of letting this particular story run wild through rumors and implications, of letting this particular chapter write itself. It kept Dylan's name out there and cost not a penny.

Billy James was a respected executive at Columbia Records at the time. He confirms that Dylan would speak to the press when asked. "Bob was easy for me to work with. He was amenable to requests I made of him. Bob was OK doing interviews. He was not difficult in that regard. He would not have been with me if he didn't want to do what I was recommending him to do. He was not difficult to deal with.

"Early on he fabricated a history for himself which I accepted as the Gospel Truth," says James. "No one had ever done that before or since to the extent Bob did in that fabulous interview he did for me around 1961, where he told me about growing up with uncles who were gamblers and working the streets of Chicago and in little Texas towns. Bob did just fine in interviews." [1]

So Dylan would have spoken to the press had there been something he particularly wanted to say, some message he wanted to get out to his fans or the media. He could have spoken to a single journalist and cleared up – or created – as many myths and fabrications as he wanted. But the decision was made to keep quiet. This only served to fuel the very fire Dylan wanted to put out, and his legendary status, much greater and more epic than the status given to other hit makers and singers of his day, continued to feed on its own mythologizing and continued to grow.

As for the public, Dylan's fans knew of Dylan's love of cycles. It had long seemed that Bob was the 1960s personality most like the iconic (and late) James Dean, a fellow rebel without a cause. Now the comparison between the two icons looked as if it could go further. It seemed as if Dylan could be the victim of a fatal crash on July 29, 1966 as Dean had been on September 30, 1955. The exact events of Bob Dylan's motorcycle accident on that bright sunny morning in July are known only to Dylan and possibly his wife Sara. She was following along behind in a family car on the way to the repair shop. It is not known whether she witnessed the accident or whether it occurred out of her sight.

What is known is that Dylan was a motorcycle lover. He not only rode motorcycles, he owned more than one, he discussed them with passion, he mentioned them in his songs, he had many a photo snapped of himself riding one – in particular the iconic photograph on the *Highway 61 Revisited* album jacket that showed him wearing a Triumph t-shirt picturing the company's 1965 model Bonneville 650cc with two carbs.

What is known is that both the San Bernardino and Oakland chapters of the hell's angels were such Dylan fans they attended his concerts and gatecrashed his parties. Or was it gatecrashed his concerts and attended his parties? They too saw in the motorcycle-loving Dylan something of an

outsider like themselves, perhaps even the James Dean figure for the 1960s that so many others saw too.

Dylan was known to ride a 500cc 'Tiger' T-100 Triumph in the Woodstock area, a 1965 model, with the telltale 'garden gate' style logo on the red/gray gas tank confirming it as a Tiger model. Dylan's Woodstock associates remember him owning a Triumph 500cc Thunderbird, a slightly smaller version of the Bonneville. However, the famous Daniel Kramer photographs of a helmetless Dylan riding a motor-cycle outside Woodstock are of a different bike, according to ex-professional rider John Samways. "The model Dylan is riding in that shot of him without a helmet is something I can identify absolutely. That is a 1964 TR6S/R, a Triumph Trophy Roadsports, and it is a 650 single-carb Triumph, which they proudly described as 'full power.' That bike is basically a Triumph Bonneville model with a single carb, although the trim on the bike is different. This is definitely the bike Dylan is riding in the famous Daniel Kramer photographs.

"Dylan's bike is a bit more sporty, perhaps, than a regular Triumph," says Samways. "They had several different grades, and the Bonneville was their top of the line in sporty bikes. I would say what Dylan is riding is the next one down."

Although British-made, the Triumph motorcycles manufactured in Coventry for the American market were selling very well in the 1960s. Even the model names such as Bonneville and Saint were specifically chosen for U.S. consumption. Bob Dylan was not the only American who felt these bikes were the equal of the homegrown Harley-Davidsons. The U.S.A. was well into the era of muscular gas-guzzling cars, and Americans primarily sought fast and potentially dangerous motorcycles. Triumph was making the models specifically for the States with smaller gas tanks, different paint jobs, stainless steel fenders, shorter mufflers, and high-rise handlebars. Dylan is also shown in photos taken around the Woodstock area riding one of these Triumphs with the higher handlebars.

Bob Dylan is not a big person and he is not tall. Like all proper '60s rock'n'rollers he is of slight build, with muscle tone not apparent in his appearance. A larger Triumph, or for that matter Harley-Davidson, is less than ideal for a man of such a physical frame. Those bikes are heavy. British motorcycle lover David Lindsey said that Ramblin' Jack Elliott revealed his A.J.S. bike, probably also a 500cc, had been left at Woodstock as it had a dodgy rear wheel. It has been reported that Dylan had driven Ramblin' Jack's A.J.S. before and it might well have been the bike left in Grossman's garage. Ramblin' Jack did leave a bike in Grossman's garage but he denies Dylan ever rode it. When I ask Elliott, he thinks carefully before stating down a transatlantic phone line: "No sir, I don't think Bob and I ever rode each other's bikes and I sure don't remember ever telling him to take my A.J.S. anywhere for repairs. No." [2]

Which leads us to the accident itself, on July 29, 1966.

Motorcycle pro John Samways, having read that Dylan's brakes were locked when he fell off the motorcycle that morning, explains what might have happened. "A lot of people riding here in the U.S.A. seem afraid of the front brake and they only use the back brake, which is easy to lock. If [Dylan] was going along and he might have been blinded by the sun and a corner was coming up, if he had locked either brake – the front or the back or both – the bike probably would have slid out from under him and he would perhaps have been behind the bike.

"Now, whether the bike went down a ditch, whether it slid into a tree, or whether it slid to a stop I don't know. But if there wasn't anything that it hit then Dylan should not have gotten hurt too much. Road rash, yes," says Samways, meaning the scabs and scrapes you would get from sliding along the asphalt. However, Samways says it would have been worse if Dylan had slid into the bike or slid down a ditch and then into the bike. "Or in some cases sometimes you slide off and fall in front of the bike and the bike hits you, and that is certainly where you can get hurt.

"I'm thinking Dylan would probably have been behind the bike if he'd have locked the brakes. The bike would simply slide out, and on those older bikes the brakes aren't so powerful that you would go over the top

of the bike's handlebars. But again, that is a possibility, and it sounds like he got hurt pretty badly. Today, we have little specific idea what the injuries were, but if he did get hurt pretty badly I would think he either hit something or he hit the bike or the bike hit him." [3]

Another aspect of what happened to Dylan that day was the very bad publicity for Triumph, who were trying to establish a greater presence in the U.S. market. Somehow they managed to keep out of the newspapers the brand and model of the motorcycle that the rock'n'roll singer was riding. Nonetheless, the company declared bankruptcy in 1976. According to David Lindsey, this may have had more to do with the fact that the Triumphs "vibrated like a lawn mower and leaked oil everywhere. But those bikes had class." [4]

Later, when the events of July 29, 1966 came up online, Peter Martin, a fellow northern Minnesota Iron Range homeboy, wrote in to a Dylan blog. He said: "I got to meet Bob Dylan at a photo show that I was in back in the mid '80s. Ramon Muxter, the headliner of the show, was an old acquaintance of Dylan, who happened to be hanging around the Twin Cities that weekend. Bob and a few pals dropped in for a look. Being an Iron Ranger myself, and having Bob looking at my pictures of motorcyclists and their bikes, I started chatting with him. We talked for a bit, and I asked him if he still rode bikes. He looked at me like I was a ghost, and said something like, 'No, I almost died on one...,' and he gave me the impression that he completely lost interest in riding when he had the accident." [5]

What is known is that Bob and wife Sara were at the Grossmans' Bearsville house on Striebel Road that fateful Friday morning in July and Bob wanted to take an old motorcycle from storage in the garage and ride it to a repair shop outside of Woodstock. Sara drove behind him in a family car.

Author Howard Sounes reported that as the Dylans left, Grossman's wife Sally was on the phone talking to her husband, who was in Manhattan, and that she continued to talk on the phone when the Dylans reappeared in her driveway a short time later.[6] The Dylans could have turned to the right or to the left at the end of the Grossmans' driveway at the southern end of Striebel Road: either way would have taken them to Woodstock. However, the shortest route would be by turning left, to go south, and shortly taking another left onto Tinker Street, driving eastward on Tinker to enter Woodstock from the west. The Grossmans' home was a very short distance (perhaps 500 feet) from the junction of Striebel Road and Tinker Street.

It is possible that the Dylans turned right out of the Grossmans' home on to Striebel Road and headed north, but they would have had to travel nearly a mile to the intersection with Glasco Turnpike, and then turn right, driving eastward and back towards their Byrdcliffe home, eventually entering Woodstock from the north. But they were not headed home; Sara Dylan brought the car to pick up Bob once he dropped his motorcycle off for repairs in Woodstock. So it stands to reason that they turned left off the Grossman property for the shorter drive to Woodstock.

Dylan said he looked into the sun while riding the bike that morning. The sun would be in the east, having yet to rise to its highest position of the day. This suggests he may have been traveling east on Tinker Street, but he could have been on almost any local road and looked momentarily into the sun: it was late morning when the accident happened and the bright summer sun would have been quite visible over the treetops.

Local police, whose phone manners confirm they have been asked this before, cannot or at least will not confirm where the accident was, but they do state emphatically that there was no police report made at the time from the scene of the accident.

Striebel Road is a steep rolling ride and Dylan was noted for being an erratic automobile driver with less than perfect eyesight. Therefore it is fair to surmise that he might also be an erratic motorcyclist with less than perfect eyesight. This together with the topographical layout of Striebel Road in particular and Sally Grossman's emphasis that the Dylans were not gone long suggests the accident most probably happened on that

brief stretch of Striebel Road between the Grossmans' and Tinker Street or just after the turn on Tinker Street as he headed east into the sun. On such a sunny morning with a motorcyclist like Bob Dylan riding a bike that needed repairs, it is not hard to imagine an accident occurring such as the facts suggest and such as John Samways described earlier.

Ramblin' Jack Elliot often rode motorcycles with Dylan in the Woodstock area in the 1960s. He remembers that Dylan loved Triumphs and was seen riding several models, although Elliott primarily remembers Dylan on a Twin Triumph 500. He had known Dylan for some time when the accident occurred, he says, having met the day he arrived from England in 1961.

"I was tickled when I did meet Bob as he was kind of a cute kid," says Elliott, "19 years old, peach-fuzz on his face, and he said he had all of my English recordings, the six LPs I recorded for a label called Topic Records in England. Bob said he liked these albums a lot and that he sure enjoyed the way I played the guitar and stuff.

"Anyway, I used to visit Bob on my motorcycle and go up that gravel driveway, and there was a sign on the tree which said, IF YOU HAVEN'T TELEPHONED YOU ARE TRESPASSING. I'd go up there and visit Bob and I then had an A.J.S. motorcycle. I went back to Europe for a brief tour in 1962 and purchased an A.J.S. 500 single motorcycle, like a Matchless single carb, and yes, I did end up parking it in [Albert Grossman's] garage. It was parked right next to Bob's Triumph and it stayed there for the winter of '65–'66. I kept it in Albert's garage as it was winter time and too cold to do any riding. It was a nice safe indoor place to leave the bike. Bob always rode his Triumph and I rode my A.J.S. and, as I said, I don't think we ever rode each other's bikes."

Elliott recalls that Dylan's bike, also in Grossman's garage, was a 500 Twin Triumph, and he thinks it may have been blue. "I remember I had been riding with Jesse Colin Young one day. I got back to Woodstock from this beautiful ride and I called Albert. I said, 'Hey, is Bob home?' And Albert said, 'Bob's in the hospital, Jack.' And I said, 'What's the matter?'

Albert said, 'Bob had an accident with his bike, the rear wheel locked up.' I asked if I could go visit Bob in the hospital and Albert said no, Bob was under sedation and not ready to receive visitors but he would be all right. So I just said, 'OK, give him my best,' and I didn't get to see Bob. Didn't go to any hospital, didn't have anyone else in Woodstock that I wanted to see, so I went back on down to New York City."

Elliott didn't see much of Dylan for some time, about three years or so. "He was then developing this Basement Tapes music but I never saw the basement or the Big Pink house where they lived." And with this, Ramblin' Jack pauses before stating reflectively: "Hmm, you know, I don't even know where it is! And we must've rode past it a few dozen times on our bikes, Bob and me." [7]

Al Aronowitz is a writer and Dylan insider (and so in thrall to Dylan's genius that he later boasted about being given the job of looking after Bob and Sara's luggage at the Isle of Wight festival). He remembers that the events of that July day had a deep effect on Dylan, who told him: "That accident came like a warning ... and I heed warnings!" Aronowitz has written that Dylan told him he broke his neck in the motorcycle accident and that Dylan claimed he had hurtled through the air when thrown from the Triumph towards the side of the road, his life flashing in front of him, thinking for sure he was about to die. [8]

Paul Williams writes confidently that Dylan's injuries were minor, a cracked vertebra (spinal bone) in the neck requiring him to wear a brace after a brief hospital visit. [9] Dylan told journalist Robert Shelton that he'd been awake for three days before he fell off his motorcycle – and if that doesn't suggest Dylan was having trouble getting back into a domestic lifestyle with his family in Woodstock and out of the write/record/tour/tour-some-more lifestyle, then nothing does or ever could. [10]

In 1987, in an *Esquire* piece, Dylan told Sam Shepard: "It was real early in the morning on the top of a hill, near Woodstock. I can't even remember how it happened. I was blinded by the sun ... I was drivin' right straight into the sun, and I looked up into it even though I remember

someone telling me a long time ago when I was a kid never to look straight at the sun. ... I went blind for a second and I kind of panicked or something. I stomped down on the brake and the rear wheel locked up on me and I went flyin'. ... [My wife] was following me in a car. She picked me up. Spent a week in the hospital, then they moved me to this doctor's house in town. In his attic. Had a bed up there in the attic with a window lookin' out. Sara stayed there with me." [11]

Dylan's bassist Rick Danko told fellow band member Levon Helm of the accident and said Dylan had hurt his neck, specifically that he had broken bones in his neck.[12] Guitarist Robbie Robertson visited Dylan in Woodstock shortly after the accident. "As I recall," he says, "it wasn't like he was in traction or anything but Bob had hurt himself and was wearing a neck brace. There wasn't much difference to me. He was still staying up all night and smoking a million cigarettes." [13]

The *New Musical Express* in London reported in August 1966 that Dylan had broken neck vertebrae and suffered a concussion. Clinton Heylin, as well researched a Dylan biographer as there is, believes "the extent of the physical damage seems to have been cracked vertebrae and mild concussion."[14] Film-maker D.A. Pennebaker visited Dylan a few days after the accident and says Dylan was in a neck brace. *Time* magazine's August 12 edition said Dylan was not wearing a crash helmet and reported "severe face and back cuts." [15]

Author Barney Hoskyns claims the accident was on Striebel Road and that Dylan "did break several vertebrae in his neck, as well as suffer concussion and bruising."[16] Howard Sounes writes that Sally Grossman believes the incident occurred on Glasco Turnpike but that a friend of Bob's who insists on anonymity claims it was on Striebel Road, just outside the Grossmans' driveway. Mrs. Grossman told Sounes that Dylan had no obvious injuries and was conscious.

All of which tells us what, exactly?

The obvious answer is that the extent of his injuries is a matter of some real dispute by Dylan's biographers. In true Dylanesque fashion, nothing was revealed. The fact remains, 40 years down the line, that none of Dylan's biographers will probably ever turn over the exact stone that uncovers the true answer as to how badly he was hurt. In today's Information Superhighway age of ruthless tabloid journalism, of celebrities being famous for being famous, the public would no doubt be able to find out chapter and verse about what Dylan's medical report said. However, in 1966 this was impossible without either someone in the know volunteering such information or a burglary charge being filed against an overzealous Dylan researcher.

It says much that Dylan and Grossman made no move whatsoever to clear up any mystery about the accident but kept the truth of the singer's injuries wrapped tightly in rumors that were soon surrounded by myths. Dylan is notorious for seldom if ever giving a straight answer.

In 1966, at a major intersection of his private life and his professional plans, he took that philosophy a step further. To all the questions being asked he gave no answers at all.

Howard Sounes reports that Dylan was not taken to the Kingston hospital 15 minutes away but to Dr. Ed Thaler's home and practice in Middletown, about an hour's drive away. The *New Musical Express* in early November claimed "this was no ordinary convalescence – [Dylan] didn't just slip away to some country retreat where he could nurse his injuries" [17] when that is pretty much exactly what he did.

Perhaps tellingly, no ambulance was called by Mrs. Dylan or by Mrs. Grossman, nor has anyone ever claimed that Dr. Thaler called in any specialists or outside medical help. Had Dylan been severely injured, surely an ambulance would have been called and he would have gone to the nearest available medical facility? Dylan stayed in Dr. Thaler's home for six weeks. Six weeks – and yet he had a family and a comfortable home an hour's drive away in Byrdcliffe. Dr. Thaler and Dylan's wife Sara denied that the reason he stayed there for so long was in an attempt to get off drugs, but it is easy to see how such a rumor could spread. Nor is it any great leap of faith to see where a 25-year-old man in some pain, moving around slowly in a neck brace upstairs at a trusted friend's home, would take some real quality time to reflect on his life and where it was going. The smart money is placed on Dylan doing precisely that, starting at the Thalers' home and then continuing this reassessment at his own home near Woodstock.

The reassessment was complex. Who was he dealing with? Why was he dealing with such people? Was the entire ballgame about being Elvis? Why were there those who hailed him as some kind of Messiah? How could he balance the long tours with family life? When would he have time to finish his novel, *Tarantula*? Was the image shown of him in the upcoming ABC-TV special, his *Eat The Document* image, the real Bob Dylan? If this special was shown on network TV across the States, that image would be further cemented in the public's collective memory bank. So was this how the artist wanted to be perceived by millions of casual TV viewers as well as his hardcore faithful?

Dylan said later: "The turning point was back in Woodstock. A little after the accident. Sitting around one night under a full moon I looked out into the bleak woods and said, 'Something's gotta change.' There was some business that had to be taken care of." [18]

And so Dylan biographers have written that the business was taken care of when actually it was not. Certainly the next part of the world tour was cancelled – but Grossman would later rearrange the dates. Dylan could play the Yale Bowl and Shea Stadium another time. The ABC-TV special was delivered but rejected. *Tarantula* publication was postponed for the foreseeable future as publishers Macmillan and artist Dylan were in agreement that it needed more work yet were in some disagreement as to what the book should actually be.

Dylan's contract with his record company was coming up for renewal, but this was not dealt with in any haste. A firm recording offer had arrived from MGM, and Dylan and Grossman were considering that, but it would take until July 1, 1967 for Dylan to re-sign with Columbia.

He took the ABC-TV footage made by Pennebaker and began shooting more film for *Eat The Document* around Woodstock as well as editing and editing and editing this sprawling mass of intriguing footage with the help of the more experienced Howard Alk. Pennebaker was more experienced than Alk at editing but dropped out of the process, even though the 1966 live tour footage had been shot by Pennebaker, a man respectfully and teasingly called 'the Eye' by Dylan. Pennebaker was exasperated by Alk's ideas about film and by Grossman's demand that he be of more help to Dylan in the editing. Pennebaker pointed out he was hired on this project to film but not to edit.

All this is definitely not dealing firmly with situations. It is not changing things. It is postponing things, pushing away projects and big decisions until they simply have to be dealt with or else.

What did change was not so much the business but Dylan himself. The rooster stopped his loud, emphatic, compelling crowing. The artist sought time out, which was granted by Grossman. Or perhaps it was demanded by Dylan while Grossman did a slow burn.

The revenue stream would dry up sooner or later if TV shows were not accepted, books were not delivered, concerts not performed, new material not recorded. This was the ever-changing 1960s and a pop music career lasting longer than three chart years was considered remarkable. If Dylan took months and months off without releasing a single every 90 days, as was the norm, then surely the mercurial pop audience would forget about him and move on? Grossman had every reason for concern.

A secondary reason for Grossman's concern, and an example of how tightly wound the 25-year-old Dylan must have been, came with the postponements and cancellations of projects that required lawyers and signed contracts, which inherently brought the possibility of advances being returned (a manager's nightmare) and lawsuits being filed against the artist (a manager's nightmare). When one signs on the dotted line the game is then afoot, as Sherlock Holmes would so accurately tell Watson, and getting out of deadlines and commitments when so much money is at stake is a near impossibility.

But there is one clear exit route that is usually accepted without dispute. If an artist is ill or incapacitated, no one can reasonably expect said artist to deliver. As contracts contain clauses for force majeure and acts of God they also more often than not contain get-out clauses in case of injury or serious illness to the artist. No one can reasonably expect an injured prima ballerina to dance; no one can expect a famous athlete to play with a broken arm; no one expects a man thrown violently off a motorcycle and with injuries requiring a lengthy convalescence to tour the world while simultaneously finishing a novel and editing a TV special. The artist has to recover first in order to work at his full capacity.

Dylan and Grossman would have recognized this. In the 1960s, a popular singer who went out of the public eye would soon be forgotten. With Dylan in 1966–67, the opposite happened. Dylan's time off after the accident and low profile gave his story a mythic proportion that neither he nor Grossman could possibly have anticipated. Just as that portion of the public devoted to pop music was absorbing the relatively new image of Dylan the curly-haired cuban-heeled lyrical genius of 'Visions Of Johanna,' and just as the public at large was finally grasping that the earlier Protest Singer was gone forever, the man born Robert Allen Zimmerman was accepting that things had to change. And so they did. First Bob Dylan changed. Changed his appearance, changed his attitudes toward work and career, and finally changed his greater goals in life. Then his music changed. Again.

# 4. You Are What You Eat The Document

*Shooting and editing two movies*

Following his July 29 motorcycle accident, Bob Dylan is reported to have spent six weeks recovering at the Middletown home of Dr. Thaler and his wife before finally moving back to his own missus and his *Hi Lo Ha* home near Woodstock, some time around the end of the second week of September '66. While his life is well documented up until then, almost nothing is known for certain about his activities during the last 100 or so days of the pivotal pop-music year of 1966. Instead, we know what he didn't do and what he was alleged to have done.

Dylan didn't perform any concerts. He didn't finish his novel *Tarantula* to his or his publisher's satisfaction. He didn't record a note in a formal recording studio where the studio clock ticked away the fee. Apparently (and let us stress that word) he did not write many songs. And he certainly did not rehearse with The Hawks, even though they were still on retainer.

He is alleged to have enjoyed family life, wisely spending quality time playing with his kids and at some point acquiring two large dogs, Hamlet and Buster, both of whom enjoyed biting people, with Buster the worst offender. Guitarist and singer Happy Traum – who would duet with Dylan on re-recordings of three Basement Tapes cuts on the popular 1971 collection *Greatest Hits Vol.II* – said later: "I never met such a dedicated family man. … Dylan shut out the world of show business and all the Manhattan craziness and turned into such an ordinary guy that he was actually a little boring to be around."[1]

It is known that at some point in August the Dylans received Allen Ginsberg, who arrived with a trunk full of poetry books he thought Dylan would enjoy reading. So Dylan had his family and he had his books. For some people that is enough. For Dylan clearly it was enough for a while. Then the old creative restlessness began to make itself known again.

The artistic drive and curiosity – which allowed him to think that a world tour, a novel, and a TV special were three things he could accomplish while also writing and recording new songs – became the itch that had to be scratched. Walking his daughter to the school-bus stop every morning was a typical dad's chore for millions but for Dylan it was a new experience to enjoy. It helped put him on a different clock than his

regular cycle of writing, touring, and recording. But what was he to do with the rest of the day?

Dylan had his family in Byrdcliffe at *Hi Lo Ha*. His manager Albert Grossman lived three miles west near Bearsville. Late 1966 saw his dear friend Bob Neuwirth in and out of the house on various missions both social and creative. Al Kooper remembers a visit chez Dylan around this time with Dylan's old Minneapolis compadre Tony Glover on hand. Photographer Barry Feinstein saw Grossman on business in New York City, was called up to Woodstock for a visit, and liked the area so much he bought property there. Other friends from the old days were occasionally about but there was no open-house policy at *Hi Lo Ha*. In fact a new sign next to Hamlet and Buster's kennel clearly stated PRIVATE PROPERTY. NO TRESPASSING.

Perhaps the longest shadow was cast by neither visiting man nor biting beast but D. A. Pennebaker's footage of the 1966 world tour. Pennebaker and Neuwirth made a rough cut of the film at Dylan's request but Dylan felt the result was too close to *Dont Look Back* and decided he would attempt an edit. He set up a film-editing suite in a spare room at his home. (Pennebaker has recalled asking Grossman's office for a copy of his original cut for posterity and never receiving one, and fears his original cut is therefore lost forever as Dylan used parts of it for his edit. However, some of Pennebaker's work survives in the 45-minute short film he edited out of *Eat The Document* footage, *Something Is Happening*.)

Dylan's tour was off, the pressure for new songs was seemingly gone for now, the book was postponed indefinitely – so why not take a crack at this footage left lying around? Whether this was Dylan's curiosity getting the better of him, his creative juices flowing again, or a simple case of Boys With Toys will never be proven in a court of law, but Bob Dylan did decide to be a film editor. With Pennebaker elsewhere and Neuwirth making plans to live in a commune (which he did in 1967) Dylan knew he needed an ally, someone more experienced in cinema, to work alongside him as he learned the basics of synchronization, match cuts, thematic continuity, and all the other fundamental rules of editing film.

Howard Alk – the imposing figure later seen standing against the car to the rear of Dylan on the *No Direction Home* package – was an old friend of Dylan's from Chicago. He was soon recruited to help Bob edit the footage for the proposed *Eat The Document* film – which ABC-TV would eventually reject when they saw it, claiming it was "incomprehensible" and that if it was shown as intended as part of their *Stage '66* series it would pale beside the other offerings that television season. The film remains formally unreleased at the time of writing, although it has been screened at film festivals and special showings.

Alk's credentials are not without merit. Together with director Paul Sills and actor Bernard Sahlins he founded Chicago's Second City theatre company, which later gave the world stars such as John Belushi, Bill Murray, Gilda Radner, and Mike Myers, the great satirical comic behind super spy Austin Powers. A graduate of the University of Chicago, Alk was a performer with little talent but a warehouse full of chutzpah and a quick wit that enabled him to go onstage and seemingly get away with anything. He played the guitar and sang. He was involved in the avant-garde art scene and the local folk clubs in Chicago. Those clubs drew him into the orbit of folk-club owner and folk-act manager Albert Grossman.

In 1959, Alk was film editor on the short documentary *Cry Of Jazz*. Early 1963 found him operating The Bear, a music venue not named after Albert Grossman. Nonetheless, he took Grossman's phone call and booked the relatively unknown Bob Dylan for two nights in April for almost no fee but some necessary local exposure. (It could be argued this is a rare example of someone getting the better of Grossman.)

Grossman somehow bonded with Alk during negotiations, and on the two concert nights in April, Dylan too made lifelong friends with the burly Alk. Alk later helped edit Murray Lerner's wonderful musical documentary film *Festival*. Anyone who saw that had to be impressed as Dylan, Howlin' Wolf, Son House, Joan Baez, and many more gave stirring performances, memorably presented and preserved.

Pennebaker used Alk as a cameraman on *Dont Look Back* in 1965. The following year saw the two involved in film again, but with the roles

somewhat changed, as Alk and Pennebaker were hired at Dylan's behest for what became *Eat The Document*. This time around it would be Bob's film and not Pennebaker's.

Alk and Dylan had tinkered with some of the footage in June 1966 before the motorcycle accident put the project on hold. Sometime in October or November the idea of editing the Pennebaker tour footage again began to sound like a good one to Dylan, and Alk was formally recalled to Woodstock from New York City to help the one-time Spokesperson For A Generation do something new with this life, something different with his time. Those hours after walking his daughter to the bus stop for school had to be filled. His backing band were sitting in the Gramercy Park Hotel and wondering when they would next be called to rehearse. They were still on retainer and their hours had to be filled as well.

Robbie Robertson remembers those very days. "I went up from New York as Bob was editing footage from the tour. I was staying at his place and I would help him out on it sometimes. He went on a vacation with his family for a couple of weeks and I worked on the film with Howard Alk at that time. [Dylan and Alk] were experimenting with something where they were just trying to kinda see what happens in the film via this experiment. I would go up to Bob's house from New York City for a few days here and there and we'd play some music or talk about stuff. He and Howard would show me some things in the film. I would work on a little music on my own. That was kinda the process for right then."[2]

Dylan decided to shoot additional scenes for *Eat The Document*. Curiously, his interest was dwindling in Pennebaker's dramatic performance footage from the 1966 tour, which so fascinates and dazzles all those who have seen it to this very day. Instead, he wanted to create original scenes, as if he were an experienced cinematic auteur.

The Hawks were rehearsing as best they could in New York City, with no permanent drummer, and demoing songs at photographer Barry Feinstein's place. Feinstein had shot the memorable jacket picture for the *Times They Are A-Changin'* album and had been on part of the '66 world tour taking photographs. He confirms that The Hawks certainly did use his studio.

"I wanted to help them out, and they were getting on their feet musically, so why not? I suppose they were close enough for Albert [Grossman] to keep his eye on them from his office not too far away. Oddly, I never really did hear the stuff Robbie, Ricky [Danko], and Richard [Manuel] were cutting in my photography studio. I didn't hear the demos done there, although they used something from my studio on their recent boxed set. Which sounded good. I should have paid more attention! I just told those guys they could use the studio at night, after hours when I was not there. This studio was on East 73rd Street between York and the river." [3]

*The Band: A Musical History* was an impressive boxed-set collection released in 2005 that does indeed include a Richard Manuel song, 'Beautiful Thing,' from Feinstein's photography studio. The accompanying credit states it was recorded there in fall 1966. Only Rick Danko and Richard Manuel are on the demo and the song is less than two minutes long, but you can hear the beauty they are striving for, the very human ache in Manuel's voice, and how The Hawks' R&B is starting to fade away as a newer sound takes a tentative step forward.

"There was a certain madness when we were first playing with Bob," says Robbie Robertson. "The phenomenon, this musical revolution that was going on. People made it into something which took the innocence right out of it, but it also made something happen and that is what a good revolution does. But the revolution doesn't go on forever. Things do change because of it and that's good." [4]

While living in New York City, The Hawks became involved in another separate film project that did nonetheless overlap to some extent with *Eat The Document.* Peter Yarrow of Peter Paul & Mary was a good friend of Dylan and The Hawks, and by all accounts he was a warm, generous man who, like his friend Bob, wanted to try his hand at film-making. Mary Travers was the 'Mary' of PP&M, and she was then married to Barry Feinstein.

Peter Paul & Mary were an influential act throughout pop's most potent decade. In 1963, remember, the bestselling LPs in the U.S.A. were *West Side*

*Story* and the first two PP&M records. Even after The Beatles appeared the following year, annual sales figures showed three PP&M LPs in the Top 12 bestselling albums. Even after Dylan went electric, the trio's largely acoustic sound remained well represented in the charts for years thanks to a string of hit singles. Yarrow was harmonizing all the way to the bank, and as an artist who was growing and changing like his friend Dylan he felt compelled to document the 1960s scene.

It would be a cultural contribution. Yarrow hired Feinstein to film a Hell's Angels meeting, figuring that the Angels were a good representative of the decade's breakaway flavor. Subsequently, Feinstein filmed the Los Angeles Teenage Fair, a dropout house of runaways in California, and a Mothers Of Invention concert. He shot an old Woodstock artist named Clarence Schmidt at his bizarre home, and the Human Be-in of January 14, 1967 in San Francisco, plus an enormous African-American talking nonsense on the phone who insisted on being referred to as Super Spade (and who, in a sad but true example of the '60s dream gone wrong, was not long afterwards murdered by professional drug dealers in San Francisco).

If the juxtaposition of all that sounds a bit like *Eat The Document* or possibly *Renaldo & Clara*'s sharp cuts and dramatic turns, this may well be explained by the fact that Howard Alk was the film editor for this project. It was *You Are What You Eat*.

Barry Feinstein rates Alk as a good film-maker. "He was great, even. He was inventive, and he proved that with his editing of some of my footage for the film I directed, *You Are What You Eat*, and with his work on political films he did later and on *Renaldo & Clara* and his *Hard Rain* TV special with Bob."

Feinstein says that he directed *You Are What You Eat*. "I just thought that in this particular period, everyone was in make-up and seemingly everyone interesting was in costume, and that this would make a great documentary of the time. We thought we'd have a lot on the Hell's Angels, and they are in the film, but a lot of it is here in Woodstock, with locals like Clarence Schmidt."

Four of The Hawks had a screen credit in *You Are What You Eat*, explains

Feinstein, because they played behind Tiny Tim. "This was recorded in New York when they were off the road after working with Bob. Tim duets with [his girlfriend] Eleanor Baruchian. The footage of Tiny Tim singing was shot in my photography studio in New York, the same one in which [The Hawks] were cutting demos at night. The screaming girls at The Beatles concert were not from Shea Stadium, as many people think, but from their last concert, the one at Candlestick Park in San Francisco." [5]

Peter Yarrow knew The Hawks from the road before they had hooked up with Dylan and says he got them to back up Tiny Tim in *You Are What You Eat*. "I was friendly with all of them. In different ways. Garth was such a gentle, book-ish, amazing musician. Levon was a bit of a hellion. Robbie was straight and brilliant and the one I related to most directly. Rick was an amazing bassist and a free spirit and a bit of a hellion. Richard was just all heart; what a sweetheart. I was close to them but this was external to my relationship to Bob." [6]

Again it was cinema and not music that was bringing together the cast of characters who would later make the Basement Tapes, *John Wesley Harding*, and the classic first two LPs by The Band.

Several bootleg releases of Basement Tapes material cut by Dylan and The Hawks (as they were still known) contain material with Tiny Tim's unmistakable lead vocals, but Robertson denies emphatically that this had anything to do with the later Basement Tapes sessions in and around Woodstock. "We were all still living in New York and we hadn't moved up to Woodstock yet, not at this point," he says. "Albert Grossman knew we were just a little frustrated in the city trying to get places rented where we could make some music and work on some music, because you were always disturbing somebody. We didn't have a soundproof isolation-booth kinda place we could go to in order to play."

Feinstein's photography studio proved a useful location for them. "If we worked there at night there was no one next door at the other offices, so we were not bothering anybody. We did a little bit, but it was just Rick, Richard, and me, and then finally Garth [Hudson] came. When Garth came, that's when we had more of a recording possibility. That's when we did the stuff with Tiny Tim, at Barry's studio in New York City." [7]

Recording behind Tiny Tim for the soundtrack of *You Are What You Eat* got the drummer-less Hawks working again. Thanks to the startling keyboard work of Garth Hudson on some of the Tiny Tim material, it is this music that is clearly the template for their later incarnation as The Band, where a more restrained and less R&B style is heard – a style they would develop on the Basement Tapes.

Mr. Tim, as Dylan called him, appears in the film as he essays 'Memphis' in a vocal style that both Chuck Berry and Leonard Chess might query. He subsequently duets warmly and sincerely with his girlfriend Eleanor Baruchian on Sonny & Cher's 'I Got You Babe.' As Feinstein confirms, Tim also sings 'Be My Baby' while Feinstein's footage of The Beatles' final concert performance is shown.

Tim's fourth song is Al Jolson's 'Climb Upon My Knee, Sonny Boy' and it provides the highlight of a wildly disjointed film. Written by Jolson, Buddy DeSylva, Lew Brown, and the great Ray Henderson in 1928, it was recorded by Ruth Etting in September of that year in New York City for Dylan's future label, Columbia Records. Etting was so popular in her day that she was promoted as America's Sweetheart, and even the later legendary version of the song by Jolson never quite captured the parental love evident in Etting's earlier recording. Tiny Tim was adept at taking songs from the early 20th century and presenting them to the 1960s audience – his signature song 'Tiptoe Through The Tulips' had been a huge hit for Nick Lucas in 1929. Tim was Dylan's guest at Byrdcliffe for several evenings in early 1967. The two most unusual voices of the decade would dine and then discuss the music of 40 years earlier.

Tiny Tim's sincere reading of 'Climb Upon My Knee, Sonny Boy' is heard while the film shows a young man in the communal Greta Garbo Home for Boys & Girls ingesting some ghastly drug that causes him to writhe and moan in great and obvious discomfort. It is the most striking scene in *You Are What You Eat* and an image that the few who saw the movie are unlikely to forget. Oddly, only 'Be My Baby' and 'I Got You Babe' appeared on the soundtrack LP in 1968. Perhaps even more oddly, the drummer credited on the CD reissue of *You Are What You Eat*, Bill LaVorgna, was Judy Garland's longstanding drummer at the time – hardly the makings of a Hawk.

Record producer John Simon was and is one of the leading talents in his field and was a primary force behind the first two Band LPs. He picks up the tale. "I had been a producer at Columbia Records and Al Kooper, then of Blood Sweat & Tears, told me it would make sense for me to be a freelance record producer rather than be on staff." Simon did not know that such a position existed or that royalties existed. The first album he worked on as a freelance was *Child Is Father To The Man* by Blood Sweat & Tears.

"Two different people had recommended me to Peter Yarrow to do the score to a movie called *You Are What You Eat*, sort of a documentary about the 1960s which started out as a documentary about the Hell's Angels." Simon says that the focus of the film changed when the team went to film the Angels and instead discovered a love-in. "So they said, OK, this will be a documentary about the '60s. And in the course of that I met Albert Grossman, who was Peter Yarrow's manager, as manager of Peter Paul & Mary."

Grossman suggested a deal: he needed someone to produce some of his artists; Simon needed some business help. "At the same time I had met the guys in The Hawks," says Simon, "because Robbie Robertson was a particular friend of film editor Howard Alk's. They had worked together on *Eat The Document*." [8] Simon had worked briefly with Robertson on March 8, 1965 in Columbia Studio A when ex-Chico Hamilton jazzman Charles Lloyd invited the guitarist to play on the last track of his *Of Course, Of Course* LP, a song with a very Band title: 'Third Floor Richard.' Simon was producing and Roy Halee was the engineer. The song Robertson allegedly plays on is archetypal New York City "yeah, man" jazz. One can imagine the participants all wearing berets and sporting goatees. Gabor Szabo was the guitarist on the LP and it sounds more than a bit like Szabo on 'Third Floor Richard,' and no second guitar is audible. Two cuts earlier, the song 'Goin' To Memphis' (also a Band-sounding title) begins with some guitar that also might be Robertson.

As producer on the Tiny Tim sessions, Simon confirms that members of

The Hawks did back up the singer on Mr. Tim's contributions to *You Are What You Eat*. Simon maintains that those tracks were recorded in a formal New York City studio and certainly not in Woodstock or even at Feinstein's photography studio.

Wherever they were recording, Albert Grossman knew The Hawks were still drawing a weekly salary and wanted them to work to earn it. So Tiny Tim was not the only singer they backed up while cooling their heels in New York City.

Carly Simon had some success with her sister Lucy in a folk duo logically called The Simon Sisters, long before she became a regular hit maker in the 1970s. Signed to Kapp Records, the duo graced the charts in 1964 with Lucy's musical arrangement of Eugene Field's 'Winkin', Blinkin' And Nod.' Somehow, younger sister Carly, stumbling around with little direction as a soloist, caught the eye of Grossman. "Once Lucy was married I got involved with manager Albert Grossman," she says. "Without my dear sister's protection, I was a sitting duck. [Grossman] offered me his body in exchange for worldly success. Sadly, his body was not the kind you would easily sell yourself for. My record, produced by Bob Johnston, was shelved, which was a shame because it was actually quite good."

Simon recalls that Grossman had Dylan re-write an Eric von Schmidt song for her, 'Baby Let Me Follow You Down.' It was a good, funky song, she says. "I was backed by Robbie Robertson, Paul Griffin, Mike Bloomfield, and Levon Helm. But that ended up on the shelf too. Then followed another attempt at commerciality, in which Grossman teamed me up with Richie Havens as Carly & The Deacon, but this team never made it into the studio."

Simon is being forthright but leaving out some details. She had discussed her upcoming session with Dylan in the week before his motorcycle accident. "I remember feeling I was being groomed as a female Dylan," she says, "so I met with Dylan in Albert's office after Bob had rewritten some of the words [to 'Baby Let Me Follow You Down']. This was about a week before his famous motorcycle accident, and he seemed like he was very high on speed: very, very wasted and talking incoherently, saying a lot about God and Jesus and how I would have to go down to Nashville [mimics Dylan's voice]: 'Hey … you know … oh … you … Nashville … the players … are just … you gotta … just, just … believe me!' And he stretched out his arms as if he were nailed to a cross, repeating, 'Believe me!' over and over." [9]

Grossman had seen The Simon Sisters perform in New York City and indeed had in mind that what the world really needed was a female counterpoint to Bob Dylan. Although writer and Band archivist Peter Viney maintains that the Carly Simon sessions arranged by Grossman were held in September 1967, this would have conflicted with The Hawks' own demo sessions. No way would a professional like Grossman let what looked like a hot property – the act soon to be The Band – become sidetracked into a session with an untested solo singer when he knew Warner Bros. and Capitol were currently expressing interest in his new group.

In late 1966, however, Messrs Robertson and the rest were looking for any decent excuse to get in the studio. And if Simon had discussed her upcoming Hawks–Grossman session with Dylan in the week before his motorcycle accident, then surely this would date the session to September 1966. Simon agreed it was 1966 in the lengthy 1973 *Rolling Stone* interview that she and James Taylor, her husband of the time, gave to Stuart Werbin. "I wasn't into writing songs at all then," she said. "We did a song that Dylan … changed the lyrics around for me, 'Baby Let Me Follow You Down,' it's really a guy's song, and [we did] a song that Bob Johnston wrote with Wes Farrell called 'Goodbye Lovin' Man,' a song they'd never heard me sing until I got into the studio. It was just one of those 'all right, we'll make a B-side quick.' … I just wasn't ready to be molded, even though I tried out of desperation because I wanted to be wanted." [10]

Grossman was no producer, as his demos done a year later for The Hawks would illustrate, but he did have taste and a finger on the pulse of the public's heartbeat. A photocopy of a faded session log reveals that the September 1966 N.Y.C. session for Carly Simon had a line-up of Robbie Robertson and Mike Bloomfield on electric guitars, Simon herself on

acoustic, "Ricky" Danko on bass, Richard Manuel, Al Kooper, and Paul Griffin on assorted keyboards, and Levon Helm on drums.

According to an eyewitness, Simon finally found the courage to stand up to Grossman and they had a very frank exchange of opinions as to the direction of the session. Grossman walked. Possibly he was not used to such a strong dispute from an artist so green – and from the tender gender, too. He brought in Bob Johnston to finish the recordings, the perfect producer if you wanted to get another Dylan of any gender. Four songs were completed by Johnston and company, including 'Baby Let Me Follow You Down' and 'Goodbye Lovin' Man.' Columbia turned them all down and the four finished tracks presumably languish in the Sony Music vaults to this very day (although Simon's take on 'Baby Let Me Follow You Down' has surfaced on a rare bootleg CD).

With this sad ending to what could have been a spectacularly stellar beginning to a young woman's career, The Hawks returned to Feinstein's photography studio for more demos, to the Gramercy Park Hotel for more rest, and to *You Are What You Eat* for piecemeal work doing whatever was required.

*You Are What You Eat* is less than a cinematic masterpiece but in many ways the ultimate late-1960s film, although *Eat The Document* might be up for that title as well. It's worth listening to dancer and scenester Carl Franzoni in conversation with John Trubee for the ultimate '60s summation of the film and the inventive and explosive era that Dylan had helped create (and from which he was now beginning to distance himself).

Franzoni was a member of Vito Paulekas's dance troupe, a prototype group of young California hippies who originally danced along wildly to The Byrds at Ciro's before moving on to Love and then The Mothers Of Invention. In *You Are What You Eat* they are seen dancing to the Mothers during a late-1966 gig by Zappa's band at the Shrine Auditorium in Hollywood. Feinstein was using a handheld camera with no sound-sync, so the music heard in the film at this point is a prototype jazzy hippie jam between Michael Bloomfield's new band The Electric Flag and John Simon.

"If you ever see this movie you'll understand what 'freaks' are," says Franzoni. "It'll let you see the L.A. freaks, the San Francisco freaks, and the

New York freaks. It was like a documentary and it was about the makings of what freaks were about. And it had a philosophy, a very definite philosophy: that you are free-spirited, artistic. ... There's a vignette the cameraman does in the lobby of this hotel, and he's talking to some of these kids, and they're so loaded they're ..." and at this point Franzoni imitates a speedfreak blabbering. "The logo for the movie is my tongue. That's where The Rolling Stones got the idea for the tongue. They were gonna buy the movie ... but they declined."

Franzoni says that *You Are What You Eat*, which played in third rate movie houses, ends with himself, Paulekas, and a friend called Sheldon Jarman onstage with Frank Zappa, amid black light and strobes. "So you only see us in part, here and there, and we're moving so fast it is almost an unbelievable thing that you're seeing. And the audience sees this crazy thing that's happening in front of them. This music, this powerful music ... I'm sure it's a blues number, because it's as high as it can go, and the flash of this light. ... Barry Feinstein is onstage with other cameras and they're shooting from all angles as this thing ends." [11]

In his liner notes to the 1997 soundtrack CD of *You Are What You Eat*, Peter Yarrow writes in a style reminiscent of the tone used by Howard Alk in his accompanying notes to the 1971 debut of *Eat The Document* in New York. "*You Are What You Eat* was a film production journey that lived the essence of the subject matter that it explored," writes Yarrow. "It is a documentary that was itself a fiction, embodying the spirit of 1960s non - linear thinking; a break with past process and society's rules. The process was inherently MTV in reverse, the sound track being added to a mélange of footage, shot in the crucible of experimentation of that era: the late 1960s immediately before the anti-Vietnam War movement exploded on the American scene. There was a reckless abandon, an innocence, and an excessiveness to the film which was haunted by the evolving tragedy of the legacy of drugs. ... The film's truth, if there was any, would be in the space created by this push-pull. The film-to-music relationship implied a kind of 'absurdity,' absurd in the sense of Dadaism. One was invited, if not compelled, to view and experience events with fresh eyes." [12]

For many, Dylan embodied the spirit of 1960s non-linear thinking and the breaking with past processes and society's rules – whether he enjoyed such a position or not. Further, his music compelled many to view and experience events with fresh eyes. Yet while clearly on the same boulevard as his artistic friends, he seemed to be traveling against the traffic as they flowed alongside it.

John Simon writes in the same 1997 soundtrack reissue: "Working on *You Are What You Eat* was my first experience in the town of Woodstock. Barry Feinstein had shot many, many reels of film. Howard Alk, the film editor, and I stayed in a house with two film-editing machines called Moviolas. Our task was to make sections of a good movie from what we saw. ... After *You Are What You Eat* I changed from a suit-wearing company man to a '60s Woodstock hippie and I never looked back!"[13] Don't look back, indeed. But another Woodstock artist-in-residence was about to start wearing suits.

*You Are What You Eat* is everything that post-motorcycle-accident Bob Dylan was trying to get away from. The soundtrack featured not just Tiny Tim but Harper's Bizarre, Paul Butterfield, Peter Yarrow, and some psychedelic freak-out jamming courtesy of the Electric Flag, dubbed onto the footage of Zappa's Mothers at the Shrine.

The credits for *You Are What You Eat* list appearances by Dylan cronies David Crosby, singer and songwriter John Herald, Donovan's wife-to-be Linda Lawrence, and such 1967 scene-makers as Chet Helms, Frank Zappa, Barry McGuire, Green & Stone (managers of Buffalo Springfieldand Sonny & Cher), and, curiously, songwriters Jerry Leiber and Mike Stoller, best known for writing hits for The Coasters and Elvis Presley. One might think with all these familiar names and all these friends involved, and with Howard Alk responsible for editing the footage, that Dylan The Sixties Icon would at least be comfortable with *You Are What You Eat*. Alk even edited the footage in a style he must have admired, as the pair used this very method on *Eat The Document* and again to an extent on *Renaldo & Clara*.

However, Dylan was changing his lifestyle and his appearance. He was slowly changing his image and would soon audibly change his music, even if the public would not hear that music for some time. "I had been in a motorcycle accident and I'd been hurt," Dylan would write later in his *Chronicles*, "but I recovered. Truth was that I wanted to get out of the rat race. Having children changed my life and segregated me from just about everybody and everything that was going on. Outside of my family, nothing held any real interest for me and I was seeing everything through different glasses."

Admittedly, anything Dylan says can be taken with a grain of salt. He is a past master of the put-on and put-down. His interviews are as full of left turns, unchallenged data, and surprising personal viewpoints as any in the history of the entertainment industry. Still, only a paragraph after the above sentences in *Chronicles*, he continues: "I had a wife and children whom I loved more than anything else in the world. I was trying to provide for them, keeping out of trouble, but the big bugs in the press kept promoting me as the mouthpiece, spokesman, or even conscience of a generation." See? I told you. "That was funny. All I'd ever done was sing songs that were dead straight and expressed powerful new realities. I had very little in common with and knew even less about a generation that I was supposed to be the voice of." [14]

Here is Dylan admitting to the change in his life and career – and a change that caught so many of his fans by surprise because they heard no new material between *Blonde On Blonde* (released May '66) and *John Wesley Harding* (December '67). No Spokesperson For A Generation, he. Fair enough. All the sweet, innocent little dear did was "sing songs that were dead straight and expressed powerful new realities." Which, bless him, he certainly did, as millions have witnessed.

Point being, m'Lord, with this knowledge to hand, can it be any wonder that the defendant was put on such a pedestal? His denial of having much in common with a generation who so warmly embraced him is more than a bit rich, since he and that generation, his own generation, had suffered the cold war together, had been through the folk boom together, had fought civil rights battles together, and had re-embraced electric rock'n'roll and the accompanying live-for-today

lifestyle that surrounded it then and now. When Dylan subsequently lost his love for the rock'n'roll lifestyle and moved toward family life, many other members of his generation were doing much the same. More and more of them left boring jobs in gray cities and left dreary classrooms in stifling universities for rural living, just at the moment the very first babies were born to these Baby Boomers, these peers of Dylan's, his own generation, his own audience. Not only did Dylan have a lot in common with this generation, he helped define them, helped shape their views. His songs inspired them, his lyrics were the favorite poetry of their days, and if he is not putting us on here ("all I'd ever done was sing songs..."), which this master of put-ons might just be, then he is kidding himself.

"Whatever the counterculture was, I'd seen enough of it," he writes in *Chronicles*.[15] Yes, the counterculture still fascinated millions who looked to it as an alternative and it fascinated dear Dylan friends like Yarrow, Alk, and Feinstein who felt called upon to document it in *You Are What You Eat*. But Dylan was beginning to make it clear he wanted in with the new and out with the old. He was not fascinated by the counterculture, he was frightened by it, by its disregard for the America that he so loved and by its dismissal of the family at the exact moment Dylan was proudly enjoying his new family. He was understandably irritated and frightened by those countercultural victims who trespassed on his property seeking answers from him at any given hour of the day.

So: in with the new for him, a new that was really the old; and out with the old, an old that to everyone else in the country seemed quite new and revolutionary. No more the galvanizing of R&B music with Beat-poetry lyrics. No more Anello & Davide boots. Not in his music, not in his films and TV specials.

If this new Dylan was uninterested in the groundbreaking, iconic performances and sounds that Pennebaker filmed of the old Carnaby Street-suited Dylan on his world tour of 1966, one can only imagine what His Bobness thought of a film, made by and featuring his friends, where hippie girls blowing bubble gum are juxtaposed against white-helmeted riot police, where long-haired boys enthusiastically eat flowers picked from a public park's flower bed, where Clarence Schmidt appears shirtless outside his whacked-out home of tin and aluminum in Woodstock. A film where dancer Carl Franzoni spins around ballroom floors like a chicken on narcotics while sticking his lengthy tongue out at every pretty girl within range, where marijuana is smoked while someone on the soundtrack vigorously wiggles the oscillator switch on a Moog synthesizer, and where a bare-chested Howard Alk takes his self-portrait on a Nikon in the southern California desert. A film where Indian music plays while topless women dance during a psychedelic light show – tellingly, this is one of the longest sustained scenes in the movie – and a young Rodney Bingenheimer stands motionless at the Teenage Fair.

All of Dylan's friends were still living in the 1960s that Dylan's music and attitude created. How could they not be? But the man himself had moved on. Bob Dylan was moving as far away from psychedelic light shows as was possible in both his private and professional lives, and every member of his entire private universe was in danger of becoming Mr. Jones. Even if they didn't know it.

Change was nothing new to Bob Dylan. His fans might have been startled when he adopted a new stance, but he had seemingly found the right professional home at Columbia. The record company's publicity guru Billy James had recently moved over to Columbia's subsidiary label Epic, where he was manager of Information Services. "It was not difficult for me to deal with Bob when he changed an image or his music," says James. "Why? Because I thought the guy was great. But it does present a challenge for marketing people. Yet every great artist has their period of change, of transition. I had been trained as an actor early on and had been a working actor, so I was attuned to and aware of the creative process and how creative people adapted and changed. So Bob's going from one style to another and changing his appearance was OK with me. And by the way, Goddard Leiberson, the president of Columbia at the time, thought the world of him." [16]

*You Are What You Eat* had assembled many of the characters involved in some of the most influential and pivotal music of the decade. Howard Alk, most of The Hawks, John Simon, and Albert Grossman all found

themselves becoming involved in the next chapter of Bob Dylan's musical journey, a chapter that would gain in importance as time slipped slowly forward.

Dylan once complained in an interview of "a time when psychedelic music was seemingly taking over the universe." [17] That psychedelic music was at least partially inspired by Dylan's outlandish stance and his sometimes unfathomably beautiful and poetic lyrics. Yet as 1966 drew to a close and psychedelia's banner year of 1967 rolled in, Dylan was moving to a music that would eventually sound the death knell of light shows, of painted women dancing in cages by the stage and 20-minute versions of folk songs, of Carnaby Street jackets and black boots with cuban heels. Lord John clothes would be a thing of the past and the Lord Our God would be somewhere in his present.

One man had the vision responsible for such a change, even if he did have a little help from his friends. Those friends knew what artistic vision was when they heard it and played it. Those friends were changing themselves, reacting to the times they had helped to create as they rode shotgun around the world alongside their boss. Pretty soon they would all be living around Woodstock, New York. Those friends of his were restless. They were itching to get to work.

# 5. The Summer Of Family Love

*Gathering and setting-up in Woodstock*

Bob Dylan's motorcycle accident has come to be viewed as a pivotal moment not only in his life but in his career. One of the givens among fans is that before his motorcycle accident Dylan was prolific and did little wrong, and that afterward he suffered a period of writer's block, that his creative streak ended when he fell off his Triumph that hot July morning.

Yet 1967, the year after the accident, is far and away the most prolific of Dylan's career. He would record week after week after week with Robbie Robertson, Rick Danko, Richard Manuel, and Garth Hudson (and, before the end of the year, with Levon Helm too). It proved to be his longest sustained period of recording – and he would still find the time and enthusiasm to travel to Nashville for a few more days of recording in order to complete the dozen songs for *John Wesley Harding*.

Dylan would record at least 60 originals in Woodstock in addition to his 12 for *John Wesley Harding*. He recorded a total of at least 107 different songs in Woodstock alone – including those new Dylan originals, plus around 32 imaginative cover versions of songs by his favorite artists, a dozen of his beloved traditional folk numbers, and a handful of humorous improvisations. And he may even have recorded a few more songs. Dylan collectors worldwide are still looking for the rumored 1967 versions of 'Wild Wolf,' 'Minstrel Boy,' and possibly some other minor miracle captured by Garth Hudson during one of those summer-of-love days up in Woodstock.

Dylan's sound audibly mutated into something different from what can reasonably be called the electric folk-rock of his mid-1960s music. But he still occasionally dealt in the surrealist, witty, sometimes unfathomably poetic lyrics as he had done in his days before the motorcycle spill. Any barroom musicologist could make an argument for the entire Americana/No Depression/alt.country scene beginning right there in Woodstock some time in the first half of '67. In fact, the sole non-American song recorded during all the Basement Tapes sessions is Rimsky-Korsakov's 'Flight Of The Bumble Bee,' and even then their improvisation is hardly a traditional reading of the piece. Admittedly, no

one knew until the bootleg tapes or until the first copies of the *Great White Wonder* LP bootleg hit the shops of Los Angeles that Dylan was going through this creative purple patch. But the Basement Tapes era of 1967 will probably go down as Dylan's most powerful period of sustained songwriting greatness.

A list of the pick of the compositions is enough to impress the Bob novice and send a large tantalizing chill down the spine of the Dylan fanatic: 'This Wheel's On Fire,' 'I Shall Be Released,' 'You Ain't Goin' Nowhere,' 'Tears Of Rage,' 'Nothing Was Delivered,' 'I'm Not There (1956),' 'Sign On The Cross,' 'Down In The Flood,' 'Too Much Of Nothing,' 'Quinn The Eskimo,' and 'Million Dollar Bash.' Such a list fails to include the classic material on *John Wesley Harding* like 'All Along The Watchtower' and 'I'll Be Your Baby Tonight,' songs surely written during the latter stages of recording the Basement Tapes.

If another songwriter had written any four of these songs in their career then that person would be considered a creative force of note. Dylan wrote each song on the list and then quite a few more in less than a calendar year and perhaps in as little as six months.

A rather startling sidebar to this remarkable activity comes when you compare the fruits of 1967 to the next few years of Dylan's career. He wrote over three dozen songs that sound completely composed and sorted out before he recorded them in Woodstock, while some two dozen more Basement Tapes Dylan originals sound created on the spot or perhaps only partially written beforehand. This is a total of some 60 new Bob Dylan songs in 1967, a high-water mark of creativity for the Bard Of Hibbing. And even some of Dylan's Basement Tapes songs that are clearly improvisations and not real identifiable songs are nonetheless bursting with musical and lyrical inventiveness.

During the following calendar year his inkwell would run almost dry and, to be quite specific, his new songs in the next half-decade after the Basement Tapes would be smaller in number as well as artistically weaker when compared to that dramatic burst of creativity in '67. Depending on your point of view, it would take until November 1973 and Dylan's reunion with The Band for the *Planet Waves* album or possibly until the September 1974 sessions for *Blood On The Tracks* for Dylan to get up and running at full steam again.

Dylan's activities in '67 seem now like a tremendous recovery from the motorcycle accident and the start of a new, abundantly creative period in his songwriting career. They appear in hindsight to mark the absolute high point and an emphatic exclamation point to a six-year pattern of creative growth unparalleled by any individual in the world of modern popular music.

The year began with The Hawks still in position as Dylan's faithful backing band, a team of hired hands called upon for their daring musical support and conscious or perhaps unconscious help in cultural change. Dylan did not discharge his musical partners, even though with no concerts scheduled it would make sense to stop paying the four Hawks their retainer, as he had only record royalties to rely upon now. But these particular musicians were special to him. He had asked The Hawks to tour the world and they had. They suffered for their art in a way that damn few MTV heroes will ever know. Now he would ask them to act in a motion picture and they would.

Before Christmas '67, The Hawks too would shift their sound, moving slowly away from the declaratory R&B of 1966 and morphing with apparent effortlessness into what became, for two grand, magnificent LPs at least, the ultimate rock'n'roll communal artistic effort. This was The Band, where no one member was any more important than the next.

There was no bootleg industry in 1967, and so the year would end with no secret tapes smuggled into vinyl pressing plants during clandestine late-night visits. His future as The Most Bootlegged Artist Ever had not begun. And yet the quality of the Dylan–Band Basement Tape acetates and reel-to-reel tapes that would be passed around the record industry would create a strong underground buzz. So strong that in 1969, when a copy fell into the hands of two young men in Los Angeles, they thought they

might go into the record biz themselves. They would do so in the gleeful hippie spirit of the day and inadvertently start today's black-market million-dollar rock music bootleg industry. Bob Dylan was their first artist and Basement Tapes songs (with a few relatively minor outside additions) made up the aesthetic core of their first release.

The whole Basement Tapes episode began innocently enough, Robbie Robertson claims. "The Band didn't go up to Woodstock to do some recording. That is not really true. The guys who became The Band went up there. Rick [Danko] and Richard [Manuel] came up at one point: they were doing some additional shooting for *Eat The Document*, they were still trying other experiments with the film, and they shot some things early in the year with the snow still on the ground. I don't think they were ever used, if I recall correctly, but that's how it all started." [1]

Robertson was already in Woodstock alongside Dylan, Howard Alk, and Bob Neuwirth as the Dylan–Alk axis devised yet more ingenious ways to edit Dylan's planned film, *Eat The Document*. Dylan and Alk would continue to edit the movie for years before agreeing on a cut that was shown in 1971 at the New York Academy of Music and later that year at New York's Whitney Museum of American Art. *Eat The Document* was finally broadcast on television in 1979 on New York City's WNET station.

A bootleg DVD of the film appeared in 2003 that included the legendary limousine ride where Dylan gets a lift from John Lennon while Bob Neuwirth films away and Rolling Stones employee Tom Keylock drives. Whatever the merits of the original footage and the multiple versions edited by Alk and Dylan, the film would provide much of the backbone for Martin Scorsese's dynamic *No Direction Home* documentary of 2005, which would have ended limply without the dramatic *Eat The Document* inserts.

Rick Danko remembered later: "When I first moved up to Woodstock in 1967 I went up there with Richard Manuel and Tiny Tim to work on Bob's movie *Eat The Document*. We stayed at the Woodstock Motel for a couple of weeks and, the country boy that I am, I realized that since I left Ontario and my home neighborhood I'd been living in cities for seven years, or however long it had been, and I realized I did not have to be in cities any more."[2] It was February 1967 when Danko, Manuel, and Tiny Tim were told by Dylan to come to Woodstock to shoot additional scenes for *Eat The Document*, scenes that Dylan cryptically explained might be used for another film he was thinking about doing, something about a circus. I'll say.

Yes, The Hawks had been recording tracks in Manhattan whenever they could, sometimes in Barry Feinstein's photography studio, sometimes behind singers such as Tiny Tim or the young Carly Simon. But that was dining on humble pie after the wild ride of the 1966 world tour. They'd been without direction since Dylan fell off that Triumph in July. Their six months of restlessness and creative wandering were about to come to an end.

There was indeed snow on the ground of Ulster County that February of 1967. The creeks were frozen over and, yes, the windows were filled with frost. Tree branches groaned with the white weight of last night's snowfall and only the winter wind broke the quiet softness of the woods around Overlook Mountain, its many snakes hibernating till the warmth of spring.

Leaving Manhattan at 3:00am in order to film at sunrise, Danko and Manuel were instructed upon arrival to unpack their instruments and back up Tiny Tim musically. The three of them performed songs in the cold early morning hours and then filmed some spots of their own until three in the afternoon, when they retreated to the Grossman home off Route 212. Sally Grossman greeted them there with logs crackling and blazing on the fireplace. They warmed their hands and welcomed the hot toddies served to warm the soul.

On subsequent days they rose at 5:00am to work, filming with Dylan and Alk in the first hours of daylight. The Canadians, like Robertson before their arrival, felt at home in the Woodstock winter. Danko the farm boy and Manuel the small-town son grew to appreciate the town and were reminded of the charms of rural life after all those years on the road with Ronnie Hawkins, the years with Helm when they were Levon & The Hawks, and finally with Dylan on his world tour. The big city was out for

now and Woodstock was home. Well, not quite. Originally, Danko and Manuel lived in the Woodstock Motel, as did Tiny Tim, who was very much a part of the Dylan–Grossman circle at the time. If the days of filming curious scenes were challenging and fun, the nights at the Woodstock Motel must have reminded Danko and Manuel of the road. Comfortable it was, although surely a step down from the Gramercy Park Hotel in New York City. A touch bohemian it might have been, too, but a home?

Danko rivaled Robertson as the business mind of The Band and was always thinking about where they were going collectively. And he rivaled Garth Hudson in having The Band's best memory. "These people had this restaurant in town where I ate, as I was living in [the] motel," Danko recalled, "and the lady's husband died, unfortunately, and so they closed the restaurant down. But she told me about this pink house they were living in and that it would be available. The rent was something like $250 a month." Levon Helm wrote in his autobiography that it was $125 a month.

"It sat right in the middle of 100 acres," said Danko, "and it had a pond, and mountains were right nearby, and it had a lot of privacy. So Garth, Richard, and myself ended up renting the house, and we weren't making very much money as Bob had had the motorcycle accident."[3] It was a split-level house, not far from the hamlet of West Saugerties, that Danko recalled as "really more cotton candy, a pale magenta, than pink."[4] Nonetheless, the house was known as Big Pink.

Danko the businessman is reputed to have told Robertson and Manuel that they needed more permanent quarters than a motel and reminded them they would eventually need a place to rehearse. It was out of the question for them to rehearse in the Woodstock Motel and, lest they have the same problem they had in Manhattan, they would need their own home and their own studio with it. Renting Big Pink at 2188 Stoll Road would solve many of their problems. They would have three bedrooms, a kitchen, a garage, acres and acres to ramble in, enough flat space for touch football games, a view of Overlook Mountain, and their employer not far away. Three of them were up for it, but Robertson was never going to share this particular lease. He had met his future wife, Dominique, when the Dylan world tour played Paris on May 23 of the previous year. Dominique was a journalist at that day's memorable press conference given by Dylan at the Hotel Georges V.

Robertson was smitten with his beautiful French girlfriend and marriage was on the cards. No way would he move into a bachelor palace like Big Pink. "This scene, this place started as our place to go and write some songs and to just have the pleasure of being able to enjoy a situation to play music," says Robertson. "To really start to figure out what we were gonna do for this first [Band] record. That's what we were doing, and once we got it set up and everything, I mean there isn't a tremendous amount up there to do outside of your home life and normal chores.

"So Dylan would just come over, and it was like the clubhouse. Rick and Richard and Garth and later Levon all lived there. At one time, that is. Garth, Rick, and Richard moved into Big Pink but I moved to a different place because I had a girlfriend – and I didn't want her to see what happens!"[5]

Robbie and Dominique wisely moved a few short miles away from Big Pink, setting up domestic shop in a cabin on Sally and Albert Grossman's property. This may have been so he could liaise with Grossman easily, and surely Dominique – a newcomer to this circle of rather unusual personalities – would have felt more comfortable with the hospitable Sally Grossman nearby than with the street-gang mentality of young men in a rock group living next door. The Robertsons later moved to a house on Ricks Road, a lazy country avenue running north and south, connecting Glasco Turnpike with Route 212 and closer to Big Pink's shenanigans.

Back on Stoll Road, there was another kind of domesticity brewing. Manuel did the cooking, Hudson did the dishes, and Danko was responsible for taking out the trash, keeping logs on the fire, and the general upkeep of the house itself. All three were responsible for the grounds immediately surrounding the house and all three soon learned to love the nearby woods and the rapidly running creek, as well as the wildlife that so often strolled by their window.

They were all relaxing. They were pleased that they did not now have to play six nights a week, four sets a night at the gin joints and cheap party palaces of the East Coast, the drunken frat bashes of deep South universities, and the cold cowsheds of Ontario and Quebec, and all just in order to eat and pay rent. Now it was time for something. But what was that something?

They shot scenes for *Eat The Document* that Dylan described quickly while Alk focused hastily. It taught them rapidly that they might one day become more formal actors but that their improvisational skills were limited. Attempts at movie making added something new and made for an interesting sideline, but as Robertson put it: "Music is what we do."[6] It was only a matter of time before their attempts at imitating Dylan's favorite film, Truffaut's *Tirez Sur Le Pianiste (Shoot The Piano Player,* 1960), proved to be a side road and not the main avenue.

Within a few weeks of Danko, Hudson, and Manuel moving into Big Pink, Robertson began driving over daily. Frequently they would play football or goof around like the young men they still were, talking for hours, discussing their collective future, taking stock, and playing each other their favorite records. Their tastes included country & western (Danko), Ray Charles (Manuel), city R&B (Robertson), and Anglican church music and the avant-garde (Hudson).

Robertson was the one most aware that they needed to push further, but Danko was the one who months earlier had told Dylan quite frankly on a late night plane flight during the world tour that The Hawks didn't see themselves as just Bob Dylan's backing band and that one day they would leave their mentor and friend Bob to go and do their own thing musically.

In Big Pink they began to get out their various musical instruments and jam on old favorites, at first setting up their equipment upstairs on the ground floor, happy in the knowledge that no one near them on Stoll Road could possibly hear and complain about the racket. When filming was not scheduled they played a bit. If filming ended with the diminishing light of the shorter winter day they'd frequently retire to Big

Pink and toss around musical ideas. The four of them were back at it, experimenting with the music of their old day-job, sweating away at the coal face as they had with Ronnie Hawkins. If the change to domesticity was challenging for Dylan it was even more so for his backing band. Levon Helm had been on the road with Hawkins since 1957; earlier he had played with Conway Twitty and before that he led his own Razorback groups back home. Robertson had been with Ronnie Hawkins since 1958; Danko signed up as a Hawk in 1959; Manuel joined the act in 1961. Garth Hudson, an old man of 24 when he joined The Hawks not long after Manuel, was the last one to learn the Ronnie Hawkins rules of the road when he arrived in December 1961.

These men had endured between five and eight years of living on the road, of quick hot coffees on the run, of greasy meals in diners, of bad headaches from stale cigarette smoke, all while traveling with a hangover. They were used to moving around a lot. In Woodstock they now had a place of their own and no road to go on. They were acclimatized to a nocturnal lifestyle where they went to work in the late afternoon, worked through the dark hours, and went to bed not long before dawn. Now they would have to readjust to normal life and normal hours in Woodstock.

These residents of Big Pink would start to keep hours that, while hardly conservative to the average working stiff, were positively banker's hours compared to their previous caffeinated lifestyle. They were not discovering a new way of life but rather an old one they had intentionally discarded long ago, back when they decided to give their dreams a try instead of maintaining conventional careers or following parental wishes. They were discovering who they were spiritually in the same way they would soon discover who they now were musically.

Levon Helm was a Southern farm boy whose first instrument was guitar. He'd seen Bill Monroe & His Bluegrass Boys play live "and that really tattooed my brain." [7] He later switched to drums after inspiration from the minstrel and medicine shows that still toured through Arkansas in the years immediately after World War II. Helm performed with his

own groups and soon sat in with Conway Twitty. Then he met Ronnie Hawkins and his life changed forever.

"Let's start with Levon," says Hawkins, taking a deep breath. "Levon was from Marvell, Arkansas, and I was in Fayetteville, Arkansas. I left there to go to Memphis to be a frontman for the session guys there. By the time I got to Memphis the band had broken up about who was gonna be leader," he laughs. "I have always dealt with the most intelligent musicians. I was stuck in Memphis: I couldn't go back home as I had told half of Fayetteville I was gonna be a frontman for these hot Memphis session guys. I couldn't go home as the whole state of Arkansas must've heard 'Memphis is calling me, folks, I'm gonna be a frontman for this new band.' You can't go home after that."

Hawkins had taken guitarist Ray Paulman with him as well as Paulman's cousin, who played piano. "And the piano player knew a little drummer who had sat in with them. This fellow didn't have a set of drums but could play some guitar and he had good rhythm, and that was Levon. So we got together to practice, gigged, went up to Canada, and the Arkansas boys had to go back to marry their 14-year-old girlfriends who were pregnant. So I decided instead of going through all that trouble at the border you'd have with American boys, I would hire Canadian musicians that I had seen and that I knew had the potential of gettin' good."

Helm had more gumption than anybody Hawkins knew. "He was my right arm, my left arm, and both legs. I couldn't have made it without Levon at all. Levon learned things in leaps and bounds and knew rhythms and knew guitar anyway. All we did was audition kids who had the potential of gettin' good and eventually that's how we ended up with the Band guys. Levon was gifted, he was *gifted*. That kid coulda done anything. He had that Mississippi River in him and his Dad could play some harmonica, could play some of that funky stuff, so Levon had it in him. This black, funky music is what we all, as musicians, wanted to do." [8]

John Hammond Jr., blues musician and son of the famous producer and talent scout John Hammond, got to know The Hawks in the early 1960s. He agrees on the importance of Levon Helm. "Oh, he was wonderful on drums even way back when. He was a lyrical drummer, very imaginative, and could be outrageous in his ideas. He knew all the country blues, being from that part of the States, knew all the kind of stuff Ronnie Hawkins was into. He played very sophisticatedly when The Hawks did James Brown or Bobby Blue Bland tunes, and he could really drive songs like Little Junior Parker material." [9]

Robbie Robertson was a streetwise kid. His mother was a Mohawk who first exposed him to music on the Six Nations reservation where she grew up. He played guitar, pitching songs to singers before he was out of high school. "That is what made Ronnie Hawkins hire me at 16," he says. "It was because I wrote two songs he had recorded when I was 15. And I was writing before *that*." [10] The songs were 'Hey Boba Lu' and 'Someone Like You,' recorded by Ronnie and a version of The Hawks with Levon Helm on drums at Bell Sound Studios in New York City on October 26, 1959 (and released on the *Mr. Dynamo* album, on Roulette SR25102).

Robertson's old employer remembers hiring him like it was yesterday. "At the time I had two great guitar players," says Hawkins, "and they were Fred Carter Jr., who is now one of the highest paid session players in Nashville, and Roy Buchanan. Robbie studied under them." [11] Hawkins recalls taking on Robertson "to keep him outta trouble." The new boy effectively became Hawkins's roadie. Then Carter gave notice he was about to quit and get married and move to Nashville. Robertson was right there. Hawkins: "His momma told me that Robbie had quit school and was out on the street running around, so I gave him this little job and gave him 50 a week and room and board. He just stayed with us, learnin' and practicing."

Hawkins switched Robertson to bass and then rhythm guitar. "He got really, really good. When you're playing six or seven days a week and you are practicing every day, a young musician starts to get really good, he starts to get tight. I called Robbie 'The Duke.' He was always wearing those pinstripe suits, dressing like a stockbroker. He always wanted to do

something good and he worked at it. I always knew he was going to do something big, but my god, I didn't know he would do as well as he did. Man, he is as big as they get right now."[12]

Of all The Hawks, Rick Danko was possibly the most loved by those who knew and worked with this particular musical gang in the 1960s. Bob Neuwirth once described Danko as "a brother." He was born in the hamlet of Green's Corners, Ontario, near the town of Simcoe, in an area of Canada populated by many descendants of expatriated Southerners upset by the outcome of the War between the States. Danko grew up surrounded by picking 'n' singing in a family who loved to get together and play. So he was able to take a banjo to school to perform for his classmates in the first grade.

Danko heard legendary American DJs like John R and Wolfman Jack late at night on the radio, and this gave him a lifelong love of gospel and R&B to match his earlier love of country & western. And there was no doubt who was the king of R&B, the master of rockabilly in the Ontario area.

Danko's first fulltime professional employer remembers him fondly. "When my bass player, Rebel Paine, was gonna have to get married and do all that shit," recalls Ronnie Hawkins, "I told him he'd finish at the end of the summer. And Ricky Danko told me later he got his guys on the bill of one of our shows just so I would see him play. Shrewd move. Ricky got up there and played with his little band a couple times and I thought, 'That kid there is a guitar player, but in three months he could change over to bass if he wanted to.' So for three months I had him practicing with Rebel for about six hours a day. I had Robbie and Levon practicing with him too. One hour with each musician." Working like this for about two weeks was tough for Danko, says Hawkins. His arms became swollen from the effort and his fingers were tired. "But he made it. And of course the band didn't want him at first, they did not think this country boy was hip enough. Yet he ended up the one who was working more than anybody else. His singing was a plus too, as was his personality. He was raised on a tobacco farm but he was an apprentice butcher when I found him. Everybody liked Ricky, he had that warm, human thing. Everybody liked Ricky." [13]

John Hammond Jr. agrees. "The Hawks were all easy to get along with. Rick Danko and Levon were as effortlessly friendly as anyone you could ever meet. Very likable people. We hung out and partied and talked about blues endlessly and plans for the future. It blew my mind when they went from such a solid blues band to more of a folk-rock thing. It was a real seismic shift in a way, it was a change of tack in their sailing. I think a certain amount of that was due to Rick Danko's singing and Richard Manuel's writing and singing. Richard was a great singer. A great singer, phenomenal. A good piano player but a great singer, an unforgettable baritone, and truly a great guy." [14]

Band archivist Rob Bowman reported that Richard Manuel was considered by Helm and Danko to be their band's lead singer. Manuel too was from Ontario and he sang in the choir at his Baptist church. Like Danko, he grew up listening to country & western and discovered R&B later. A troubled soul, he is described by producer John Simon as the kind of guy who "drove 150 miles per hour in his driveway, faster on the road." [15] Levon Helm remembers him as having a go-for-it-now attitude: "Richard would wave his glass in the air, smile, and say, Spend it all." [16]

Hawkins will never forget Richard Manuel and how he hired him. "When Stan Szelest decided to go back to Buffalo and do whatever he was gonna do, I brought Richard into my band. Not because of his piano playing, because at that time he was a weak piano player, but because of his vocals. He was a strong throat." [17]

Hawkins continues: "Richard had that sadness: it was the way he phrased. It was what you call soul, and a lot of the time with me he was singing what you call Ray Charles stuff. Even though no one in the world can outdo Ray Charles, our Richard had a sound like it but nonetheless distinctly his own." [18]

The final piece of the puzzle was Garth Hudson. He was the oldest of the Hawkins crew, the last to be hired, and the greatest virtuoso talent in a talented bunch. Hudson's dual image as mad musical genius and wise old man of the mountains proved priceless to The Hawks as they mutated into The Band.

Hudson has proved to be unique in popular music. There is simply no other musician like him performing anywhere in the rock'n'roll world. "I hired Garth Hudson to teach the rest of The Hawks music, formal music," says Hawkins. "We were already outdrawing every band there was up there in the Great North, we were at the top of the list and then some, but to stay there we got to learn some more and keep it goin'. So I brought in Garth Hudson from London, Ontario, to teach music and play organ. He was not a rock'n'roller but he was a gifted musician. He was the one who was the educated musician, like a doctor's degree, like a Juilliard school of music cat, and I figured he could teach the boys some of the stuff. And he could learn a lot, too, as he was starving to death. He was over-educated in music and could not get a job."

Hawkins says this image of Hudson is pretty accurate. "You have to be a scholar to understand what in the hell he is talking about. I never did learn! I just nodded my head and grinned when he said something to me. I didn't know what he was talking about, but man, he played music no one had ever heard before. Yet it fit in, it fit in with rock'n'roll. He put those sounds out there. I used to say, goddamn, Garth, we may have something here! If it sounds good to me, it may sound good to a whole 'nother bunch o' drunks!"[19]

These five – Rick Danko, Levon Helm, Garth Hudson, Richard Manuel, and Robbie Robertson – became not merely Dylan's backup but his musical allies, his partners in crime. They journeyed to the same station but arrived on different trains, as Robertson would memorably remark. From the moment Dylan discovered them he knew they were special.

Many Dylan fanatics know the story about Albert Grossman having a very capable assistant in his office named Mary Martin from Toronto and how she directly suggested to Bob that he contact The Hawks. (Capable indeed: Martin later managed fellow Canadian Leonard Cohen.) The story goes that she played Dylan and Grossman a tape made at a Hawks gig in New Jersey, piquing Dylan's interest. Certainly the Grossman office did have a reel-to-reel tape of Levon & the Hawks, but there is some debate about whether it was a live mono recording made by Mary Martin or studio tracks cut at Hallmark in Toronto in October '64 by local DJ Duff Roman.

Al Kooper swears he knows for a stone cold fact that Martin, who had heard The Hawks play at Friar's Tavern on Toronto's Yonge Street months before, took Dylan and Grossman to a Hawks show in New Jersey and that this is where they first heard Robertson and the rest. Yet both Kooper and John Hammond Jr. had known of The Hawks beforehand, so the water gets pretty muddy when it comes to the truth behind Dylan meeting and hiring The Hawks.

Kooper remembers seeing several future members of The Band for the first time when they were backing Ronnie Hawkins on an Alan Freed TV show. Meaning Kooper would have been watching *The Big Beat* on WNEW in New York, a program shown Mondays to Fridays from 3 to 6:00pm and on Saturdays from 9 to 10:00pm.

"I primarily knew Levon and Robbie as they were being courted by my publisher, Aaron Schroeder, the guy who signed me as a writer," says Kooper. "He was offering them a deal as writers and also as a group. And that ended up sort of a disaster. But they came up to the office and I met them there – and we all remember that. Robbie was already a songwriter but so was Levon. This is 1963 or '64, way before Dylan for any of us. They were The Hawks looking for a record deal without Ronnie Hawkins." [20]

John Hammond Jr. too remembers meeting The Hawks in the early days. He recalls it all without personal fireworks. "In 1962 I started playing professionally," he says, "beginning on the West Coast and moving back east in the winter or late fall of '62. I got gigs at clubs in New York, and this led to my being signed up by Vanguard Records, which was huge. In December '62 I had a gig up in Toronto in a club called the Purple Onion on Yorkville Street, a bohemian area then and very gentrified now."

Stan Thomas, a folk singer, came to see Hammond backstage, said he

liked the show, and asked him if we wanted to come see a band at the Concord Tavern afterward. "I asked him what's the name of the band and was told it was Levon & The Hawks. So Stan brought me over after my show and I heard this band, which was just phenomenal. They were just so in touch and in tune. I mean, strictly blues and R&B. I was introduced to the guys, they called me up, I did a song with them that night, and we became really good friends. That's how I met The Hawks, the guys who became The Band."

Hammond stayed in touch with his new friends as they played many of the old Hawkins gigs, including those in and around Wildwood, New Jersey, where there were a lot of clubs and a rock'n'roll scene. "They would come through New York City and they'd call me up and I would go down and play with them a few times. They had a gig at a place called Joey Dee's Peppermint Lounge, and I sat in with them there. We were good friends and I really admired the guys. When groups like The Beatles, the Stones, The Animals and all hit the scene there was pressure on me to expand my sound – and anyway, I'd always had in the back of my mind a band like Howlin' Wolf's or Muddy Waters's or Jimmy Reed's. I was into adding an electric sound to the country blues."

In the fall of 1964, Hammond approached the Vanguard label and asked if he could have a session with some friends of his who were in New York, including The Hawks and Michael Bloomfield. "Michael was a friend from Chicago then getting his name around. Charlie Musselwhite, who I met probably in 1961 when I was driving to Chicago to hear whoever I could hear, was also invited to my session. Vanguard allowed me one session, and I invited Dylan over. I was very excited and we cut 12 songs in three hours. It was called *So Many Roads*, an album of mine out in 1965. It was at that session that I introduced The Band, then The Hawks, to Dylan. Dylan flipped out over these guys. And the next thing I knew they were recording with him."

The Hawks on this session were Robertson, Helm, and Hudson. Hammond remembers them as talented, restless, ambitious. He says they were hoping they could cash in on their R&B–blues sound but it didn't seem to be working. "You had others then playing in a similar vein, like The Animals or Them, but The Hawks knew the material a bit more first-hand and had grown up on the music at a closer range than so many of these [British Invasion] acts."

Later on, says Hammond, The Hawks' association with Dylan allowed them to focus on finding their own unique sound. "They were so talented, so ready, and so able to do what it would take to make it. When Michael Bloomfield heard Robbie play at the So Many Roads session he told me, 'Listen, I am not playing guitar.' It's a fact!" he laughs. "Robbie was one of the best blues players I had ever heard. He was so intense in his playing and his chops were really exciting. I don't know where that kind of inspiration comes from – perhaps from playing so often back then – but I was a witness to this. I saw it and heard it."

While only 12 tunes made the LP, Hammond says that they recorded maybe 25 songs, and a lot of the out-takes went on to his subsequent *Mirrors* album. He recalls how the track 'So Many Roads, So Many Trains' came together on the session. "Robbie said, Why don't we do it in stop time? We did that 'boom boom, cha cha, boom boom, cha cha' instead of the Otis Rush version that had inspired me. That's kind of a Band vibe or idea right there. We were all flexible and dynamic at this session."

He observed Garth Hudson closely at the recording. "He was already a crazily talented keyboardist. Oh yes he was. He was a genius and a terrific player. He seemed the oldest of The Hawks, the wisest, and the most adult. He also played saxophone and was really good on it. A frighteningly talented guy."

Hammond brought Robbie Robertson with him to the studio in June 1965 so they both could watch Dylan record 'Like A Rolling Stone.' Which is odd, because on Hammond's sessions, Robertson replaced Mike Bloomfield as guitarist, with Bloomfield having to shift over to piano, while at these Dylan sessions, Bloomfield was playing the lead guitar fills on 'Like A Rolling Stone.' Robertson must have been amused that the guy

who'd admitted he was not as good a guitarist as Robertson was now sitting in an expensive studio as lead guitarist for a major star of the day.

Hammond has one more anecdote about his days with The Hawks, and this too involves Robertson. During 1965, the two of them went up to the Brill Building, the famous songwriting factory in New York City. They approached Leiber & Stoller with the intention of making a demo for them. "This is Red Bird Records, George Goldner's thing. We talked them into giving us a session to make two songs, and of course we recorded 12 songs in three hours. We had a band put together by Leiber & Stoller: Charles Otis on drums, Artie Butler on piano, my friend Bill Wyman was in town so he played bass, and Brian Jones wanted to play harmonica and I said, 'Brian, sorry, I am playing harmonica.' And Robbie Robertson was unbelievable at the sessions: what a phenomenal player! It was recorded at A&R Studios. Phil Ramone was the engineer. It was about as big time as you get in 1965."

Two of the songs, 'I Can Tell' backed with 'I Wish You Would,' became a John Hammond single on Red Bird 10-047 – or, as Hammond more accurately describes it, a Bo Diddley tune backed with a Billy Boy Arnold tune. Robertson played guitar on these two songs and Rick Danko played bass on some tracks cut in the three-hour session. "It was a hit in Pittsburgh," laughs Hammond. "Thanks, Robbie. Then George Goldner, who had not met me yet, came back to New York City, and I had a big meeting with him. Leiber & Stoller were really hot on this single. Goldner said, 'Jerry, Mike! I can't promote this guy, he's *white!*'

So everything kind of went out the window. A year later I approached Atlantic and they bought the tapes from the estate of Goldner, who died, and the rest of the session, the rest of the tapes with Robbie and Rick Danko, were released as *I Can Tell* on Atlantic in 1967."[21]

Had the *I Can Tell* tapes come out on LP a year or two later, the rock world would have been able to make a more direct comparison between the R&B-obsessed Hawks and the equally soulful but country-tinged post-Basement ensemble known as The Band. Touting Robertson and Danko's involvement on an LP in 1967 would not have increased sales much, but two years further on and any album with those names in the credits would have been granted far greater scrutiny from *Rolling Stone, Crawdaddy,* the *L.A. Free Press* and the other assorted underground papers of the day. Nonetheless, *I Can Tell* and Hammond's earlier *So Many Roads* had The Hawks playing the hot, punchy R&B sound they would soon leave behind.

These rockin', bluesy Hawks had so impressed Dylan with their early work with Hammond that he nabbed them for his fall '65 tour dates and for the session on November 30, 1965 where he made a second attempt at 'Can You Please Crawl Out Your Window?' They were his band at that session in New York City at Columbia's Studio A and they were his band over a year later, traipsing around the snow outside Woodstock as Dylan directed them in semi-improvised situations from the movie script he had kept locked safely in his own mind.

Their careers were to become even more intertwined as the filming of new scenes for *Eat The Document* slowed down a little and as their natural inclination toward music began again to become more central to their daily lives.

To Dylan, who according to his autobiography viewed life as a continual history of repeated chaotic events, the world was something to keep at bay in 1967. Certainly his previous world – of touring, an attempted novel, and films – was something he wanted to keep at a distance. And he could well have had other reasons for keeping that distance.

Operation Junction City, the largest engagement to date in the Vietnam war, had been launched in February, while in the nation's capital a select committee from the U.S. House of Representatives had voted to censure and fine New York Congressman Adam Clayton Powell Jr., an African-American, for misappropriation of funds earmarked for the Education & Labor Committee that he chaired. The civil rights movement had shifted with the introduction of black power to the brew, and many American cities suffered nightmarish riots as a consequence. U.S. Federal agents did

have some good news to read about as the presumed boss of Chicago's organized crime syndicate appeared in Federal court on a series of charges. And plans for a pop music festival were underway in Los Angeles after a meeting between Mamas & Papas leader John Phillips, his wife Michelle, producer Lou Adler, entrepreneur Alan Pariser, and Beatles/Byrds/Beach Boys publicist Derek Taylor. No doubt they would seek Dylan to perform or at least to give his blessing, as The Beatles would soon give theirs.

Dylan would not be in the nation's capital that year nor appear in a Federal court. He would not be singing for the troops in Vietnam. He would never make it to Monterey for the festival. He would not be volunteering answers to the multitude or to the strangers trespassing on his property. He would be in Byrdcliffe "doing nothing, absolutely nothing" according to Robertson (when interviewed by *Daily News* journalist Michael Iachetta, who was looking for Robertson's boss).

In 1967, Dylan was definitely making appearances in Woodstock: at the greengrocer's, at the baker's, at his friend Bernard Paturel's Café Expresso, playing chess. In contrast to Robertson's disinformation to Iachetta, his old employer was doing something. He wasn't singing in public but he was definitely singing.

Garth Hudson would soon begin recording Dylan and The Hawks in Woodstock and, as we'll discover, this would take place at various locations, but notably the work was done in the basement of Big Pink. The recordings are what became known as the Basement Tapes.

In total there are allegedly 37 tape boxes, each containing a seven-inch reel of recording tape. John Simon says that Garth Hudson recorded his friends and musicians with the tape running at 7½ i.p.s. (seven and a half inches per second). At that speed, there would be approximately 20 minutes of recording time on each reel, and not every tape reel is full.

Those hoping to hear Dylan discussing anything at all on the 37 reels – be it civil rights, Vietnam, or philosophical matters – will be disappointed. His voice is heard almost exclusively singing. He does, however, at one point instruct a keen-to-tape Mr. Hudson when to turn the machine off and on other songs encourages Richard Manuel to sing this or that.

Hudson would start the tape following a nod or word from Dylan, and when the song was finished he rapidly reached over to the tape machine and turned it off. This is why there is so little studio chat, so few wasted moments, and no tuning-up heard on the Basement Tapes that have escaped so far. The tapes themselves consist of the songs and very little else. Songs are even cut off on several recordings before they come to a complete musical halt as Hudson is so anxious to save tape.

At the time of this writing, over six hours of true Basement Tape music has been unearthed, totaling at least 107 different completed performances of songs, including multiple takes of some. (This does not include most of what are accepted to be recordings that The Hawks put to tape in Woodstock without Dylan's input - see chapter 13; many Hawks/Band tracks long considered from Woodstock were in fact out-takes from later sessions in N.Y.C. and L.A.)

So, 37 reels with 107 songs averages to around three songs per 20-minute tape. That means there is hardly room for many other out-takes to exist, be they missing songs like 'Minstrel Boy' and 'Wild Wolf' or yet another take of 'You Ain't Goin' Nowhere.'

Some of the songs were officially issued on the 1975 Columbia Records two-LP set *The Basement Tapes*, although some of The Band material on that set was not from Big Pink nor from any of the other places in Woodstock where they recorded. A version of 'Quinn The Eskimo' came out ten years later on the Dylan *Biograph* collection, and on the long overdue (and quite remarkable) boxed set *The Bootleg Series, Volumes 1-3* two more Basement Tapes songs appeared, 'I Shall Be Released' and 'Santa Fe.'

That means that fewer than 20 songs totaling less than an hour from this now legendary Dylan period have reached the public at large. That's all. Meaning around five hours remain unheard by even the most observant fans. Meaning almost 100 songs, and possibly even more, are waiting in the black market as fans of Dylan, The Band, great songwriting, '60s music in general, and what we now call Americana hope and pray for

an official, remastered, souped up, all singin' and all dancin' issue of this remarkable chapter in the life of modern America's most creative songwriter.

"We were playing with absolute freedom," Robertson confided to Greil Marcus. "We weren't doing anything we thought anybody would ever hear as long as we lived. But what started in that basement, what came out of it ... and The Band came out of it, people holding hands and rocking back and forth all over the world singing 'I Shall Be Released' came out of this little conspiracy, of us amusing ourselves."[22]

Like their primary creator, these recordings have been the subject of myth and mystery, a little fact, and quite some fiction. Their stature has grown as rumor has spread and their absence is pondered. Never has a session that lasted for so long, with so many worthy out-takes, and which dictated the next few years' musical direction for both the principal singer-songwriter as well as his faithful and priceless backing band, been so discussed, so pondered over, yet so misunderstood.

Both the singer and the band were finding a new voice, a new idiom with which to perform. These two acts were more than mere pop music performers. The singer was a cultural force, whether or not he wanted that title. The backing band would soon stop backing and strike out on their own, briefly eclipsing the mere pop-music world and becoming a cultural force, much like their Hibbing-born employer. And then, this most democratic of bands would crash back down to earth, mortals after all.

The more you twist the kaleidoscope as you peer into it, the more the patterns change and the more there is to digest. In 1967, five (later six) musicians would understand that, and on every level. They dealt in such patterns, musically speaking. They were about to create a new pattern, one which reflected their pasts as well as their futures.

Ladies and gentlemen: the Basement Tapes.

# MILLION DOLLAR BASH

## 6. Clouds So Swift

*Establishing the working day*

The year 1967 turned out to be an extremely productive one for Bob Dylan as a writer and for The Hawks as musicians as they slowly but discernibly mutated into The Band. Levon Helm, who would be a late arrival to the Woodstock sessions, had been working down South and recalls that when he did arrive toward the end of '67 Richard Manuel told him Dylan had been writing "ten songs a week for months."[1]

*New York Post* journalist and scenester Al Aronowitz visited Dylan's Byrdcliffe home, *Hi Lo Ha*, and remembered Dylan writing ten new songs a week. Aronowitz also wrote for *Cheetah* – the über-hip counterculture magazine whose debut issue memorably included a foldout of Mama Cass Elliott naked – and noted there that Dylan was "rehearsing ... in his living room with Robertson's group, The Hawks."[2]

Garth Hudson recalled: "We were doing seven, eight, ten, sometimes fifteen songs a day. Some were old ballads and traditional songs, some were written by Bob, but others would be songs Bob made up as he went along. We'd play the melody [and] he'd sing a few words he'd written or else just mouth sounds or syllables. It was a pretty good way to write songs."[3]

Or as Richard Manuel told Caroline Boucher in 1971: "I don't think we'd have come off the same if we were living in the middle of New York [City]. It's an awful strain, we've recorded in New York and ... in the middle of the song the studio is shaking with the subway."[4]

It is difficult to believe that Dylan really was writing ten songs a week for months unless the quality of those songs was pretty average. As the public has not even heard anything near a ten-song-a-week output from Dylan in the intervening years and as Dylan is the most bootlegged, most faithfully archived artist of the modern era, he either wasn't writing at that rate, wasn't recording at that rate, or his own quality control prevented nine of those songs a week from being heard. Or, at the risk of starting a rumor, the possibility exists that there are even more seven-inch reels of Basement Tapes than previously imagined. But given the thoroughness of Dylan's acolytes in their continual hunt for More Bob this is hard to accept. No doubt Dylan has had his periods of pronounced productivity. David Crosby is one of many who reports that Dylan apparently does have the ability to churn out a song or prose of some sort at will. Surely this is work along the lines that Hudson describes above: songs barely "written" in the clinical sense of the word. In other words, songs not completely finished lyrically nor arranged before the tape was rolling, but songs that were ideas never completely fleshed out – or perhaps songs with nonsense lyrics from the far side of Lewis Carroll, like "the poor little chauffer was back in bed with a nose full of pus, yea! heavy and a bottle of bread."

Dylan was capable of singing something, however logical, coherent, or identifiable, the first time he opened his mouth with music playing behind him. Hudson's claim about doing up to 15 songs a day may well be l iterally true, but they did not record 15 songs in any one day, nor did they record seven or eight songs in a day. It is entirely possible that Dylan was in a restless creative spirit, as per usual when he was cooking on all burners, and had Hudson and his Canadian compatriots *try* 15 songs in one day, but they probably were not tried for very long, nor were they all recorded.

If they had worked at such a clip, the final number of Basement Tapes songs would total several hundred, given that they were rehearsing and then recording for months. It would have to be so if it is accepted that the Dylan–Hawks axis recorded "daily" for seven months off and on. Daily is the word most used in this context by Danko, Hudson, and Robertson.

Recently, Hudson told Will Hodgkinson: "The Basement Tapes were initially demos for Dylan. He would come over to the house and write funny stuff like 'Million Dollar Bash' and we would go into the basement and record it. ... Dylan would be coming round the house three or four days a week and there was a little typewriter on the coffee table in the living room that he would bash away on while we were in the basement. Richard [Manuel] wrote a song about that, 'Upstairs, Downstairs.' As far as I know that's one of those few sacred Basement Tapes songs still in the locker." [5] This makes more sense. (And note that Hudson says "few.") Dylan had the sensibilities of an artist, as his father had been told back in Hibbing during Bob's high school days. It is unlikely such a bohemian would come over daily, day in, day out, as if working in a bank, when said bohemian knew there was no clock ticking, no deadline to be held against, no particular contract to fulfill. Three or four days a week with time off for vacations and family commitments – and, as Hudson tellingly mentions, The Hawks were working too, with a Manuel original called 'Upstairs, Downstairs' waiting to be heard. This raises the possibility there are more Dylan originals to be heard – but certainly not as many as remain unheard if they recorded daily or near daily for the many months the Basement Tape sessions were held.

Besides how much work was done, another question is how much work was recorded. Dylan is heard on one particular reel telling Hudson: "You don't have to record this; you're just wasting tape." Why not record it? Obviously Hudson was gesturing toward the tape deck in some way for Dylan to comment, so Hudson must have thought something they were playing right then was worth preserving. Dylan either wasn't happy with the song or, judging by his dismissive matter-of-fact tone, it was simply another song where their rehearsal attempt didn't prove powerful enough or memorable enough for Dylan to want to waste even the low-quality tape brands that Hudson was using on the tune.

It seems they were satisfied if they could put down one good, permanent, kept-for-posterity recording per day. Which doesn't mean they didn't do other songs each day, but one completed tune committed to tape per day seems their rule of thumb.

By any measure they would move on, Dylan not being one to tarry if a song wasn't readily grasped at a session. And in moving on and in going through many songs only once or twice they might well have fooled around with 15 songs in a given day. But fooling around with a song and recording a relatively rehearsed version are two different things. The latter would have taken up a great deal more time. Robertson, who readily admits to being a lesser archivist than Hudson, remembers trying out so many things so many ways in the basement that the many sessions there soon became something of a blur. A warm, happy memory of generous days, to be sure, but a blur nonetheless.

And yes, the legendarily strong coffee that Dylan imbibed along with the strong Canadian beer and the occasional jazz cigarette that The Hawks enjoyed could easily create a blur as well as a buzz. Add to all that the memory going a little hazy due to the passing decades and no wonder the sober archivist Hudson is the musician present who remembers the most. Dylan liked to work fast in the studio, even if the studio was a basement or a living room, and when things weren't done in a handful of takes he frequently grew frustrated and moved along. One wonders if this impatience was not partially a byproduct of the strong coffee.

When Dylan's followers finally heard about the scale of recording done in Woodstock in 1967 their next question was almost as much *when* as *how*. The sessions probably began in March that year, starting as rehearsals and then recording. These were at Dylan's house, *Hi Lo Ha*, in Byrdcliffe, lasting into April and possibly to early or mid May. Then Dylan and The Hawks shifted to Big Pink on Stoll Road, working on and off until October 1967, and then they moved again, to Danko's house off Wittenberg Road. The sessions may have lasted until December, possibly even into the new year of 1968.

But none of this is by any means certain. So now let's consider some of the arguments.

June '67 was a generally accepted starting point, although Clinton Heylin has reported that they started in April and that June marked the start for the selections found on the 1975 two-LP *Basement Tapes* release.[6] In his excellent liner notes for the 2005 Band boxed set, academic Rob Bowman writes: "Every day for seven or eight months, Robertson, who had rented a house nearby, would drive over to Big Pink. For two or three hours, often in the company of Bob Dylan, everyone would write songs, throw ideas back and forth, play older songs from a multiplicity of genres, and occasionally lay some of it down on a 2-track recorder in the basement."[7]

When Bowman wrote those words he had spoken to every member of

The Band, save the late Richard Manuel, and since it is acknowledged that Basement Tapes sessions ran at least into November '67 – they had to if returning prodigal son Levon Helm is heard on drums on some cuts, and indeed he is – then this would mean that Helm is right when he wrote in his autobiography: "The boys told me that they'd been working with Bob on songs and demos since March." [8] Conceivably, Helm might be off by a month but not by two. Note also that he wrote "demos." This means they were recording. You record demos; you don't rehearse demos. You rehearse songs. Demos means the tape deck was out and the mikes set up. It is also hard to believe that everyone would wait until May or June to pick up where they left off, having not played with Dylan for so long and yet having been in Woodstock since February.

The mystery remains as to exactly when they started recording as opposed to rehearsing. Surely they could not have been recording since early or mid March? If they had, the Basement Tapes would threaten to be the audio equivalent of *War And Peace*. The inescapable conclusion is that they set up their gear and, within a short time, certainly in late April if not before, they started recording. Casually. When the time was right and the song was where they wanted it. Even if they wanted it a bit undercooked.

Rick Danko is quoted by Helm as saying: "For ten months, from March to December 1967, we all met … and played for two or three hours a day." [9] Robertson, Danko, and Manuel were in Woodstock in February, filming and editing for *Eat The Document*, although it couldn't have taken long for Danko and Manuel to realize their future was not in cinema but in music. Grossman would have known that using The Hawks as actors for extra scenes for *Document* was better than their running up hotel bills while doing next to nothing for his client Dylan in New York – but that acting was nonetheless not the best use of their time. They were musicians, he was an astute manager, and he would have communicated his anxiety about this to Dylan in private if not openly. Grossman must have been concerned about The Hawks playing extras in a movie when they could be playing their instruments and creating music with Dylan.

Such a course might allow him to re-book the cancelled tour dates. Unquestionably, a manager like Grossman would look at the calendar and think, God almighty, it's now March! They haven't worked together as a musical unit with Bob for ten months now.

It seems logical that The Hawks started to fool around musically, to rehearse informally, some time in March '67. Being actors would not take up all of their time. Dylan, Alk, and sometimes Robertson retreated to the film-editing room on occasion. By all accounts there was not much to do in Woodstock other than your day job, enjoying the scenery, and completing the various chores of day-to-day life.

"We got to like this lifestyle, chopping wood and hitting our thumb with a hammer, fixing the tape recorder or the screen door, wandering off into the woods with [Dylan's dog] Hamlet," Hudson told Martin Scorsese during *The Last Waltz*. "It was relaxed and low key. Which was something we had not enjoyed since we were children." [10]

The day job for Robertson, Danko, and Manuel was music, by now long imbedded in their DNA. It is natural to expect them to be playing as an ensemble, albeit an informal one, some time relatively soon after they all reassembled in Ulster County. Danko remembered starting on songs in March but he didn't say specifically that it was demos being recorded. Most likely they would collectively shake off some cobwebs first, mess around a bit looking for a focus and a methodology to work by, routine some old songs, and then and only then actually have Hudson, a latecomer to Woodstock, set up and record them playing with their employer.

Basement Tapes participants all remember that a steel furnace in the basement at Big Pink was sometimes put to use. The furnace was shut off if its noise interfered with the recording process. However, the recordings of what are called the Basement Tapes definitely started out at Dylan's *Hi Lo Ha* house in Byrdcliffe in a living-room styled area that The Hawks nicknamed the Red Room. This room was not red any more, although it had been during the previous tenancy. When the sessions moved to Big Pink's basement, the aforementioned steel furnace was still being used.

It makes sense if the first Basement Tapes rehearsals – not necessarily recording sessions – were started in March in the Red Room, as it wouldn't have taken much time for Sara Dylan or her husband to figure out that recording at home is one thing but recording at home when there are small children around is next to impossible. So, relatively soon they decamped and set up again at Big Pink. As the furnace was in use at Big Pink, this must have been April or early to mid May, because by June the furnace wouldn't be required: summer would be coming and the windows would be opened to let a breeze into the basement (or even the garage door opened, as Big Pink's basement was the house's garage). Given all the facts known for certain, and the temperament of the creative and business minds involved here, it stands to reason that the sessions started in late March 1967.

The Basement Tapes sessions were interrupted no fewer than five times during the course of the year for various personal and professional reasons. Work stopped cold during these breaks. Dylan certainly didn't work without his Hawks – no solo recordings have even been rumored from '67 – but the group did do some work without him, although surprisingly little in Woodstock, given the opportunity they had earlier in the year and given the shot in the arm later in the year when drummer Helm reappeared. So: the sessions probably started in March, and they definitely started in the very private home of the lead singer. *Hi Lo Ha* had the space to spare for four Canadians and one Minnesotan intent on recording. They were given a room that was a den or second living room, already dubbed the Red Room. Robbie Robertson explains: "You know what? There is a little bit of confusion and all these different people's views as to what The Basement Tapes are. The Basement Tapes refers to the basement there at Big Pink, obviously, but it also refers to a process, a homemade process. So some things we recorded at Bob's house, some things we recorded at Rick's house. Or so people tell me! Some songs we did at this Red Room, as we called it, up at Bob's place, a little bit, and then some things we recorded in the city [New York]. We were here and there, so what it really means is 'homemade' as opposed to just a single location in a formal studio. The two main places for what we now know as the Basement tapes are the Red Room at Bob's house and the basement at Big Pink. And there wasn't much done at the Red Room at Bob's. There was other stuff done over at this other house, Rick's house – but not at Clarence Schmidt's house." [11]

With the town of Woodstock containing more than its fair share of wild characters such as Clarence Schmidt, it is no surprise that confusion exists as to the artistic activities of even its most famous citizens. If the sessions started at Dylan's house in March, school was on and his daughter would be coming home some time after 3:00pm.

The Hawks may have been adapting to the country tempo but they were still not what you would call morning people. It is unlikely that Richard Manuel, for instance, awoke much before noon. These young men would struggle to arrive at Dylan's house around 1:00pm.

Dylan would have been up early with his eldest child, Maria. He had coffee, helped the household prepare for the day, and walked Maria to the bus stop. He had taken up painting after one morning meeting an artist neighbor, Bruce Dorfman, as Dorfman walked his own daughter to the school-bus stop.

They became friends and Dylan spent many happy hours painting in Dorfman's nearby studio. The quiet hours of the morning could happily be filled with oils and canvases, and soon they were. This worked out well, given The Hawks' relatively late arrival in the day.

Eventually, when the musicians did arrive, stories would be swapped, a welcoming coffee offered by Sara Dylan, and no doubt the dogs, Buster and Hamlet, would have looked for a Canadian leg to bite. Business would then drift over to the Red Room, with a bit of discussion about what to do or how best to rehearse the song they were going to put on tape. And then they went to work, not more than two and a half hours before Maria Dylan came home from school.

Dylan was besotted with his family and would have known when Maria was back and would have been curious to discover how school went. A bigger problem would have been Jesse Dylan, who was only 14 months old. Even with the relatively low volume of the Basement Tapes sessions, it would have been difficult for Jesse to nap with five musicians recording in the house. And then the Dylans would have dined as a family. So the sessions could not have gone on for very long on the days they were held at *Hi Lo Ha* in Byrdcliffe.

Surely this arrangement would soon have come to an end? Even with the possibility that Mrs. Dylan arranged to be out of the house with Jesse when the troops assembled each day, and even with Maria going over to a friend's house for a play date after school, this is no way to maintain the closeness of a young family, much less the peace and tranquility of a home. Nonetheless, as Robertson says, "Music is what we do."[12] Even though these early sessions were dominated by covers and traditional folk songs, things were slowly heating up and at some point they recorded a few originals in the Red Room.

This was where and when these talented musicians all eased back into recording at the same time as, with the exception of Dylan, they all eased out of the movie business. What they eased into at first was the sound of young men singing like old men on old songs, since the Red Room sessions do consist primarily of covers and past favorites, with a few improvisational songs also captured on tape. These seemingly improvisational songs reflect Dylan's recent cinematic techniques more than they do his previous songwriting style. In the past, Dylan had frequently worked fast on recording his material in the studio, yet he could be meticulous about the lyrics, tinkering with the words until the last moment. Either the Bard of Byrdcliffe was saving his best material or he hadn't written any of the year's forthcoming classics yet. So, the tenor of these earliest Basement Tapes is that of old men musing over a directionless past.

Yet they were not old men. Instead, they seemed adrift in an ever-

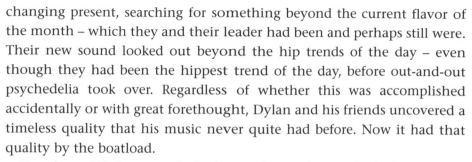

changing present, searching for something beyond the current flavor of the month – which they and their leader had been and perhaps still were. Their new sound looked out beyond the hip trends of the day – even though they had been the hippest trend of the day, before out-and-out psychedelia took over. Regardless of whether this was accomplished accidentally or with great forethought, Dylan and his friends uncovered a timeless quality that his music never quite had before. Now it had that quality by the boatload.

How long did they spend playing and recording each day? Robertson and Danko said that they worked two to four hours a day at first, a pattern that seemed to continue throughout the year. Dylan had his pleasant distractions of a young family nearby and, as Howard Alk would remind him periodically, a film in need of editing. Robertson had a wife close to hand and, not infrequently, spent time editing with Dylan as well as sometimes visiting Grossman to absorb as much information about the record business as he could.

Their previous nominal leader, Levon Helm, was not around to crack the whip. Helm had quit the employ of Dylan in New York City during the last day of November 1965.

He was tired of the booing he'd heard while drumming for Dylan, was upset The Hawks were again someone's backing band instead of going it on their own, and bravely admitted later in his autobiography that he didn't really like Dylan's mid-1960s music.

So without a bandleader to drive them on, how long could they have worked at recording each day in Woodstock? Dylan, even in a comfy living room or a basement with a steel furnace, was not one to overstay his time in any recording studio. And in all the books, magazine articles, interviews, and offhand comments from and about the participants in the years since these organic recordings were made, not one player has ever claimed that they worked extremely late in the studio or complained that they worked long hours in the studio. Dylan likes to get in, get it done, and get out. Oddly, it seems they wasted little time when recording, even though time was in abundance. Yet when it came down to work, they really did work. A session in Nashville, Los Angeles, or New York City in those days was three hours long, stopping right there. The musicians' union agreement stated that union musicians were required to take a break before another three-hour session could start later. That's approximately how long the Basement Tapes sessions were on the days they were held: three hours.

That's three hours of actual work, not including their arrival, small talk, catching up, and first gratis hospitable coffee and light refreshment from the hosts. And not including the initial goofing off where young rock musicians are seemingly required to musically satirize a particularly ghastly popular song of the day before getting down to business. Three hours of real work, then.

As any rock musician save a member of The Grateful Dead will tell you, any time you play past three hours on the trot it is beginning to become too much like hard work. You take a break. Jann Wenner asked Dylan in 1969 if he got to work frequently with The Band out in the country (presumably meaning Woodstock). "Work?" said Dylan. "Well, *work* is something else. Sure, we're always running over old material. New material ... and different kinds of material. Testing out this and that." [13] There in 25 words is a great description of the Basement Tapes sessions from The Man Himself. Old material, new material, different kinds of material, testing out this and that. Bingo. Note he didn't say whose old material, as it certainly wasn't his.

Having sessions that usually lasted only two to four hours a day meant that, for the most part, fatigue was not a problem. Certainly, substances imbibed were making the musicians sound audibly tired on certain selections, but material such as 'This Wheel's On Fire,' 'Tears Of Rage,' 'Sign On The Cross,' and so on often benefits from the ageless tenor  provided by a certain weariness that is evident in Dylan's vocal.

With the musicians only working these few hours a day and with five breaks in the calendar year of 1967 due to family, professional, and other commitments, the sessions could indeed have lasted longer than the seven months that most Dylanologists claim for them.

And even with a starting date of March or April, it is shocking to remember that this particular group of musicians had not worked together regularly since the Royal Albert Hall concerts that ended the last leg of Dylan's world tour back in May of 1966.

There were serious cobwebs for Dylan in particular to clear out of the way. This is perhaps why the Dylan originals recorded in the Red Room and which musically kicked off the year for him are pretty much improvisational and not the formal, dynamically arranged poetics of the past few years.

As we've noted, the Basement Tapes music that has leaked out to the black market is remarkably devoid of false starts and half-completed versions. Relative to the amount of work done, very few half-completed versions are heard. There are several reasons for this. One of the underlying themes of those remarkably creative days is that, time and time again, the players demonstrated how well they knew each other's musical habits. Even Dylan, for so long a soloist onstage, was now attuned to the ensemble's inner workings. This is evident on the few asides and instructions heard before, after, and sometimes even during the songs themselves, as Dylan pushes for a better this or that from their collective performance.

The musicians worked until they had what they wanted, or at least until they had sketched the tune's outline, until they knew the bare bones of the song they would perform. Frequently, they would improvise as they read Dylan's hands for the chord changes on an instantaneous song – frequently based on some old folk, R&B, or C&W classic they had enjoyed in times past.

They knew intimately from playing this kind of music for so long how the arrangements should go. You hear them laugh. You even hear Dylan laugh at some of his more audacious or absurd improvisational lyrics inflicted upon a slightly changed traditional folk tune. Remarkably enough, the reason there are few false starts or incomplete tapes is because – wait for it – they were trying to save tape. That Garth Hudson was recording on budget-line tape brands such as Shamrock and Bel-Cleer tells a story in itself. That he started recording only seconds before a given song's start, switching off the recorder even before some songs have finished resounding their final chord, tells the same tale again. Equally telling, Hudson halves the recording speed to 3¾ inches per second from 7½ i.p.s. in the Red Room. Possibly this is to save tape; probably it's because these warm-up cover versions and almost-improvised originals were not worth the faster tape speed. Certainly somebody thought this way.

If someone today found the long wooden box that Garth Hudson built and the many seven-inch reels of tape, recorded in '67 and stored inside, it would still be impossible to know exactly which songs on those tapes were recorded where. Not exactly, anyway. Hudson was a deft engineer but he did not keep strict session details about the dates, locations, and who played what on which take. To be fair to Hudson, he did remember many of the recording particulars later, as did Danko. But they kept no official log of the proceedings.

Robertson says they weren't making a record, they were just fooling around and had the attitude that no one was ever going to hear what they were up to. How right he was back then and how wrong he is now. They did make a record, even if it took until 1975 for Robertson, ironically enough, to be the one to complete and compile it. Millions eventually heard it. Several critics declared it the album of the year, even though it was not the year their publications had in mind.

So, they had to start some place, and the Red Room it was. Whether anyone else was listening or not, or ever would, four Canadians and a Minnesota bohemian were listening intently to one another. They were consciously not continuing with the challenging, sometimes harsh sound of the 1966 world tour. Knowing they were not going back on the road any time soon meant that the four restless Canadians never rehearsed a single song from Dylan's impressive back catalog. Not one. This was a time for planting seeds. This was the sound of retrenchment and advancement at the same time, of discovery and of nuance, of grace and gracelessness. And all found in the 12-note scale.

# MILLION DOLLAR BASH

## 7. Now You Must Provide Some Answer

*Recordings in the Red Room at Hi Lo Ha*

The first batch of Basement Tapes recordings were allegedly recorded in the so-called Red Room at Dylan's *Hi Lo Ha* home in Byrdcliffe, starting around March 1967 and continuing into late April or early/mid May. What follows is my view of each of the songs. The title is followed by the composer, specified if not Bob Dylan, then the length of the recording, who played which instruments, and what it sounded like.

The Red Room songs have a fresh, rough feel about them and they have a particular sound, a sound heard across these first 22 selections recorded in 1967, as winter slowly began to give way to spring across the Catskills.

The world will have to live with the fact that it will never know exactly which Basement Tapes tune was taped when and where. The 22 recordings here all have a similar sonic feel to them and were probably cut at 3¾ i.p.s. in mono, with Dylan frequently playing on an acoustic 12-string guitar.

The feel of the music that Dylan, Danko, Hudson, Manuel, and Robertson made in the Red Room is relaxed and yet restless. Or as Dylan memorably and famously told Jann Wenner: "Fact, I'd do it all over again. You know, that's really the way to do a recording, in a peaceful, relaxed setting, in somebody's basement. With the windows open … and a dog lying on the floor." [1]

Or in somebody's recently painted living room, with kids crawling around on the floor just down the hall.

## LOCK YOUR DOOR
0:20
**Bob Dylan** vocal, acoustic guitar, **Rick Danko** bass, **Garth Hudson** organ, Richard Manuel drums, **Robbie Robertson** electric guitar
• This 20-second snippet shows Hudson already coming to grips with the recording equipment. Sounding like part of a longer, somewhat improvised song, it ends when someone fails to wind back the tape far enough to erase all of 'Lock Your Door' for the following song, 'Baby, Won't You Be My Baby.'

## BABY, WON'T YOU BE MY BABY

2:47

**Dylan** vocal, piano **Danko** bass, **Hudson** organ, **Manuel** drums,
**Robertson** electric guitar.

• Clearly, Dylan has written most of these lyrics beforehand: they flow
well, with a formal mid-tempo blues structure like 'Call Letter Blues'/
'Meet Me In The Morning' or a cross between 'She Belongs To Me' and
'Leopard-Skin Pill-Box Hat.' With work, this really would have been
something. As it is, it's relaxed and laidback, with Manuel already proving
to be a surprisingly decent timekeeper for a man just beginning on the skins.

Ends abruptly as Hudson goes into a solo. Damn.

## TRY ME, LITTLE GIRL

1:36

**Dylan** vocal, acoustic guitar(?), **Danko** bass, **Hudson** organ, **Manuel**
piano, **Robertson** electric guitar.

• This is just over a minute and a half of mixed up confusion. As the
acoustic guitar is often inaudible during these sessions, it is possible
Manuel is upstairs chatting to Sara and the kids while Dylan is playing the
piano. The vocal fairly well follows the piano playing on this cut,
suggesting maybe a first-attempt number, with the singer playing the ivories.

The rest of the band gallops along as best they can, but it would have been
wonderful to have a second or third take of this, as Dylan sounds
excited – even if the lyric is slight and primarily an excuse to shake a tail feather.

The song actually ends at 1:31 with five seconds following of the piano
and organ dicking about on some other riff.

## ONE MAN'S LOSS

3:48

**Dylan** vocal, piano, **Danko** bass, **Hudson** organ, **Manuel** drums,
**Robertson** electric guitar.

• Dylan may be winging it here, and although Manuel may be learning the drums (check out the rudimentary but successful fill at 1:17) he already has style. The Fab Four tried stuff like this at Twickenham in early 1969 when they did 'Dig It' but this is slower, more Pentecostal, more pleading. Note that the choruses to these improvised, hardly-sketched-out tunes are usually quite definite; it is in the verses where Dylan lets memory run free and imagination take flight.

Terribly recorded, this must be one of the earlier things put to tape. Nonetheless, its sound earmarks it as originating from the same place as the other songs here.

Dylan's vocal is distant: his microphone might be off and the listener is only hearing his vocal bleeding through the other mikes. If this is indeed one of the first things recorded, Hudson may simply have forgotten to turn him up.

Dylan also seems to have the echo pedal on his piano depressed continuously – or perhaps someone placed tacks on the hammers of the piano for that tinny honky-tonk sound.

## YOUNG BUT DAILY GROWING
(Traditional)
5:37
**Dylan** vocal, acoustic 12-string guitar, **Danko** bass, **Manuel** lap steel guitar.
• This is a Child ballad (a traditional song collected by Francis Child in the 19th century) and a Dylan favorite, which he knew back in Minnesota and performed at Carnegie Hall's Chapter Room on November 4, 1961. His friend and fellow balladeer Liam Clancy of The Clancy Brothers often sang this one onstage, sober, and frequently essayed it at the White Horse Tavern in New York City after a few pints of the dark stuff.

The song is a variant of two British broadside ballads intertwined down the years: 'The Trees They Do Grow High' and 'My Bonny Lad Is Young But He Is Growing,' the latter published by H. Such in London some time between 1849 and 1862.

Robertson and his Canadians might not have been folkies but they may have known the song: a version was collected in Newfoundland by musicologist Ken Peacock, who noted this intriguing little ballad as very difficult to trace. Many scholars feel it is of Scottish origin, citing as evidence the arranged marriage of Elizabeth Innes to young Urquhart of Craigston who died young in 1634. Arranged marriages, sometimes of male minors to a woman very much their senior, were a fairly common practice among well-to-do families of this and earlier periods.

It is as close a glimpse of Dylan solo acoustic as any tape made in Woodstock provides.

### BONNIE SHIP THE DIAMOND

(Traditional)

3:24

**Dylan** vocal, acoustic 12-string guitar, **Danko** bass, **Hudson** organ, **Robertson** electric guitar.

• The Diamond was a Canadian whaler, built in Québec in 1801 and sailed to Scotland to join the Aberdeen fleet in 1812. The Aberdeen Journal of March 18, 1812 reports: "The fine new Ship Diamond ... with Captain Gibbon in command, sailed on Thursday last, for the Davis Strait Whale Fishery."

The ship went on a yearly voyage until 1819, when she was caught in the early autumn ice while staying out too late in the whaling season. This time the crew were saved. In a situation repeated today, over-fishing off Greenland during the early 19th century had a devastating toll on the whale stocks. A new hunting ground, the South-West Fishery, was discovered in the region of the Davis Strait and it was mostly here that the Diamond fished.

In 1830, the Diamond, the Eliza Swan, and the Resolution along with 17 other whaling ships were caught in the ice of Melville Bay on the west coast of Greenland. The ships were lost and many sailors died.

Dylan is utterly committed to the lyric and, after a stilted, hoarse start, clears both his throat and his mind to focus on a tragic tale of men doing dangerous work in some of the world's coldest and most unforgiving seas. Sadly, dropout occurs on one channel from 1:23 to 1:26, which sounds like the result of tape oxidation. Manuel sits mutely on the drums with only a hi-hat tap at the end giving away his presence. Robertson and Danko are stumbling somewhat early on. It's true that, as Robertson has said, this music was not the train they came in on, but by the end all the coals are burning. If there is a God in Providence, a second take of this will turn up one day.

A quite musically accomplished though less dramatic version of the song appears on Roger McGuinn's 2001 CD set *Treasures From The Folk Den*, where he performs it with Judy Collins.

## THE HILLS OF MEXICO
(Traditional)
3:01
**Dylan** vocal, acoustic 12-string guitar, **Danko** bass, **Hudson** organ, **Manuel** random snare hits, a few hi-hat taps, **Robertson** electric guitar.
• Any song is bound to be intriguing that begins in a town called Griffin and ends with Dylan saying, "You don't have to take [tape?] this one down, Garth … you don't haveta … you're just wasting tape."

McGuinn did this one, too, as 'Buffalo Skinners' on his *Folk Den Vol. 2*, sounding like he got his version from Pete Seeger's take on it. Dylan, whose vocal finds no joy in buffalo hunting at all, sounds like he got his take on the song from Woody Guthrie. It's a folk-circuit staple, and everyone from Arlo Guthrie to Roscoe Holcomb and Burl Ives has had a crack at it.

On this and the previous song, Hudson stealthily enters after over a minute and a half of the song is done, Robertson enters at the two-minute mark, and right when it jells Dylan tells Hudson not to worry about taping it.

It sounds like Dylan couldn't remember the next part of the lyric and stopped the song in frustration.

What remains is what folk music would sound like if the early Velvet Underground were told by Tom Wilson to forget Warhol and the drugs and to try playing this old cowboy ballad instead.

**DOWN ON ME**
(Traditional)
0:39
**Dylan** vocal, acoustic 12-string guitar, **Danko** bass, harmony vocal,
**Manuel** very soft harmony vocal, **Robertson** electric guitar.
• It ends with Dylan musing aloud, "Yeah, that could be done," after a
three-part harmony between him, Danko, and Manuel falls apart.

Dylan would have known it anyway, but it appeared on records by two of
his friends, Odetta's *My Eyes Have Seen* (Vanguard, 1960) and Eric von
Schmidt's *The Folk Blues Of Eric Von Schmidt* (Prestige, 1963). The von
Schmidt LP appears next to Dylan in the montage on the cover of *Bringing
It All Back Home*. Whether or not Dylan learned the song in the green
pastures of Harvard University is anybody's guess.

Manuel (or Hudson) drops something off his chair at 0:19.

**I CAN'T MAKE IT ALONE**
3:30
**Dylan** vocal, piano, **Danko** bass, **Hudson** organ, **Manuel** nearly
inaudible lap steel guitar, **Robertson** electric guitar.
• This has got to be the first or second pass after a brief run-through: it is only
the pianist (surely Dylan) who seems to know the song with any confidence.

Manuel's lap steel is a drifting, ethereal ghost, like Brian Jones's
autoharp on 'You Got The Silver.' Manuel is sitting on the drum stool,
meaning he is furthest away from the tape recorder. This was done on
purpose, because drums are loud enough acoustically to be heard without
amplification or the close placement of mikes. Unfortunately, this means
that when Manuel plays other instruments from his perch on the drum
stool, some of his musical contributions are difficult to hear. It is possible
his lap steel is in reality Dylan's pedal steel guitar, a gift given to Bob that
none of them mastered. But if it is being used here, Manuel is shunning
the pedals (which instantly change the tuning of the strings lying
horizontally above) and simply sliding the steel bar up and down

he strings to the appropriate pitched position. Or in this case the approximate pitched position. Dylan must in some way have been frustrated by this song or their performance of it as they do not return to it. This is odd, because it is a promising tune that would have fit musically and thematically into the late-summer sessions that provided the lion's share of his contributions to the 1975 two-disc vinyl long-player set.

## DON'T YOU TRY ME NOW
3:11
**Dylan** vocal, piano, **Danko** bass, **Hudson** organ, **Manuel** pedal steel guitar, **Robertson** electric guitar.
• Another bluesy, 1950s, almost Fats Domino R&B workout, with Dylan on piano playing a slower version of his 'Hero Blues' riffing. For a 1960s icon, His Bobness has a huge love of the previous decade's rock'n'roll and effortlessly writes songs in that style.

Robertson enters late, again, suggesting he has another task at the sessions beside playing on the songs. The Hawks certainly would have come in on this train and, listening to this rarity among Dylan songs, one with a distinct middle eight, it is apparent that the best vocalist to cover it would be either Ronnie Hawkins – who could no doubt do the best ever last-set-of-the-evening, 3:00am, I've-been-drinking, show-off Duke-Peacock vocal in history – or Bobby Blue Bland, who invented just that genre anyway.

Richard Manuel is definitely on Dylan's pedal steel here as he attempts a few primitive pedal movements toward the end.

The last three seconds are an impatient Dylan banging a few piano chords, anxious for the next song. The man works fast.

## ONE FOR THE ROAD
4:47
**Dylan** vocal, acoustic guitar, **Danko** bass, **Hudson** organ, **Manuel** piano, **Robertson** electric guitar.
• Not the Sinatra saloon classic but a tune that takes up where Frank left

off. Dylan and Robertson used to laugh about which singers should get demos of which songs, but surely manager Grossman could and would have instructed someone to get this to Sinatra – a saloon singer who would soon be cutting songs such as 'Mrs. Robinson' and 'Something' in an attempt to reach out to a younger audience.

A lot of this is improvised, so the lyrics are not strictly logical but still noteworthy. How the players followed Dylan changing the chords towards the end is anybody's guess. Surely they were staring at his hands?

The song is worthy of a decent cover version and, to its real credit, is quite memorable enough on its own, although repeated listenings reveal it to be a template for another Dylan Basement Tapes classic, 'Sign On The Cross.'

### I'M ALRIGHT
0:58
**Dylan** vocal, acoustic guitar, **Danko** bass, harmony vocal, **Hudson** organ, **Manuel** piano, **Robertson** electric guitar.
• Another drinking song, this one sadly unfinished. Perfect for The Faces, back when Rod Stewart and Ronnie Lane were mates and still speaking to one another. The Hawks with Ronnie Hawkins singing could have cut this song up and spun it out five ways from Sunday. Ends while the performance is still on. Damn.

### SONG FOR CANADA
(Ian Tyson, Sylvia Fricker)
4:21
**Dylan** vocal, acoustic 12-string guitar, **Danko** bass, harmony vocal, **Hudson** organ, **Manuel** piano, **Robertson** guitar.
• So this is where 'Open The Door, Homer' came from. The melodic frame and chord sequence suggest this is the template for the Dylan original.

"One single river, rolling in eternity, two nations in this land that lies along its shore, but just one river rolling free." Ian Tyson was a real

Canadian cowboy and his (then) wife Sylvia Fricker was a folk musician. They met playing coffeehouses in Toronto and in the early 1960s signed up to be managed by Albert Grossman. Both were talented. Ian wrote the Canadian folk anthem 'Four Strong Winds,' memorably covered by Neil Young, and 'Someday Soon,' well known in the Judy Collins version. Sylvia wrote 'You Were On My Mind,' the archetypal '60s folk–pop classic, for The We Five.

Dylan also recorded Ian Tyson's 'The French Girl' as well as 'Four Strong Winds' later this year at Big Pink, but the score was evened at three-all when Ian & Sylvia covered a trio of Basement Tapes songs the following year.

Many CD collections and books refer to this song as 'One Single River' but the title is 'Song For Canada.' The Hawks may not be folkies, but perhaps remembering they're Canadians too (or possibly hearing the song as a proud statement of the Great White North) they are down with it, playing confidently, with grace, and ending on a dime. They respectfully wait a few quiet moments at the end before you hear Hudson's chair squeak as he leans over to turn off the tape recorder.

## PEOPLE GET READY
(Curtis Mayfield)
3:24
**Dylan** vocal, acoustic 12-string guitar, **Danko** bass, harmony vocal, **Manuel** piano, tenor harmony vocal, **Robertson** electric guitar.
• Dylan would record this later for *Renaldo & Clara* as well as the *Flashback* soundtrack. His 12-string is getting progressively further out of tune, adding to the sense that this is the correct order in which these songs were recorded. But why does Hudson sit out for most of this, hitting only a few chords?

Dylan anxiously picks a few McGuinn-like doodles at the top before coming in too early with his singing. Without stopping playing they try again, and the gospel masterpiece by Robertson's main man and quiet guitar hero – Curtis Mayfield of The Impressions from Chicago – is

sincerely essayed by sinners who convincingly sound like they believe The Word. Certainly one of them does. There was a huge Bible displayed on a book stand in Dylan's *Hi Lo Ha* home, its pages wrinkled and dog-eared from someone's studying the text.

Dylan duets with his favorite harmony man, Rick Danko, but on key lines such as "…the Kingdom's throne" and "…you just thank the Lord" it's Manuel who underpins the whole message with a beautifully soft vocal part. (Robertson might be singing along softly at points such as "…get on board" as the overtones from the harmonies are quite strong at such points.)

At 2:12 Dylan plays a tender if slightly clumsy lead guitar solo on his acoustic 12-string. At 3:18 Bob bumps his guitar on his chair.

This songs touches the heart: they're singing and playing like they mean it. And dig this: everybody seems to know the words by heart. Later, Van Morrison would use The Impressions' original as a starting point for his own 'Tupelo Honey' – and you know Van The Man would have loved to have been in the Red Room singing along on this one. But he didn't live in Woodstock yet. Had he heard this was going on, he'd have moved there sooner.

## I DON'T HURT ANYMORE
(Don Robertson, Jack Rollins)
2:24
**Dylan** vocal, acoustic 12-string guitar, **Danko** bass, harmony vocal,
**Manuel** piano, **Robertson** electric guitar.
• "Let us try it once, Garth … raise away [erase away?], Garth." CBS Records ran an ad campaign two years earlier based on the slogan Nobody Sings Dylan Like Dylan. It would appear that no one gives instructions like Dylan, either. *Raise away*? Where is Hudson, anyway? Why doesn't anyone tell the singer to tune his 12-string?

The song was a major hit for Hank Snow in 1954, spending 20 weeks at Number 1 on the country chart. Eddy Arnold got a minor hit out of it in 1956 and Faron Young revived it in the 1960s. In 2005, Martina McBride covered it for the CMT generation of fans. Dylan and Danko, the two biggest true country fans in any room, be it Red or pink or whatever, sing it like two enthusiastic drinking buddies. Which perhaps they were that day. Dylan holds nothing back, the Hibbing youngster in him happily singing a favorite of his long-gone youth.

Only Levon Helm's presence would have made this any better. Helm's forthright attitude might also have gotten Dylan to tune.

Fans of The Hawks were shocked when *Music From Big Pink* appeared and Ronnie Hawkins's old R&B crew were heard playing C&W. Had they heard this back in 1967 they would have understood.

Dylan later covered Hank Snow's Number 2 C&W hit of 1963, 'Ninety Miles An Hour (Down A Dead End Street).'

## BE CAREFUL OF STONES THAT YOU THROW
(Bonnie Dodd)
3:15
**Dylan** vocal, acoustic 12-string guitar, **Danko** bass, harmony vocal,
**Hudson** organ, **Manuel** a few soft lap steel passes, tinkling piano,
**Robertson** electric guitar.
• "Now is there a tune you can play to that?" Dylan asks. "That pea is on[?] down the road ... let's put it up in D." Manuel says something about "down the road" and Dylan laughs.

Bonnie Dodd played pedal steel for Tex Ritter and, briefly, for Bob Wills. Little Jimmy Dickens cut this at the end of the 1940s, but without much action, and legendary Nashville publisher Fred Rose loved the song and wanted a hit. Rose was publisher, mother confessor, and father figure to Hank Williams, and he got Hank to cover it in his Luke The Drifter persona.

Williams's recitation was better than Dylan's but Dylan still sounds sincere. Part of the difference is that Dylan is audibly surrounded by drinkers on a tune whose lyrics mention the evils of drink. Williams was a drinker, yet one who sounded thoughtful, pious, and sober on his recording of this somber ballad. Dylan only has the first quality here: thoughtfulness.

Dion's folk–country cover of this reached Number 31 on the pop charts in 1963 during his own spell with Columbia Records and Hank Williams Jr. took it to Number 37 on the country charts in 1969 when he was still slick-haired and showbiz.

### BABY, AIN'T THAT FINE
(Dallas Frazier)
2:05
**Dylan** vocal, acoustic 12-string guitar, **Danko** bass, harmony vocal, **Hudson** organ, **Manuel** piano, **Robertson** electric guitar.
• Hudson turns on the recorder once the song is started, so the very beginning is missing – or perhaps on this seven-inch reel the long fade of 'One Man's Loss' (or perhaps a second pass at it?) ran over the start of this one.

With Dylan sounding like the great Doug Sahm working it out with his Tex-Mex pals on the west side of his hometown, San Antonio, the Dylan fan who hears this can easily connect the dots to Sir Doug and Bob singing 'Wallflower' on October 9, 1972 at Atlantic Studios in New York City.

Fred Rose had the publishing on this one, too, from the pen of the guy who wrote 'I'm A People,' 'Elvira,' 'There Goes My Everything,' 'Beneath Still Waters,' and the immortal 'Mohair Sam.' Also a memorable duet in 1966 between Gene Pitney and Melba Montgomery. Dylan has great taste.

### ROCK, SALT & NAILS
(Bruce Phillips)
4:34
**Dylan** vocal, acoustic 12-string guitar, **Danko** bass, harmony vocal
**Hudson** organ, **Manuel** piano, **Robertson** electric guitar.
• A slow oft-covered country ballad by U.Utah (Bruce) Phillips, this was the title track of Steve Young's groundbreaking 1969 LP for A&M (the one with 'Seven Bridges Road' on it) and more recently was covered by

alt.country heroes Buddy & Julie Miller. A favorite in the bluegrass world thanks to a Flatt & Scruggs cover in '65, it has been cut as a fast jig. But here, after inquiring if Hudson is ready, Dylan sings it like he sang 'Moonshiner' back in August of 1963 for Tom Wilson: slowly and with great feeling. He doesn't sound tired; he sounds ageless. And so do his friends. "If the ladies were squirrels, with their high bushy tails / I'd fill up my shotgun, with rock, salt, and nails." Mercy.

Why isn't Hudson louder? Didn't they play this stuff back soon after they cut it to check it out? "Is that, ahh, is that tough ... to do another one?" Dylan inquires at the end. "Yeah," someone says.

## A FOOL SUCH AS I
(Bill Trader)
2:48
**Dylan** vocal, acoustic 12-string guitar, **Danko** bass, harmony vocal
**Manuel** piano, **Robertson** electric guitar.
● Columbia released an April 1969 version of this on their ghastly *Dylan* from 1973, an album comprised mainly of out-takes from *Self Portrait*. This is way mo' betta, even if you can practically smell the green smoke.

It's another song first cut by Hank Snow, who released it on a single in 1952. Admittedly, Dylan and co may have learned it from Elvis's 1959 version, although Carl Dobkins Jr. cut it around then too, as did Jim Reeves.

Dylan starts this one too low, moves up the capo on his acoustic, and tries again. He gets the recitation quite right, Robertson plays the unobtrusive but supportive guitar, which is his bread and butter, and Danko shows why Dylan liked to sing with him so much – but where oh where is Hudson?

## SILHOUETTES
(Frank C. Slay Jr., Bob Crewe)
0:20
**Dylan** vocal, acoustic guitar, **Danko** bass, harmony vocal, **Hudson**
organ, **Manuel** piano, harmony vocal, **Robertson** electric guitar.
● The Diamonds battled it out with The Rays on the U.S. charts in 1957

with this, but The Rays won, hitting Number 3 with this classic slice of teen Americana when all seemed malted milkshakes and sock hops. Perhaps America may never have been that way, but then nostalgia ain't what it once was either. Hudson slowly fades this one in and it ends in giggles, directly giving way to the next song.

## BRING IT ON HOME

2:59

**Dylan** vocal, acoustic guitar, **Danko** bass, **Hudson** organ, **Manuel** piano, vocal, Robertson electric guitar.

• After some insistent strums of the acoustic guitar, Manuel announces, "Got that one," and, leaning away from the mike, states: "C'mon home, baby." Which is enough to get the gang going on a Bo Diddley beat.

"Richard, Richard, take a verse ... sing a verse," says Dylan. Manuel replies, "What's the song?" Dylan: "Any song, man ... sing a verse! You know that song."

The beat continues to build as Manuel mumbles: "You know I can't ... I can't hear that." They press on regardless. "OK, I'll sing a verse," says Dylan reluctantly, improvising lyrics around the title phrase. This is 'Who Do You Love?' crossed with 'Tombstone Blues.'

The sound is that of Johnny Cash's Tennessee Three paying tribute to Bo Diddley and Bo's maracas player Jerome Green. Green was a former jazz tuba player who toured with the former Elias McDaniel between 1950 and 1964, shaking his maracas and performing verbal jousts with Diddley on such memorable slices of urban life as 'Say Man,' 'Bring It To Jerome,' and 'Down Home Special.'

Animals lead singer Eric Burdon remembers Green as fond of drink and yet so concerned about getting fired for drinking on the job that he had a friend make him two new maracas. Each was capable of hiding a small whiskey bottle inside.

This type of song is the common ground of The Hawks and Dylan. At 2:10, Robertson starts riffing as if The Hawks are once again behind

Ronnie Hawkins and it's the fourth set of the night at Lucy's Orbit Lounge. At 2:21, Dylan finally leaves the title alone and starts singing improvised lyrics of which Hawkins and Allen Ginsberg would have approved: "A two-three parlor in the pool and a hot rod for your pay." Then again, you can hardly hear what Dylan is singing because the song is in collapsed mono with very little separation. Perhaps he is singing something else. But why let that stop the fun of listening? A grapefruit rots in the hot sun, I fought the law and the law won. Hudson fades this like a pro.

## I CAN'T COME IN WITH A BROKEN HEART
2:44
**Dylan** vocal, piano, **Danko** bass, **Hudson** tambourine, **Robertson** electric guitar.
• They want to rock but are trying to find the groove. There is drop-out from 0:19 to 0:25 and they start again. Someone apologizes at 0:39. Dylan halts things and at 0:46 they try yet again. Another one-chord groove, another 'Sittin' On A Barbed Wire Fence.' In light of the story of Robertson walking out of a 1965 Velvet Underground gig in N.Y.C. after only five minutes, it is ironic how much this sounds like the Velvets learning 'I Can't Stand It.'

With whips, chains, flashing strobes, and lyrics about drug use and sadomasochism, there would have been much for Impressions fan Robertson to find alien and extremely unsettling about the Velvets. His personal artistic journey was in the other direction.

Nonetheless, Dylan with the embryonic Band and The Velvet Underground could each make a one-chord Diddley-like drone song out of thin air.

With the limited musical room in which the Velvets' guitars could move and with Lou Reed at this early stage mimicking Dylan's vocal style, the connection is easy to hear.

## THE KING OF FRANCE

3:24

**Dylan** vocal, electric piano, **Danko** bass, **Hudson** tambourine, **Robertson** electric guitar.

• Is this Manuel on electric piano and Hudson slapping the tambourine? It is possible. The keyboard, which sounds like a Fender Rhodes electric piano, follows the vocal closely, and there is no keyboard soloing, with a right-hand fluff at 0:26 as the chords change, so it suggests Dylan on the ivories. The poor, distorted mono-ish sound quality makes this frustrating to hear. It sounds like a good song with a good chord structure and an intriguing Dylan lyric about the king of France coming to the U.S.A. to tell all the New World types just what it is all about. Only Dylan and Danko know the song well: it sounds like they were working on it beforehand and then called for reinforcements. But if this performance seems loose, perhaps that's because Jack Daniels is sittin' in. Sounds like it.

This would seem to mark the end of the sessions at the Red Room in Dylan's *Hi Lo Ha* home at Byrdcliffe. From here on out the sound quality gets better. Hudson's engineering skills become more developed – or at least he is more familiar with the equipment to hand – and the sessions gain a focus that they didn't have before.

Or perhaps that's all conjecture. Maybe this is simply the point where Sara Dylan put her foot down and asked everyone to leave the house and to take those noisy amps and guitars when you go. One could hardly blame her.

Besides, much of the Basement Tapes tale is conjecture, any known and accepted facts notwithstanding. That is part of the great mystery of these recordings. Quoting Robbie Robertson directly, facts aren't always the most interesting. No doubt the Bob Dylan so attuned to the folk world of Roscoe Holcomb and Dock Boggs would agree.

MILLION DOLLAR
BASH

# 8. Lost Time Is Not Found Again

*The recording gear they used*

The Red Room recordings chez Dylan were the first Basement Tapes sessions, the first musical work that the Dylan–Hawks team had done since the end of the '66 world tour, and the beginning of the most productive year of Dylan's songwriting career.

This is fact. So much of the rest of the Basement Tapes story is mystery and myth. So much of the rest of the story is undocumented and it is unlikely that the whole truth and nothing but the truth will ever be revealed. It seems the preponderance of ill-prepared and poorly manufactured bootleg records will forever cause Dylan's loyal and faithful fans to mistake Paradise for that home across the road.

With no one in the Big Pink basement so much as cracking a smile, much less the code of silence that has surrounded so much of the sessions, it is left to those recording experts who knew Dylan, who knew The Hawks, and who have worked with them since to piece together as best we can just what happened to get the music recorded.

There are reasons both human and technological that have allowed and caused this timeless music to continue to affect its target audience, 40 years and more since it was recorded on to magnetic tape. Unlike the more magical and age-old realm of creation – the one in which you find songwriting, musicianship, and performance – the technical realm of recording is finite and quite tied to the technology of the hour.

It is relatively easy to identify what could have been accomplished as well as to identify what could not possibly have been done in the Red Room, in the basement of Big Pink at 2188 Stoll Road, and at Rick Danko's house off Wittenberg Road. The technology available leads us straight to some facts and directs us toward others before stopping short of certainty. But one thing is for certain: Garth Hudson proved an excellent engineer, a fine tape op, and an all-around technical wiz. His deep internal logic and his linear thinking skills are almost as much the story of the Basement Tapes' sound as Dylan's songs or The Hawks' playing.

Hudson was the only person in the various rooms where the Basement Tapes were made who could have recorded them. He had made many,

many recordings before – one estimate is thousands of tapes – of polka bands in union halls, ice skaters performing, birds chirping happily at dawn or plaintively at dusk, calypso music, and the rest.

To record the Basement Tapes would have been no stretch for Hudson. He needed the three basic elements of recording in 1967: some microphones; a mixer to organize what those microphones capture; and a tape recorder to connect the mixer to. As we'll see, he may also have needed some kind of artificial reverb device. Hudson probably plugged his microphones into two small mixer boxes and then plugged those into a 2-track tape recorder.

We have two technical guides, Joel Bernstein and Rob Fraboni, to put some more detail into this outline. Bernstein needs little introduction in the rock world: he is a world-class archivist, a recording engineer, a folk musician, and a noted photographer. In particular, he is the archivist for Neil Young and Joni Mitchell, although for decades he has worked with all of Crosby Stills Nash & Young and during the latter part of the 1970s worked for Bob Dylan in Santa Monica.

With Neil Young – who owns a 29-song reel-to-reel copy of the original Basement Tapes – Joel Bernstein has been exposed to the music that Dylan and The Hawks made in 1967 as much as anyone outside the people who actually created that music all those years ago.

Bernstein met Garth Hudson in 1984 in San Francisco at the Great American Music Hall. He told Hudson he'd been listening to Young's reel of the Basement Tapes. At which point Hudson looked archly at Bernstein and said, "Oh, really?"

Bernstein told Hudson that the reel was Elliot Mazer's copy. Mazer, who produced many Neil Young albums, starting with 1972's *Harvest*, had gotten his Basement Tapes reel from Albert Grossman back in 1968. Mazer was working for the manager and was given the chore by Hudson of dubbing a safety copy. Later, Mazer took the tape to Young when he went out to work with him in 1971, knowing that Young would love to hear what his friends had been up to in that basement.

Bernstein remembers that Young would have him play one of those safety copies on the big speakers in the studio for inspiration. "I once had Clinton Heylin and Greil Marcus sitting on my couch listening to this copy," says Bernstein. "Greil had never heard anything like it. If you think about it, here is a man who did the original liner notes for the 1975 set, a man very familiar with the material, and he was understandably thinking he'd heard it all before. But his jaw fell open, he was completely gobsmacked from the first playback, because he'd never heard the Basement Tapes spread so wide before, not until I played him and Clinton the original, this 15 i.p.s. copy. Garth really did a great job on those original tapes."

When Bernstein met Hudson in the 1980s he naturally took the opportunity to ask some technical questions. "Garth told me that some of the equipment he used for recording the Basement Tapes was Peter Paul & Mary's P.A. equipment," says Bernstein. PP&M were also managed by Albert Grossman.

It has been said that the gear was left over from the '66 tour. "No, it was definitely not stuff left over from the Dylan world tour," says Bernstein, "not as I understand it or as Garth said to me. How could it be left over from a tour of Europe by anybody? First of all, there is not a lot of equipment you are going to be taking to Europe on a tour, aside from your guitar and a guitar amp. You are probably not taking microphones at that point." Also, adds Bernstein, the electrical AC power rating is different between the U.S. and Europe. "So my point is, how much equipment are you gonna take on a Dylan European tour and bring back home to the U.S.A.? I would say next to nothing. Guitars, yes. But back in 1967 technology had limits that it doesn't have today."

Bernstein explains that Peter Paul & Mary often used a custom three-microphone stand, seen in some live photographs of the trio from the 1960s. "Most of the mikes they used were very good ones. Garth mentioned they used a Neumann U47, maybe a Telefunken, but a classic, a real classic." Some PP&M live shots show the three-mike system with

two U47s and a separate guitar mike, a Neumann KM-56.

The Neumann and Telefunken U47 mikes are essentially the same unit with a different brandname. "Today, they cost many thousands of dollars," says Bernstein. "They are a microphone that people justifiably cherish. Those mid-1960s live photos of Peter Paul & Mary would show you those mikes, and this was a way, way better system than most people were using at the time. Garth is certainly looking for the best mikes he can use. I am pretty sure the U47 is used to record Bob's vocal on the Basement Tapes, because on the Neil [Young] reel it sounds so fantastic. This is a way, way better system than most people were using at the time."[1]

Bernstein suggests that Peter Yarrow of Peter Paul & Mary might know more about the subject. But Yarrow's memory isn't perfect. He remembers PP&M using some of the very equipment that Bernstein describes, and Garth Hudson says they borrowed from folk's finest trio. Did The Hawks record on equipment Peter Paul & Mary loaned them? "Not to my knowledge," says Yarrow, "but it is quite possible. The microphones we were using up to that time we were not using any more, and they could have been loaned to the guys by someone for use in the basement."[2]

Rob Fraboni is one of the engineers who cleaned up and mixed the Basement Tapes for release on the Columbia two-LP set of 1975. He worked with Dylan and The Band on *Planet Waves* and on *The Last Waltz*. He's also worked in the studio for John Lennon, The Raspberries, Patti LaBelle, The Beach Boys, The Rolling Stones, Joe Cocker, and Eric Clapton.

Fraboni insists that Hudson used only two or three microphones on the Basement Tapes sessions. "I was always mystified by the rather elusive quality Garth captured. I couldn't figure out what it was. And then I discovered what it was: it was because there were very few mikes."

One of Fraboni's favorite recordings of all time is 'Louie, Louie' by The Kingsmen, and this, he discovered, was made with one microphone. He argues that too many microphones mess up the sound, that technically the phase relationships become too complex, and that something less tangible is lost. "It messes with this spiritual thing in a way that takes the integrity away. This is what it is about this stuff which is go great, the fact that Garth did this recording so simply, yet he captured this spiritual thing. From an engineering point of view that really captured me." [3]

Joel Bernstein, however, thinks there may have been up to six microphones. Perhaps two vocal mikes, for Dylan and whoever else is singing, one acoustic-guitar mike, one mike on the guitar amp, one on the bass amp, and one on the organ. The drums and the piano do not seem to have been miked but were loud enough to bleed into the other mikes. (On some songs, Dylan's acoustic guitar sounds like it is not miked but is still heard because it is bleeding into his vocal mike.) Rick Danko appeared to bolster Bernstein's argument in a late-1980s interview when he mentioned that there were perhaps five inputs: "Garth ran the tape recorder and we had a little mixing board with four or five inputs going into the 2-track machine." [4]

In the basement at Big Pink, not long after Levon Helm returned late in 1967, Hudson would produce and record a group of musicians from India called The Bengali Bauls, invited to Woodstock by Grossman. On the back of the *Bengali Bauls ... At Big Pink* album (Buddah BDS 5050) a technical note says the microphones that producer Hudson used were Norelco D-24 models. (These are Austrian-made AKG mikes, branded Norelco for U.S. distribution.) Perhaps Hudson used them for the Basement Tapes recordings too, in addition to those borrowed from Peter Paul & Mary? And later, perhaps Peter Paul & Mary took their microphones back to use themselves and Hudson was left with the D-24s for the Bengali Bauls album?

Bernstein remembers that when he talked to Hudson in 1984 there was also some discussion of the 'conscience' mike, a round-the-neck microphone such as a game-show emcee might have worn. This is what Dylan and The Hawks called the Voice Of Conscience microphone. "There is a Beat influence here," says Bernstein, "the idea being that every once in a while someone would walk up to the conscience mike and say something, or perhaps put it on and say something. Particularly in The Hawks' segment of recordings from Woodstock, we hear these pronouncements, things a bit like that wonderful moment in *The Last*

*Waltz* where you hear [Beat poet] Lawrence Ferlinghetti talking. There's a sort of line from the Beats to that moment. That's the conscience mike." Richard Manuel's asides on 'See You Later, Alligator' and his mournful answers to Dylan and Danko on 'I'm Your Teenage Prayer' are examples of the Voice Of Conscience mike picking up absurd verbal contributions (and 'Teenage Prayer' is so full of 1950s pastiche and verbal nonsense it sounds like the early Mothers Of Invention).

So we have our microphones. The next requirement in the audio chain is a mixer of some sort. When he met Hudson in 1984, Bernstein asked if it was true that he had a couple of tube mixers that he fed into the tape deck. "And Garth said yes, they were Altec tube mixers." These would probably be Altec 1567A mixers. Check out some 1960s studio photos and you will see racks of Altec gear. The 1567A was one of the most popular little mixer boxes during the mono era, both for location and studio recording. It was not like modern mixers, with faders and an array of switches, but a simple box, like a small hi-fi amp, with knobs on the front and connectors on the back. Hudson certainly would have been familiar with them. And this tallies with the technical note on the Bengali Bauls album, which specifies two 1567A mixers. Peter Yarrow confirms that Peter Paul & Mary used the Altec 1567A in their P.A. set-up.

"So, the signal from each mike goes into a tube Altec mixer," says Bernstein. Each of the two 1567As had four inputs and one output. Using two of these mixers, one into each side of the stereo on the tape recorder, Hudson could easily have employed six mikes. "I think that is all they needed," Bernstein says. "I don't think there was anything more going on there at any one time."

Now we know about the microphones and the little mixers. But how did they get a tape recorder into the Red Room or the Big Pink basement in 1967? Forty years ago, studio-quality tape machines were large, bulky, and awkward to move. Bernstein says the answer is that they used a smaller professional tape machine.

"The model tape deck they were using was an Ampex 602," says Bernstein. "This came out around 1957, although they are probably using a newer version. There are only a few models they could have used: there were not so many options at the time. I am sure they used what is known as a suitcase model, a portable deck that could only hold up to seven-inch reels, which indeed we know is what they used, and which could only record at 3¾ or 7½ i.p.s. [inches per second tape-speed], and again we know those are the two speeds used on the Basement Tapes. The Red Room reels sound like 3¾ mono, but they were setting up – they haven't played in a long time and they were figuring out what to do." [5]

The Bengali Bauls album credits Hudson as using an Ampex 400 tape recorder, but this particular model had a poor reputation and probably was not the one he used for the Basement Tapes. Rob Fraboni is more specific – and after all, he helped transfer the tapes to LP release in 1975. He says that the Big Pink tapes were certainly not made on the Revox tape recorder shown on the cover of that *Basement Tapes* two-LP set. "They were done on an old Ampex, a beige colored machine," he says, probably referring to the 602. "It's funny: that Revox is in the Cleveland Rock & Roll Hall Of Fame where it says it was the machine the Basement Tapes were recorded on. That is not true. The Ampex machine actually used is gone now: Garth lost it in a fire." [6]

So there we have the basic recording set-up: the microphones, the mixers, and the tape recorder. One further sonic point: there is audible reverb on Dylan's voice. Where is that from? Hudson told tape archivist Joel Bernstein that it came from a mechanical reverb box called an Echorec. "My feeling is that you have Bob on a U47 mike to a Guild Echorec," says Bernstein, "and then that output is going to a channel on a mixer on that side of the tape deck, giving you the beautiful reverb which you hear on Bob's voice." [7]

The Italian-made Binson Echorec offered a tape-echo effect using magnetic metal discs, providing the desired effect but without the hassle and fragility of tape itself. Syd Barrett used one on the early Pink Floyd recordings on both his voice and his guitar, particularly his Hawaiian-like slide playing, and Hendrix owned two. Guild of New York City

manufactured the unit for U.S. consumption. We need to call a brief technical time-out here. Echo, reverb, and delay are sonic cousins but not the same thing. 'Reverb' (short for reverberation) was a common effect found on many amps and P.A. systems 40 years ago but never quite excited the listener in the same way that true echo or delay did. Reverb allows the sound, the individual sonic signal, to reverberate, to resound, or be repeatedly reflected for a given amount of time. 'Delay,' however, does exactly what it says on the tin: the sound (that is, the sonic signal) is delayed in time so it lasts a bit longer. 'Echo' is repetition of a sound. The echo component on gadgets such as the Echorec allowed a greater and morecomplete reverberation than a mere reverb component on a guitar amplifier did.

To play back the recorded music they needed some monitor speakers. The ones used for the Basement Tapes sessions were Klipschorn units, says Bernstein, and yet another part of the Peter Paul & Mary P.A. system. "They are huge corner cabinets, designed so that when you put them in the corner the face points diagonally out to you, face out from the corner at an angle, and you were making a huge 'infinite baffle' of the corner itself. On purpose." This means that the corner and walls of the room would add to the speaker's efficiency, extending its low-end reproduction. "It had a claim to fame that it could produce the lowest known organ note, a 32-cycle note which no speaker that you could buy for your house at the time was able to reproduce."

If the equipment was this good, how is it the myth continues that they used thrown-together gear and hand-me-down items? Both Bernstein and Fraboni agree that the sound quality on the original tapes is quite good. On that 1975 two-LP *Basement Tapes* set the sound is obviously way better than the average mid-1960s demo. Nonetheless, the story persists that Hudson was recording on mediocre equipment at best. He was not.

Why do some Basement Tape songs have distortion, yet so many of the recordings sound as clean as clean can be, with a surprisingly strong signal engineered by Mr. Hudson? After all, he was not a trained professional recording engineer. "It is simply remarkable to me what

Garth did," says Bernstein. "I can see the rest of the guys going onto the lawn and having a smoke while Garth – the drug-free one who is on a natural high – is working on the equipment in the basement, listening to playbacks, doing this and that to sweeten the recorded sound."

Bernstein says that after the Red Room mono recordings, Hudson moved to recording two individual tracks, using one mixer to feed mikes to the left side and the other to the right. In this way, there is no common or 'summed' mono information in the centre of the stereo picture. "Most people are unaware of this, as they haven't heard an early enough copy of the Basement Tapes. The last time I transferred Neil Young's Basement Tapes collection I reviewed it cut by cut, song by song, and I set the level so each cut peaked at zero." In other words, he balanced the two tracks so they played back at equal levels.

"What I found to my amazement is that if you do that, then Garth mixed them perfectly. Each cut, every time. And that if you were down a little one side or another it radically changed the mix. On the mono versions, which we've heard from *Great White Wonder* forward, I can hear things where I think, Oh man, they're leaning on the left channel too hard! The bootleggers created their own problems here, their own distortion and so on. But when you even the levels, which almost nobody has done, well then it's perfect. The version of 'I'm Not There' which has circulated has a distorted bass on it. But the version I transferred is completely clean: the bass is not distorted at all. Not at all. And that's Garth. He did a great job. It really is one of his finest moments how he kept everything clean sonically." [8]

Rob Fraboni agrees that Hudson did a fine job of engineering as well as capturing a certain sound quality and a feel peculiar to The Hawks' cultural relationship to Americana. Fraboni is quite a fan of the Basement Tapes, as smitten by them as Bernstein or Neil Young. Unlike Band members Hudson and Robertson, who feel the Basement Tapes are simply another episode in their professional careers.

Robertson: "This is way back in the past, and to me it is just one of those artistic periods, like your blue period or your cubist period. Simply one of those stops along the journey that happened, a chapter in the professional life of The Band." [9]

Fraboni: "They did things like 'King Of France' and our singer is seemingly on speed and he's just rapping and talking, he plays and talks and plays and talks. We didn't put any of that on the 1975 record but some of that stuff is really incredible. I don't know how much of that has been bootlegged but there is some great stuff there. I put songs like 'Banks Of The Royal Canal (The Auld Triangle)' on a tape for myself, and some other things too, even some of the Red Room stuff. I made reel-to-reels, about three hours' worth, for myself to enjoy of the Basement Tapes. Terrific stuff." [10]

Another valuable result of the way Hudson recorded the material is that the various set-ups of musicians and singers and instruments in relation to the microphones and the resulting 2-track tape provide an audio clue to the three recording locations: Red Room, Big Pink, or Danko's place. This is the primary methodology used for grouping songs together in this book: certain songs sound the same because of where and how they were recorded and engineered.

The combination of Hudson as engineer, Dylan as ringmaster, Robertson as shop steward, and the intuitive playing of Danko and Manuel and their oh-so-sympathetic harmonies – all this proved that they were up and running. To use Danko's phrase, they were starting to get things done.

They would increase their groundspeed with the move from the Red Room to Big Pink. It was at Big Pink that what otherwise might have been an interesting sidebar to Dylan's career became an important story behind his ever-growing legend. It was there that The Hawks began audibly and identifiably to become The Band, creating a legend of their own. And it was there that Hudson and his friends perfected the informal recording set-up and process that would serve them so well on those legendary first two Band LPs, and which Dylan would also use for later albums such as *Oh Mercy*.

Others would follow this template, but Big Pink was the sounding of a gun that started a race still being run.

MILLION DOLLAR
BASH

## 9. Building Big Ships And Boats
*Moving to Big Pink*

As the sessions moved over from the Red Room at *Hi Lo Ha* to Stoll Road and Big Pink's basement, everyone had to pitch in, whether they lived there or not. Garth Hudson needed help moving the equipment and setting it up. It was less of a cozy domestic scene than *Hi Lo Ha* as there was – ahem – little feminine influence visible in a home in the woods leased to three road-hardened rock'n'roll musicians: Hudson, Rick Danko, and Richard Manuel.

Danko described the routine at Big Pink. Bob Dylan and Robbie Robertson would come on over from their homes nearby. "Bob would show up like clockwork around noon."[1] Dylan would always let himself in if no one was up and he'd put on a pot of his high-octane coffee and immediately retreat to a typewriter set up on a table, typing furiously on whatever new idea came into his head.

Hudson said: "It amazed me, [Dylan's] writing ability, how he could come in, sit down at the typewriter and write a song. Also what was amazing was that almost every one of those songs was funny."[2]

Hudson also remembered Dylan making up songs as he went along: The Hawks playing a sketched-out melody behind him and Dylan singing what few words he had or mouthing sounds and syllables until specific inspiration grabbed hold of him again. Robertson says they had been night owls for years. "But when you are up in the country and out in the mountains it affects you a little bit differently. The idea was not: 'Let's get started when the sun goes down.' That is urban thinking, artists in a garret someplace. Like most people, you get started around noon or something like that. We were up and about and ready to work by then."[3]

Dylan had continuing problems with Hamlet, and it was at this time that the dog who loved to bite people was thrust upon Danko, who took him in. Soon, no Big Pink session was complete without Hamlet in attendance.

"I helped sort out the basement as it was very ..." A pause follows, and you can no doubt imagine Robbie Robertson smiling as he strives to recall the exact way it felt. "What I did was make the set-up in the Big Pink basement sorta: OK, let's put the piano over here, get the drums down there, put the recording thing here on this table so Garth can see it and

reach it. I kinda helped sort out the place." All of this was, says Robertson, the opposite of every known rule of recording. The exact opposite of the 'correct' way to record. For a start, he recalls, the basement at Big Pink had a cement floor. "Cinder block, concrete-block walls, and a steel furnace. It was everything you shouldn't have when you are recording. You don't want hard surfaces, you don't want a furnace, you don't want metal things in the room, because that ruins everything. So we compromised and put down this big rug – and that was the extent of the acoustical treatment of the room."

Robertson also makes one very important point about the layout of Big Pink. The basement was in fact a garage, and the garage door was used only for bringing equipment in and out, not cars. The main entrance to Big Pink was effectively on the second floor, up a grassy slope to the left of the building. The garage door led into the basement, which was a one-room garage. The basement was, he says, only used for making music. So while we've all been calling these recordings the Basement Tapes for years, they really should be the Garage Tapes.

"Garth set up these microphones," Robertson continues, "and very early on we came to thinking there were not a lot of people doing recordings like this. Les Paul was a pioneer in this area, of setting up some gear somewhere, with a little echo unit or something like that, and just getting a vibe out of it, out of the room, the sound there."

Robertson says that this was where their new style of playing came from. "What it was, you would set up in a circle, and so we could balance the instruments. No monitors, no nothing, except if you played too loud you couldn't hear the vocal and that meant you were playing too loud. Because we were sitting in a circle looking at one another. And so it became like, hey, this is the way to play music! Everybody was in on it – we are not all off in separate rooms with earphones where you cannot see one another and you cannot visually figure out this or that. That's the way most people recorded. Not us, not Bob."

They came to the conclusion very early on, Robertson remembers, that there was something so natural about this method of recording. "You just let the sound follow it and whatever it represents, the sound of the song, the song itself, the instruments. It was all a happy accident. But if you find the right accident then you are on to something. All the guys could see each other! So you could react to that musically and emotionally." [4]

The informality of recording at Big Pink proved to be an antidote to the tense scheduling, the required formality, and the constant clock-watching that came with recording at a major studio, particularly a studio in an urban environment. Their informal approach proved to be a much imitated technique, used later by The Beatles, U2, Dylan, R.E.M., Jackson Browne, and countless others.

When asked, decades after the fact, if he ever thought the Big Pink method of home recording would become so imitated, Robertson says no, he didn't dream it would happen. "And I didn't really care about it, either. I just did not think like that, like, 'Whoa, this could be setting an example for the future!' All we were trying to do then was get something down on tape so we could remember it."

But he agrees that the Basement Tapes era was when The Hawks/Band learned to record. "I gotta say again how important the circle is, the idea of musicians near each other, making eye contact and reacting to the physical. It is all of that sittin' and singin' in a circle, that kind of music."

That kind of music, as Robertson calls it, came not only from a number of musical influences but a number of techniques: flat out improvisation; the typewriter on the Big Pink coffee table beckoning Dylan to create; the playing of a song that the ensemble half-remembered until another song sprang from their fumbling around; and Dylan's habit of impulsively playing piano songs on the guitar and his guitar songs on the piano. All of this once Hudson said they were ready to record.

"A lot of songs were written with only a typewriter," recalls Robertson. "It wasn't a technique, necessarily; it was more like taking a stab at some ideas and things via a typewriter. But Bob wrote a lot of songs like that, tapping away at a typewriter. That's why you get long songs, because you are just typing away and your hand doesn't get tired of writing." Robertson laughs at that, and then continues. "So Bob could write ten verses to something and it was only a matter of running out of paper then.

Also, a lot of these tunes were tunes that Bob knew, that we didn't know, or they were tunes we did know and we were just having some fun."

Robertson readily agrees that it was Dylan introducing them to folk music in more than a few instances. "He would play songs, songs I had never heard, and after we'd heard it or played it I would say, 'Did you write that?' And he would say no, that's an old song by blah-blah-blah, and frequently he would tell a little story of the song or what was behind the song. And that was interesting, learning some of these old-timey songs."

And The Hawks were still more of a rootin', tootin' R&B act? "Yes, except in some cases where we knew about some other things, a lotta different things. We knew about mountain music, for example. The Stanley Brothers are on there."

This is a reference to 'If I Lose,' an early, classic string-band song recorded by North Carolina's Charlie Poole in New York City in 1927 and later recorded by Ralph Stanley and his brother Carter in the 1960s for Tommy Hill at Starday. However, there is some debate about where The Band's version was recorded, as it may be an N.Y.C. demo for their first LP and not a Basement Tapes cut.

"We played in a circle," Robertson continues, "like mountain musicians sittin' where they can hear each other, someone singing lead and someone singing a harmony, maybe, and you would just play at that volume. That gives you something right there. When everybody plugs in and turns up and the monitors are turned on, after a while there is something that is left behind."

Robertson has never denied it was anything but an informative time, a great ride for everyone on the bus. "To be on the front lines with Dylan where we are trading experiences … he taught me a lot about folk music. None of the guys in The Band were about folk music. We were not from that side of the tracks. Folk music was from coffee houses, where people sipped cappuccinos. Where we played as The Hawks, nobody was sipping cappuccino, I'll tell ya. We were playing hardcore bars.

"Our experience was to help Bob learn to play in a band. It is much different from playing on your own, where you only have to follow your own tempo, your own meter. Now we were hooked up with a guy who was changing the course of songwriting during this period, and there is no question about his opening of those gates. He was opening those gates for me as well as everyone else." [5]

When Robertson and The Band later recorded the *Music From Big Pink* album, they still would set up in a small circle. "And we used the same kind of mike on everything. A little bit of an anti-studio approach. And we realized what was comfortable to us was turning wherever we were into a studio. Like the Big Pink technique." [6]

Perhaps Robertson and the guys in The Hawks were unaware at the time of the impact of their informal recording methods at Big Pink (and then elsewhere for the first Band albums). But did they not recognize this later on, perhaps when they spoke to fellow musicians? The classic example is the attempt that The Beatles made in January 1969 in Twickenham, England, to film *Let It Be* while recording in the honest, live, no-frills, no-overdubs, down-home way that The Hawks/Band did for the Basement Tapes and their early post-Dylan recordings.

Robertson says that various Beatles did tell him it was an influence. "Songs in there which were ... you know, John Lennon told me 'Don't Let Me Down' was a direct attempt to do what The Band was doing. And George Harrison told me stories about that too. Starting with the Basement Tapes and then into *Big Pink* and our second album, you can see our recording technique was that we never went into a recording studio, that we brought the atmosphere to us. We were the first ones making the records without a recording studio.

"Even years ago when I did my first solo album and I went to Dublin to work with U2, they were recording at Adam Clayton's house with all the equipment set up in the living room and so forth. They just went, 'OK ... does this look familiar? Where do you think we got this idea from?' Now, this technique is as common as any recording technique in music. So that was another thing The Band contributed to, and The Beatles were the first ones to follow in those footsteps." [7]

As we've heard, the steel furnace was in use in the Big Pink basement and could interfere with the home recordings that Hudson was making so meticulously on the equipment he had to hand. So it is reasonable to

estimate that it was April or early to mid May when the five musicians upped stakes at the Red Room and moved to Stoll Road and the basement of Big Pink.

We know that the sound reproduction clears up in Big Pink as Hudson gets to grips with the machinery and continues to learn on the job. Things began to run smoother as summer approached. They were all learning on the job. They were audibly replacing the youthful Beat poetic/rebellion/alienation anthems of the 1966 world tour with mysterious though familiar melodies and lyrics about local characters and biblical references. All of this backed by a warm ensemble performance that suggested family, friends, community, and home.

As Garth Hudson recently told Will Hodginkson: "The Band was born in Big Pink. When we moved to [that] house ... we stopped playing 12-bar blues, stopped jamming, and concentrated on songs. We'd been playing blues and rock'n'roll, and all of a sudden here we were in a pink house in a beautiful place in beautiful hills near a flower-power village, and that music wasn't suitable any more. We were in a perfect situation to take a new direction. ... That's the way with a good family: they encourage everyone to work on whatever they're best at .... The Band was about being centered. We were representing history, family, and mankind."

The spirit of the sessions was not one of us-against-the-world, as had been heard so loudly and proudly the year before, but of friends witnessing or describing a Saturday night party in their small hometown. A strange small town full of oddball characters, perhaps, but a small town of neighbors all enjoying themselves nonetheless.

It was no longer music that pumped you up, it was music that invited you in. Typically of Dylan, it was music that requested the listener to think. Not demanded, not required, but effortlessly requested the listener to think. It was a music that left more than a few things blowin' in the new trade winds of 1967 America.

Robertson said the early sessions had two purposes: one was "killing time" and the other was Dylan educating his Hawks a little bit as regards traditional folk music. You hear that in these songs; they come from a particular place and time.

**MILLION DOLLAR BASH**

# 10. Tiny Montgomery Says Hello

*Recordings in the Big Pink basement*

Bob Dylan and The Hawks moved from the Red Room at Dylan's house to the basement in Big Pink around April or early/mid May 1967. With a few breaks, they would stay there until October and the return of Levon Helm.

Rick Danko said: "Bob would come over and bang songs out on [a] typewriter and we'd go down to the basement and make some music up for them. It was a good collaboration. From that we got to get our own writing chops together a bit, and it was a good thing … . I think that is the way life is and how you get involved and you get things done." [1]

What follows is my view of each of the songs from Big Pink itself – the Basement Tape songs actually recorded in the basement. As usual, the title is followed by the composer, specified if not Bob Dylan, then the length of the recording, who played which instruments, and what it sounded like.

## NINE HUNDRED MILES
(Traditional)
0:46
**Bob Dylan** vocal, mandolin, **Rick Danko** harmony vocal, fiddle, **Richard Manuel** snare with brushes, **Robbie Robertson** acoustic bass.
• Someone has let the worm out of the tequila bottle on this one. If it didn't sound like an early Basement Tapes recording, then the temptation would be to say that 'Nine Hundred Miles' is a song on which Levon Helm played. It features his other instrument, mandolin, and is the type of material he always loved playing. As it is, the smart money says Danko is singing harmony and playing the fiddle, because the fiddle kicks back in when his harmony ends and we know thatDanko did have some fiddle-playing abilities.

A simple bass part suggests a relative novice is on acoustic bass, and this would suggest Robertson, a man whom Ronnie Hawkins started out on bass. He is further away from the mikes than anyone save the drummer, and this drummer's primitive pattern suggests Manuel still pushing on the learning curve.

So who is on mandolin? Either Dylan or Garth Hudson, as Helm is in the Gulf Of Mexico working a proper job. Hudson is not known for his prowess on stringed instruments, and the rhythmic attack from the right hand on the strings suggests Dylan's style of playing. And Dylan would play mandolin overdubs during the *Blood On The Tracks* sessions, so the finger points to Bob, a man who frequently namedrops bluegrass mandolinist Bill Monroe in interviews.

'Nine Hundred Miles' ends early, not due to any lack of enthusiasm on the part of the players but because it fades into the next cut. This suggests that no one cared enough about it to bother preserving it, that much of the song was simply erased when Hudson rewound back into the section of the tape reel where it sat.

The original was recorded by Fiddlin' John Carson in the 1920s, Riley Puckett a bit after that, and Dylan might have learned it from Woody Guthrie's version. Roger McGuinn uploaded his version onto the web for one of Project Gutenberg's online e-books.

## GOIN' DOWN THE ROAD FEELIN' BAD
(Woody Guthrie, Lee Hays)
3:15
**Dylan** vocal, piano, **Danko** harmony vocal, bass, **Garth Hudson** organ, **Manuel** hi-hat, sidestick.
• It is possible Manuel is on piano and Robertson on drums, but the piano solo is fairly primitive, which suggests Dylan, and the drums are fairly tight, which suggests Manuel, who was learning fast. Robertson perhaps wasn't around at the Big Pink house at the time; his musical presence is undetected here.

Originally recorded in 1923 by Henry Whittier as 'Lonesome Road Blues,' the song was also recorded by early country stars Ernest Stoneman and Fiddlin' John Carson, although Dylan is singing lyrics primarily from the Guthrie version. Dylan would also be familiar with Elizabeth Cotten's version on Folkways but doesn't sing her version's lyrics. Woody wrote, or re-wrote, this with his friend from The Weavers, Lee Hays. Big Bill Broonzy did a great version of it, as did The Grateful Dead many times and many years later.

The band sounds enthusiastic so there must still be some tequila left in the bottle: no one, not even Dylan, makes coffee that strong.

## SPANISH IS THE LOVING TONGUE
(Charles Badger Clark, Billy Simon)
3:56
**Dylan** vocal, acoustic 12-string guitar, **Danko** bass, **Hudson** organ,
**Manuel** piano, **Robertson** electric guitar.
• The greatest of all the West's cowboy love songs, if not the greatest cowboy ballad ever, this is the work of one Charles Badger Clark, who first published it in 1915 as a poem, *A Border Affair.* It described the impossibility of a white cowboy giving his heart to a Mexican woman. Songwriter Billy Simon added the melody years later for a sheet-music firm.

McGuinn got to this one too, as did Emmylou Harris and many others, but no one has sung it with more commitment than Bob Dylan. Here he gives one of his best vocals on the entire Basement Tapes, his sincerity never remotely questioned. The musicians are learning it as they play but this is nonetheless a charming performance. Dylan attempts to break hearts with an achingly sincere vocal; with more rehearsal there would not have been a dry eye in the house. Or the basement.

Dylan recorded it again on April 24, 1969 in Nashville during a period of writer's block and the result was a poor version released on the out-takes LP *Dylan* in 1973. He played it again on the Rolling Thunder Review tour; the solo version of just Dylan and piano, found on *Masterpieces*, is almost as committed a vocal as heard that day in Big Pink's basement garage but, alas, not quite.

## PO' LAZARUS
(Traditional)
0:58
**Dylan** vocal, acoustic 12-string guitar, **Danko** harmony vocal, bass,
**Manuel** piano, **Robertson** electric guitar.
• "You come in on the second line all the time, it's very easy," Dylan instructs Danko. "It goes like this."

Though it runs out before Hudson can sort out his part, it's a shame, shame, shame the tape was stopped (the swoosh sound indicates the machine was turned off) because this song has one of the most

interesting stories behind it as could ever be imagined. One day in 1959, a Mississippi state penitentiary inmate named James Carter led some fellow prisoners in singing 'Po' Lazarus,' a melancholic old work song about a man pursued and eventually shot by the sheriff. Mr. Carter, a sharecropper's son who soon forgot about singing it that day, also forgot about the song and forgot about the man who captured it on tape, Alan Lomax.

Carter forgot about it until February 2002, when he was presented with a check for $20,000 for the use of the song in the movie *O Brother, Where Art Thou?*. The film's producers used the version of 'Po' Lazarus' that Carter had recorded in prison for Lomax, the famous musical archivist who traveled the South with his tape recorder.

For over a year, as the movie's soundtrack album sold millions of copies, its producers searched for Carter, age 76, to pay him his royalties. The $20,000 payment was the first of what would surely total over six figures, and yet Carter had never heard of the album or the movie. He earns royalties for being the lead performer on the Lomax recording – and as 'Po' Lazarus' is in the public domain, he also earns songwriter royalties. Songwriter royalties are directed to the performer/arranger once the copyright expires.

Mr. Carter's wildly improbable, hilarious story sounds like one of Dylan's absurdist Basement Tapes lyrics. The performance that Dylan starts here sounds promising and could no doubt have used Carter's input, his enthusiasm, and the never-say-die spirit that carried him out of a ghastly jail term and back into society. It is a pity that this Big Pink version didn't carry on to a happy ending too and that the tape didn't roll on to capture a complete version.

## ON A RAINY AFTERNOON
2:45
**Dylan** vocal, acoustic guitar, **Danko** bass, **Hudson** keyboards, **Manuel** piano, **Robertson** electric guitar.
• Is this Hudson on a Clavinet that sounds like a mandolin? (The Hohner Clavinet was an electric keyboard with an unusual string-based sound.)

Perhaps it is Robertson on bass with Danko on mandolin. Danko was a bit of a fiddler, and a mandolin and a fiddle have the same string layout in the same tuning. The difference is that the fiddle has no frets and is bowed; the mandolin has frets and is picked. They are sister instruments. Obviously Dylan and Hudson liked this one; it is allowed a respectful fade.

Dylan was recorded on Robert Shelton's tape recorder on May 19, 1966 in a Glaswegian hotel room, playing a song with Robbie Robertson on acoustic guitars that had the same title (also known as 'Does She Need Me'), but this is not that song.

Slightly distorted sound here, so if Joel Bernstein's "set the peak level at zero" theory is correct (see chapter 8) then this would be a cleaned-up, rockin' little record you'd want your jockey to play. In other words, if Hudson did mix things perfectly "every time" and a modern engineer did so with existing tapes, then this would sound like a pounding outtake from *Highway 61 Revisited*.

A good number to play for those who thought Dylan had by this time left the highway for the gamblers.

### COME ALL YE FAIR AND TENDER LADIES
2:05
**Dylan** vocal, acoustic guitar, **Danko** mandolin, **Manuel** bass, **Robertson** electric guitar.

• In a session where songs grew out of songs, this is really a Dylan original based on the traditional 'Come All Ye Fair And Tender Maidens' (also known as 'Silver Dagger'). After the first few lines he is no more singing 'Silver Dagger' than he is singing 'Home, Home On The Range.'

There is a rudimentary mandolin being played by Danko that makes you wonder where Hudson might be. It seems Manuel is playing the very faint bass, which starts and stops presumably because the musician holding it isn't sure how to play it.

Dylan is winging it here, calling out the chords, improvising lyrics, and trying to get something out of something heard and sang years before in the folk clubs. They sound, ahh ... very happy here. As Danko told Barney Hoskyns about the sessions: "Well, we were [frequently drunk and stoned].

Most of us were single at the time and I am sure we had our share of experimenting with drugs and alcohol and the rest of it. Red meat, vegetarian fare, whatever." [2] Or as Dylan says on the tape while he struggles with his tuning: "This guitar ain't made to do this type of music."

## UNDER CONTROL
3:21
**Dylan** vocal, acoustic guitar, **Danko** bass, **Hudson** organ, **Manuel** piano, **Robertson** electric guitar.
• Barely in control, this song sounds like Dylan's 'Sittin' On A Barbed Wire Fence' with John Lee Hooker playing and singing Dylan's parts. "Please hold the chord, please hand[?] the sound," Dylan sings/intones at one point.

The sound is no longer a crowded mono: Hudson has them in stereo here. This might suggest it is one of the first Big Pink songs where they are audibly on top of their recorded sound, or perhaps this is the beginning of a new batch of recordings from the gang after a short break.

It's yet another song that sounds like a *Highway 61 Revisited* studio warm-up if not out-take. Proof that Dylan still had piss and vinegar in him or at the very least a pot of his kickass coffee.

## OL' ROISIN THE BEAU
(Traditional)
4:46
**Dylan** vocal, out-of-tune acoustic guitar, harmonica, **Danko** bass, harmony vocal, **Hudson** Clavinet, organ, **Manuel** piano, **Robertson** electric guitar.
• A song about drinking or a song for drinking? A song about a drunk or a song sung by a drunk? Be it 'Ol' Roisin The Beau,' 'Rosin The Beau,' or 'Ol' Rosin, The Beau,' this early 19th century Irish melody started as a drinking song, became the melody for no fewer than eight political campaigns in pre-Civil War America, was transformed, remarkably, into a temperance song by reformists, and made it to the music-hall stage in several different musicals. Whatever the title, this song remained a popular American folk ballad for over 50 years. That, friends, is a hit song.

Dylan recognizes all this and more, staying faithful to the swaying melody which is oh so perfect for saloon singalongs back at The Rose & Crown when the shutters are pulled down tightly and the pub's supposed to be shut.

This is probably a first take, and Dylan seems to have had more than his share of oat sodas – but that's fine on a song such as this. Place your bets he learned this from a Clancy Brothers & Tommy Makem concert or perhaps even from Liam or Paddy Clancy face to face in the back room at the White Horse Tavern. For tipsy men playing a drunken song about a drunk drinking, it's admirable that they end with a noticeably sober neatness.

Of particular note is Hudson, a man who set up several keyboards in the basement. He plays at least two them here, first Clavinet and then organ. (There are no overdubs on the Basement Tapes.) With Manuel playing some fine piano, this song illustrates the twin-keyboardist approach of The Hawks about as well as anything in their later Band catalog.

## I'M GUILTY OF LOVING YOU
1:05
**Dylan** vocal, acoustic guitar, **Danko** bass, **Hudson** organ, **Manuel** piano, **Robertson** electric guitar.
• Another one they should not have stopped taping or should not have partially erased with a careless rewind.

Hudson is really on top of the sound by this point. The mood is late-night reflective before too much alcohol pushes emotions over into melancholic self-pity. It takes only one listen to Manuel's piano for a Baby Boomer to recognize this song as the outgrowth of the guys fooling around with 'Last Date,' a Number 2 pop hit for Nashville pianist Floyd Cramer in 1960.

Equally interesting is the simple fact that by now Dylan is discarding original material that other artists would be thrilled to have written, and discarding this strong material before he has had a chance to give it the first reflective glance, much less the second and more polished run-through. Don't look back indeed.

**JOHNNY TODD**
(Traditional)
2:00
**Dylan** vocal, acoustic 12-string guitar, **Danko** bass, **Hudson** organ,
**Manuel** piano, **Robertson** electric guitar.
• They know this one and the sound on it is fine. They respect it, too, as
it is allowed a dignified fade at the end where other songs, such as 'I'm
Guilty Of Loving You,' are partially erased or stopped abruptly.

Where Dylan learned it is a story left untold here, but 'Johnny Todd'
is a sailor's song emanating from Liverpool. Children sang it there at
playtime as accompaniment to skipping rope, and the reference to "the
Liverpool side" means across the River Mersey from Birkenhead. Folklorist
Frank Kidman collected this from a singer who couldn't remember all the
words, so it could be argued Kidman helped write it when he fleshed out
the lyrics with his own.

Marlene Dietrich put it in her cabaret act after hearing Ewan MacColl's
version, and the song's Britishness was strengthened to the nth degree
when two members of the Liverpool Philharmonic Orchestra rearranged
the tune as the theme song of the popular U.K. 1960s/'70s TV show *Z Cars*.

As the song ends you can hear Dylan rattling a sheet of paper, probably
the 'Johnny Todd' lyrics.

**COOL WATER**
(Bob Nolan)
2:59
**Dylan** vocal, acoustic 12-string guitar, **Danko** bass, **Hudson** Clavinet,
**Manuel** piano, **Robertson** electric guitar.
• This Sons Of The Pioneers 1941 classic was a hit for Frankie Laine in
Britain in 1955, but Dylan sings it as sincerely as Bob Nolan's Pioneers did
and much more believably than Laine. The search for water turns into a
search for survival in the song. The entire shootin' match adds up to a
priceless metaphor as well as a country standard.

These Canadians may have shown Dylan some hot R&B, but here he
again shows at least three of them – Danko already being a C&W

fan – that the true sincerity found in the best country music can be as powerful and emotive as Hubert Sumlin playing behind Howlin' Wolf on a Friday night at the Checkerboard Lounge. The very beginning is missing. Damn. Damn!

## THE BANKS OF THE ROYAL CANAL (THE AULD TRIANGLE)
(Brendan Behan)
5:41
**Dylan** vocal, acoustic 12-string guitar, **Danko** bass, harmony vocal, **Hudson** Clavinet, organ, **Manuel** piano, **Robertson** electric guitar.
• Perhaps that is Manuel on harmony and not Danko, but no matter. The song was written as 'The Auld Triangle' by Brendan Behan for his play *The Quare Fellow* to introduce the story about the occurrences in a prison on the day a convict is set to be executed. Behan used Mountjoy Prison as the setting for the play as he was once incarcerated there for his Republican beliefs.

The song has also become known as 'The Banks Of The Royal Canal,' and Dylan certainly would have known the song from seeing The Clancy Brothers & Tommy Makem in New York City – a song like this was their bread and butter – or it is possible he may have have heard it earlier in Minnesota.

The pristine recording by Hudson enhances the performance greatly. These are the best sounding Basement Tapes recordings of 1967. The ending is tight, save for a harmless doodle from Robertson's guitar, and Dylan suddenly chimes in with a satisfied conclusion: "All right, let's try this one."

Robertson has said on several occasions how songs such as this were too collegiate, too Pete Seeger, too white for him and his fellow Hawks' taste, but that these very same songs somehow became alive and were much more palatable when Dylan sang them and told a little story about them. Listening to Dylan sing here and listening to the dignified manner in which the once R&B-saturated Hawks follow him is proof that Robertson was not joking about Dylan singing folk standards – and proof that Mick and Keith got it right when they sang that it's the singer, not the song.

## BELSHAZZAR
(Johnny Cash)
3:03
**Dylan** vocal, acoustic guitar, **Danko** bass, harmony vocal, **Hudson** organ, **Robertson** electric guitar.

• Two takes of this one. "Are you … did you record the last one?" Dylan asks Hudson. After a too cautious beginning and some drop-out in the right channel they switch keys and carry on.

Belshazzar, the king who rejoiced when 70 years had passed and the Jews were not redeemed, thought he was rid of the Jews forever, thought the Jews would remain stateless forever. Dylan loves his biblical fables, and this one is from the Book of Daniel.

Johnny Cash recorded his song about the great but ill-fated king in 1957 for Sun Records. There were few artists in the record industry whom Dylan respected more than The Man In Black. Can this really be Cash's first ever composition, as is alleged? It certainly is a fine start to anyone's songwriting career.

Listen to the otherworldly riffing that Hudson comes up with at 1:51 to 1:56. Have mercy! Cash might have disagreed but Dylan's committed vocal almost makes this a Beat poem set to a rock rhythm.

Manuel is inaudible here; perhaps he is still in bed upstairs. If he is, he can't be asleep as the guys are swinging like a suspension bridge in an earthquake on this one.

## I FORGOT TO REMEMBER TO FORGET
(Stan Kesler, Charlie Feathers)
3:14
**Dylan** vocal, acoustic guitar, **Danko** bass, **Hudson** organ, **Robertson** electric guitar.

• Elvis did a fine job on this song by his fellow Sun artist Charlie Feathers, and The Beatles took their cue from the King when they had George sing it live on BBC Radio on May 18, 1964 as part of their *From Us To You* broadcast. But Dylan puts the breaks on the tempo and gets introspective. It sounds like a spiritual and not a rockabilly tune here.

Hudson again excels: listen to his organ swells behind Robertson's playing from 1:48 to 2:04. Those swells are a solo, a song, a symphony all in themselves. Sweet. A pity they are followed directly afterward by a group confusing a chord change.

A clean recording by Hudson, a nice performance by all, with a respectfully slow ending. You can even hear Hudson move in his chair at 3:14. Perhaps he was getting up to look for Manuel.

D.A. Pennebaker's documentary film *Dont Look Back* debuted at the seedy Presidio Theatre in San Francisco on May 17, or, to put it another way, at about the time these very songs were being recorded in Woodstock. In September, the movie opened in New York City and was seen on general release in larger American cities from that point.

Today, *Dont Look Back* is considered an important work, a valuable document, and certainly one of the greatest music movies ever filmed. It's now available on DVD with an hour-long companion film, *Bob Dylan '65 Revisited*, which Pennebaker created some 40 years after the fact from the out-takes of *Dont Look Back*.

At the time of its first showing, however, the movie, like Dylan, was considered controversial. While trade papers such as *Variety* loved the film and it garnered grand reviews in magazines such as *The New Yorker* and Newsweek, the voices of Middle America saw it in a less favorable light. *The Cleveland Plain Dealer's* reviewer wrote: "This is a cheap, in part dirty movie, if it is a movie at all. It is a chopped up 'story' of Bob Dylan's stormy visit to England. It is certainly not for moviegoers who bathe and/or shave. It is 'underground' and should be buried at once. Burn a rag, as was once said of filth."[3]

*The Atlanta Journal* was not much kinder. "The variety of audience who can best appreciate the film are likely to be bearded and small and completely in tune with Dylan's message. ... The whole effect struck me as a sort of boring, off-color home movie of the neighborhood's biggest brat blowing his nose for 90 minutes."[4]

Back in Woodstock, Dylan continued work on the recording and rehearsing of old country songs and folk favorites with The Hawks. He made no concession to the opening or subsequent national distribution of a movie about his acoustic tour of the U.K. some two years earlier. Once again, he would not look back.

### YOU WIN AGAIN
(Hank Williams)
2:39
**Dylan** vocal, acoustic guitar, **Danko** bass, **Hudson** organ, **Robertson** electric guitar.

• Starts abruptly, leaving the first line of the song, "The news is out," lost to posterity. A pity. Dylan's vocal sounds more like Jerry Lee Lewis's version than Hank Williams's, and if Manuel had been there to add piano it might have made the connection to Lewis even more clear.

Everyone obviously knows the song, although Robertson is not, strictly musically speaking, a Nashville picker. His style can be twangy, it can be gospel and sensitive, but he faithfully practiced R&B for hours as a teen and it shows. As an ensemble, these Canadians don't sound as excited on this Hank Williams standard as they so audibly are on some of the other Basement Tapes cuts. Maybe they were waiting to cover some Chess Records stuff that Dylan too loved as he was growing up, just like his friends from north of the border. That moment would never come. They would place those riffs elsewhere in the basement.

### STILL IN TOWN
(Johnny Cash)
3:03
**Dylan** vocal, acoustic guitar, **Danko** bass, **Hudson** organ, **Robertson** electric guitar.

• The very beginning of this is cut off. Whether that is a black-market mistake or Hudson hitting the record button too late is not known, but the former seems more probable than the latter.

This is a Johnny Cash original from his excellent *I Walk The Line* LP of 1964, a Number 1 country album (and 53 on the Billboard pop charts) whose tracks included such classic Cash as 'Folsom Prison Blues,' 'Give My

Love To Rose,' 'Hey Porter,' 'I Still Miss Someone,' the Dylan-inspired 'Understand Your Man,' and the title song. Dylan obviously owned this LP, and possibly Danko knew it as well as Dylan.

Robertson's playing is wonderfully sympathetic here. He sounds like he learned some country licks overnight or at least made Dylan show him the song before they turned the tape on. There is a smoothness here that seems to say they are all into the music, enjoying the song. Only a duff chord at the end from Dylan mars it in any way.

There is a muffled comment from Dylan at the end that suggests an improvement to the song. If there are really as many seven-inch reels from Big Pink as some have claimed there must be another version of this.

## WALTZING WITH SIN
(Red Hayes, Sonny Burns)
3:21
**Dylan** vocal, acoustic guitar, **Danko** bass, **Hudson** organ, **Robertson** electric guitar.
• Dylan starts, then stops the band at 0:29. Manuel giggles and, after fumbling around for ten seconds, they pick it up again.

This sounds like the Cowboy Copas version, cut not long before his fatal March 5, 1963 plane crash with Patsy Cline and Hawkshaw Hawkins.

At 1:54, Dylan says, "Let's try it again," but they keep on truckin'. At 2:49, Hudson plays some typically astounding swoops on his keyboard, so listen up, listen up! It is a fine authentic-sounding version, and can be seen as the prototype for 'Long Black Veil' on The Band's *Music From Big Pink* debut, but still makes pretty grim listening in light of the sad ending of Copas and his fellow country stars.

## BIG RIVER
(Johnny Cash)
2:30
**Dylan** vocal, acoustic guitar, **Danko** bass, **Hudson** organ, **Robertson** electric guitar.
• The first version found on a Basement Tape reel lasts only 50 seconds;

this second one is two minutes and a half. It's faster, in a higher key, and tougher and more real somehow.

It also could serve as a rhythmic, lyrical, and vocal prototype for 'Honky Tonk Women' by The Rolling Stones.

This take is a cleanly recorded stereo version with Dylan's vocal panned to the right (for the reasons Joel Bernstein described in chapter 8 about two independent tape channels with no audio in common), so if Hudson was somehow limited by the technology to hand, by now he had managed to be able to figure out a way to defeat his machines and get a consistently clean sound with all of the instruments audible in his 'stereo' spread.

At 2:21, a puzzled Dylan asks Hudson: "Do we have any room ... any reel ... why don't you shut it off ... shut it off now, why don't you shut it off ... do we have room for anything?" They did. And with that room they recorded yet another Johnny Cash song.

**FOLSOM PRISON BLUES**
(Johnny Cash)
2:42
**Dylan** vocal, acoustic guitar, **Danko** bass, harmony vocal, **Hudson** organ, **Robertson** electric guitar.
• Originally recorded by Johnny Cash in 1955 at Sun. From Dylan's opening strums on his acoustic it sounds like a *Bringing It All Back Home* warm-up number. Speed this up and you would have 'Maggie's Farm' or 'Bob Dylan's 115th Dream.'

Where was Richard Manuel on this reel? He has gone AWOL for several songs. Danko sings harmony with the same emphatic shouting style that he had employed on the 1966 world tour for the chorus of 'One Too Many Mornings.'

There is drop-out at 2:14 in the right channel. There is Robertson playing in the original hellfire-and-brimstone style where he and Mike Bloomfield were rivals. That would soon change when Robertson moved to Curtis Mayfield-styled playing, but just listen to him here. And ask Hudson to turn him up.

## THE BELLS OF RHYMNEY
(Idris Davies, Pete Seeger)

3:12

**Dylan** vocal, acoustic guitar, **Danko** bass, **Hudson** organ, **Robertson** electric guitar.

• Idris Davies was a coal miner in Wales and a friend of poet Dylan Thomas. Davies too was a young poet, in the town of Rhymney, a typical coal-mining town maybe 50 yards wide yet stretching on and on in length. After the failure of the British general strike of 1926, Davies, then a teenager, became absolutely determined to leave the coal mines. So he studied at night for four years and became a school teacher in London.

He published three slim volumes of poetry. His friend Thomas admired his writing and so had this particular piece reprinted. In many ways it is the author's epitaph: tragically, Davies died of cancer at 44.

The towns mentioned in the song are found in the south-eastern part of Wales. Each locality's worried, grieving citizenry are described by the bells of their fair town: bells are sad representing grief, brown representing work, black representing mourning, and loud as they ring with anger.

In the song, the silver bells of Wye, a prosperous place, ask her poor sister towns why they worry. Her sisters worry because they have to: they are not prosperous. Davies is making the point that poor people always worry while the better off can afford not to worry.

Pete Seeger put a melody to the poem while on tour in Montreal in the 1950s, using a melody based on 'Twinkle, Twinkle Little Star.' Just as The Byrds did in their majestic rendition of the song on their first LP, *Mr. Tambourine Man*, Dylan mispronounces the word Rhymney. (The Welsh call the town RUM-ney.)

Robertson has no reason to fear folk music or this kind of song. While the song is Welsh and The Hawks were Canadian, Robertson would in the near future write songs not all that far from this. They too would be great, although they would have a stronger rhythm.

The slightly country-like jog that Dylan's acoustic guitar gives the song is at odds with the lyrics and with his own sincere vocal.

At 1:55 Dylan sings "the bad bells of Rhymney." It's the *sad* bells of Rhymney, Bob.

## I'M A FOOL FOR YOU
3:55
**Dylan** vocal, acoustic guitar, **Danko** bass, **Hudson** organ, **Manuel** piano, **Robertson** electric guitar.

• Richard Manuel returns, so this has to be a new dawn, a new day. At 1:03, Dylan calls out for a D chord and Hudson hears it as C and Manuel hears it as a B. Train wreck. "I'm sorry, I'm playing in this funny key … this key," says Dylan. They are improvising as Dylan calls out chords several times and yet it nonetheless still sounds musical – and it will be as long as the musicians can hear him call out the proper chords.

Surely they could have gotten a Ferlin Husky cover on this one? Dan Penn made a career out of such lazy-day love laments. So did Dylan's old accompanist John Sebastian in The Lovin' Spoonful. Nor is this far away from an early Tim Hardin effort.

In stereo and clean sounding, this is without question a candidate for the expanded Basement Tapes reissue with which The Almighty will one day bless His People.

## NEXT TIME ON THE HIGHWAY
2:17
**Dylan** vocal, acoustic guitar, **Danko** bass, **Hudson** organ, **Manuel** piano, **Robertson** electric guitar.

• Another song with a fragment of the beginning missing. Does Hudson have these fragments in his own archives?

Back to the *Bringing It All Back Home* sound as this may be 'Tell Me Mama' in disguise. If Dylan had been on an electric guitar and if Bobby Gregg (who played on *Bringing It All Back Home* and *Highway 61 Revisited*) or Levon Helm had been present to drum, and if the tempo were a tad faster, this would rock like the rock of ages. As it is, it shakes like jelly on a plate. Which, for those not familiar with the blues, is a good thing.

Dylan weds several traditional blues couplets (called floating verses in the trade) and gets something going easily enough; this is, after all, The Hawks' musical home territory.

Robertson plays with the volume knob on his Telecaster and gets a wailing, bluesy sound like George Harrison did on 'I Need You' or 'Yes It Is.'

Dylan issues vulgar instructions to Manuel at 1:45 but Manuel's piano is barely, barely audible and he seems to be sitting out large portions of the song for some reason, although the lower-register keys are heard clearly twice. Perhaps he was physically exhausted. Or perhaps the Joel Bernstein Theory Of Hudson Recording is correct (chapter 8) and when a clean copy of 'Next Time On The Highway' appears, a copy which peaks at zero, we will hear Mr. Manuel's piano in all its glory.

## TUPELO
(John Lee Hooker)
2:21
**Dylan** vocal, acoustic guitar, **Danko** bass, **Hudson** organ, **Manuel** piano, **Robertson** electric guitar.
• A faithful reproduction of the John Lee Hooker sound as the band vamp on one chord. From country to R&B, these musicians are conducting a master class in both dishevelment and American Musics.

Dylan's acoustic is in tune and he plays Hooker's classic bluesy bastardization of the Mother Maybelle Carter scratch-lick very well. This is our boys visiting the Delta lyrically, musically, and as culturally as they can while in the Catskills.

Dylan messes up the words and is more or less compelled to re-write the song. He sticks to the original theme Hooker used and comes up with something Hooker would have recognized as a nice imitation and a sincere form of flattery. Dylan's voice is in a lower register and is not that far from its *Nashville Skyline* mode.

It falls apart at 2:14, but Hudson would have faded it by then anyway. After a few seconds of silence some *Goon Show*-sounding gibberish is heard.

Hooker recorded this in 1960 and it remains one of his many evocative, lazy, sensual drones, another modal masterpiece. Dylan has said in several interviews that he never forgot opening for Hooker in his early N.Y.C. folkie days, and here he proves those gigs and that singer really left a mark on him. He proves too that back then at those Hooker shows he was listening intently, already soaking it up to use, in his own form, at a later date.

## THEY GOTTA QUIT KICKIN' MY DAWG AROUN'
(Webb M. Oungst, Cy Perkins)
2:42
**Dylan** vocal, acoustic guitar, **Danko** bass, backing vocal, **Hudson** organ, **Manuel** backing vocal, **Robertson** electric guitar, backing vocal.

• Alan Lomax said the song's origins are not clear and may predate the American Civil War, but Stratton Hammon of the UCLA Folklore & Mythology Department tells us that this was a 19th century copyright for African-American songwriter James Bland, an artist who provides a link between the popular songs of the 1860s and the much more commercialized parlor music of the 1890s.

Bland, born of free Negro parents in New York City, was musically well educated and a graduate of Howard University in Washington, DC. He joined a Negro minstrel-show company and wrote more than 700 songs for minstrel use, copyrighting only a few.

Equaled perhaps only by Stephen Foster in his gift for melody, Bland turned out good songs by the dozen, although many were credited to assumed names. 'Carry Me Back To Old Virginny' was a Bland song (and once the state of Virginia's official song, but no longer so due to its references to massa and darkies). So too was 'Oh Dem Golden Slippers.'

'They Gotta Quit Kickin' My Dog Around' was in Bland's act for at least a decade. Like Foster many years before, Bland died broke and alone: Foster in the Bowery in N.Y.C. and Bland in Philadelphia in 1911. Dylan would have known this about Foster and may have been aware of Bland's sad death too. Most likely Dylan got the song from Gid Tanner & The Skillet Lickers or possibly the J.E. Mainer version, as both recordings would have been on the radar of the Harry Smith crowd.

This Big Pink basement version starts with Dylan and cohorts discussing the background vocals and single-note harmony. Manuel instructs Robertson and Danko as to what they should sing. They get out there with the song straight away, then they go further, then further than that, until their singing sounds like a cross between *Beach Boys Party!* and the early Mothers Of Invention satirical material.

### SEE YOU LATER, ALLIGATOR
(Robert Charles Guidry)
1:34
**Dylan** vocal, out-of-tune guitar, **Danko** bass, backing vocal, **Hudson** organ, **Manuel** answering vocal, **Robertson** backing vocal, laughter.
• Based on Bill Haley's hit version of 'See You Later, Alligator,' what is heard here is really an excuse to have a laugh and talk nonsense. And they certainly do laugh and talk nonsense – including the line, "See you later, Allen Ginsberg." As Ginsberg was a friend of everyone at Big Pink, Robertson today feels sheepish about this song as he doesn't want anyone to think they were making light of their friend.

Dylan audibly breaks a string at 1:24 and yells "Oh!" Then he says, "Let me pick up my cigarette," as Hudson allows the Guild Echorec too much gain and it creates a whirring sound. When this sound unexpectedly leaps in, a sonic slip-up, the listener receives a strong signal that these boys are extremely well oiled and feeling no pain.

Someone plays a Swannee whistle with great enthusiasm. That's the plastic child's toy with the slide in it like a trombone. The Voice Of Conscience mike, which according to some was in the middle of the room where anyone could swing it their way and say something important, is in full use here. So are their imaginations.

Robert Guidry is the real name of songwriter Bobby Charles, who also wrote 'Walking To New Orleans.' Charles appeared on *The Last Waltz* soundtrack and was a Bearsville recording artist, signed by no less than Albert Grossman and with a 1972 LP release on the label where he was backed by members of The Band and produced by the great John Simon. Again, this Big Pink song contains little of Guidry's: his original composition is used only for a laugh and some nonsense.

## TINY MONTGOMERY

2:54

**Dylan** vocal, acoustic 12-string guitar, **Danko** bass, tenor backing vocal, **Hudson** organ, **Manuel** bass backing vocal, **Robertson** electric guitar, baritone backing vocal.

• This was a good enough recording to be placed by Robertson and Rob Fraboni on the 1975 *Basement Tapes* two-LP set released on Columbia Records. With Dylan's vocal split far right and the same instrumental relationship as heard in the dozen and more songs before it, this proves the previous tunes with the same sonic layout are from Big Pink as well, since the recording of 'Tiny Montgomery' has never been claimed by anyone to have been from the earlier Red Room sessions or from the final sessions at Danko's house.

Hudson starts this one a nanosecond too slow: Dylan's guitar is caught in its downbeat. (Robertson and Fraboni got around this on the reissue by fading in the song quickly from Dylan's opening guitar strum. And a fade at the end obscures the clumsy ending of this Big Pink complete tape.) There is a swooping sound at the same time. Possibly Manuel is holding the lap steel and, after this opening flourish, it seems he puts it aside to concentrate on singing. There is a wooden 'clack' sound at 0:46 that may well be the keyboardist placing the lap steel down on a hard surface. Manuel is heard goofing off vocally with grunts and groans but none of his usual instruments are heard: no piano, drums, or harmonica are present on the track, yet his voice is there. Discuss.

This isn't merely the sound of a bunch of veteran rockers having fun, no way; for here we are witness to Dylan finding his muse again, or at least looking for it. Earlier Basement Tapes songs were largely covers with some semi-improvised Dylan originals and attempts at this or that sonic experiment. Dylan is singing some absurd stuff here, yes, and was not yet back to straight narratives, but he isn't hesitating in his vocal. These are words he has written down beforehand.

And this is a good enough *song* to audibly inspire four tired Canadians one day in '67. The guys hit a true groove. No drums are needed for these musicians to swing as one big happy ensemble. As they so frequently said on *American Bandstand*, I'd give it a 95 'cos you can dance to it.

'Tiny Montgomery' was also a good enough song to be covered quite creatively by Coulson Dean McGuinness Flint in 1972, a cover version that caused the young Billy Bragg to wonder where on earth the Dylan original was. Three years later he found out.

### THE SPANISH SONG (take one)
3:05
**Dylan** vocal, really out-of-tune acoustic guitar, **Danko** bass, **Hudson** organ, **Manuel** backing vocal, piano, **Robertson** tambourine.

• Also known as 'Luisa.' This reel has another brief *Goon Show* doodle before they get down to business. Greil Marcus thinks this is from late in the year. The British call this sort of a song a piss-take. The Brits also use the phrase "drunk as Lords." Both terms are appropriate here.

Dylan hits D, G, and A major in an almost random order, makes up lyrics about a Spanish babe, and generally sounds like he's having a great time, as do his friends.

There is audible laughter on this song but Bob's out there as well, really out there. Listen as the backing vocals egg him on. He could have sung about The Frito Bandito or Cinco de Mayo and it would have made little difference to the song – and his drunken friends wouldn't have noticed. We've got the lemon and we've got the salt but we're running out of tequila.

### THE SPANISH SONG (take two)
2:10
Same line-up as take one.

• The song is funny to hear and very entertaining, but one can only imagine what the reaction to this would be from Mexican musicians who play traditional Latin American music for a living. On the other hand, as Robertson has said many times over the years, they never thought anyone would hear this music. They thought they were making it for themselves. Which they are here, for this is more a party tape made by some guys at the frat house or a wacky audition tape for a satirical radio revue such as the *National Lampoon Radio Hour* in the U.S.A. or the *Goons* in Britain. This is not the career direction for anyone involved. It is Canadian beer run rampant. The Lord works in mysterious ways. So does Dylan.

## I'M YOUR TEENAGE PRAYER
3:53
**Dylan** vocal, acoustic 12-string guitar, **Danko** bass, tenor harmony vocal, **Hudson** organ, **Manuel** drums, backing vocal asides, **Robertson** electric guitar.
• A false start, then it kicks in again at 0:26, Manuel getting the hang of the drums and using the Voice Of Conscience microphone while he does so. Danko sings his harmony part straight and Robertson and Hudson perform like this was the most serious song in the world, while Manuel is clearly on the sauce more than the others.

The 1950s influence is reminiscent of a jam session between Flash Cadillac & The Continental Kids and Ruben & The Jets as Manuel's jocular asides finally cause Dylan to laugh and the sound distorts. Meaning someone down the line dubbed this one too hot (with more volume than the receiving machine can handle) and saturated the signal, or Hudson was too busy performing and neglected to mind the store when it was first put on tape.

## FOUR STRONG WINDS
(Ian Tyson)
3:39
**Dylan** vocal, acoustic 12-string guitar, **Danko** bass, harmony vocal, **Hudson** organ, **Manuel** drums, **Robertson** electric guitar.
• Written by Ian Tyson of Ian & Sylvia, who were managed by Albert Grossman, this was about the seasonal movement of workers around Canada. Tyson wrote it in 1961; it was published in 1963 and appeared on Ian & Sylvia's *Four Strong Winds* LP in 1964.

It has been covered by Canadians Neil Young and Hank Snow, Brits like The Seekers, Chad & Jeremy, Teenage Fanclub, and The Searchers, as well as Americans such as Judy Collins, Flatt & Scruggs, John Denver, The Kingston Trio, Johnny Cash, and Bobby Bare. In fact, Bobby

Bare had a sizeable C&W hit with it in 1964. While the track never quite jells, Danko's vocals do give it a sensitive air. Robertson has expressed concern over this type of folk song, this type of folk music from Yorkville (the bohemian Toronto coffeehouse district of his youth, which is today quite gentrified). But other than Manuel learning drums while on the job, this is a valid take of a proud anthem of a modest people who've built a strong multi-cultural country while remaining officially bilingual. Dylan respects this and it is only the liquid prescriptions of Doctor Forty Percent that get in the way.

**THE FRENCH GIRL** (take one)
(Ian Tyson, Sylvia Fricker)
2:31
**Dylan** vocal, acoustic 12-string guitar, **Danko** bass, **Hudson** organ, **Manuel** drums, **Robertson** electric guitar.
• Gene Clark did a fine version of this Ian & Sylvia song some three months before Dylan and his friends got to it. Clark's take is the opposite of what is heard here: his is a tight, well-arranged, orchestrated pop version of the song. This first Big Pink version is a dirge. Dylan stops them and they raise the key but he still has trouble ahead of him.

**THE FRENCH GIRL** (take two)
(Ian Tyson, Sylvia Fricker)
2:57
Same line-up as take one.
• Still too slow a take, and they lose the gospel spirit they had going on 'Four Strong Winds.' Robertson's folk-music fears are realized as they never find a groove nor the proper sensitive backing for such a tale of failed romance.

Dylan, who gets his feathers ruffled when a cover version of one of his songs changes his lyrics even slightly, misses some lyrics here. But surely this was never intended as anything but a warm-up number, because a spate of Dylan originals – and all-time killer Dylan originals at that – are right around the corner waiting to be put on magnetic tape.

What is heard is reminiscent of the Dylan music released (some would say allowed to escape) on albums of studio out-takes such as *Self-Portrait* and the ghastly 1973 collection, now thankfully deleted, entitled *Dylan*.

## JOSHUA GONE BARBADOS
(Eric von Schmidt)
2:42
**Dylan** vocal, acoustic 12-string guitar, **Danko** bass, **Hudson** organ, **Manuel** piano, **Robertson** electric guitar.
• Eric von Schmidt was a Dylan buddy early on, and it is a pity this wasn't fully rehearsed and formally released in his lifetime. The gang captures the calypso–Caribbean feel without resorting to cabaret blackface, and that's something. At 2:40 Dylan stops them with: "That's enough … it's a very long song." He might be out of lyrics or he might be anxious to move on to the stuff that he has been banging out on the typewriter upstairs.

## I'M IN THE MOOD
(John Lee Hooker)
1:54
Dylan vocal, acoustic 12-string guitar, **Danko** bass, **Hudson** organ, **Manuel** piano, Voice Of Conscience vocal, **Robertson** electric guitar.
• "Whaddaya say we hear some of that, Garth?" smiles a pretty lubricated Dylan at the very end.

Manuel contributes a surprisingly bluesy, Lafayette Leak-styled piano along with some equally surprisingly goofy vocal asides.

At 1:11 Dylan picks up the tempo for no reason other than Dr. Feelgood tells him to. Dylan is playing that Hooker-cum-Maybelle Carter scratch-lick at the top and the song is all the better for it, but it never recovers from his tempo change.

'I'm In The Mood' was included on Hooker's 1959 *I'm John Lee Hooker* album on Vee Jay. Hooker's estate recently released a DVD titled *I'm In The Mood For Love* but this nonetheless features the same song; the original title is 'I'm In The Mood.'

## THE ALL AMERICAN BOY
(Bobby Bare, Orville Lunsford)
3:55
**Dylan** vocal, acoustic 12-string guitar, **Danko** bass, **Hudson** organ, **Manuel** piano, Voice Of Conscience vocal asides, **Robertson** electric guitar.
• How sweet it is that Dylan's acoustic is out of tune on a song that begins with him singing: "Well, I bought me a guitar / Put it in tune."

Author Bobby Bare has been in country music since the 1950s. After no real luck at selling his own songs, he finally signed to Capitol, recording rock'n'roll songs without success. Right before his Army induction papers came through he wrote a song called 'The All American Boy' and made a demo for pal Bill Parsons to learn. Parsons did learn the song but, due to a mix up, Fraternity Records issued the demo cut by Bare. The single reached Number 2 on the *Billboard* Hot 100, although it was wrongly credited to Parsons.

Bare wrote the song as an obvious satire of Elvis Presley's relationship with Col. Tom Parker. Dylanologists feel this Basement version, which abandons much of Bare's original lyric, is a not-so-hidden dig at Albert Grossman, who Dylan was then discovering had taken greater percentages of his publishing than he'd thought previously. As with 'Dear Landlord' on *John Wesley Harding*, some of Dylan's faithful hear the singer covertly saying there must be some way out of here, sang the joker to the thief. But Dylan lived this particular nightmare of pop music fame as much as the character in this song did. So he isn't joking. Or is he? He couldn't have been joking that much. He had his take of this song copyrighted in 1973.

## SIGN ON THE CROSS
7:18
**Dylan** vocal, piano, **Danko** bass, harmony vocal, **Hudson** organ,
**Manuel** drums, harmony vocal, **Robertson** electric guitar.
• Along with 'I'm Not There (1956)' this acclaimed selection is generally considered by Dylan aficionados as not merely one of his best songs from the basement sessions nor merely one of his best unreleased songs from

any era but – get ready – one of Dylan's best songs, period, and one of his best vocals, period and full stop.

This masterpiece would have been recorded when *Sgt. Pepper's Lonely Hearts Club Band* was taking over the airwaves, at the very moment when the alienated counter-culture was brandishing its creative muscle and was sweeping aside so many societal mores and folkways. A new artistic movement was reaching its creative peak – and was thinking its leader, who had previously seemed so fearless, was still with them, leading the charge. But Dylan, the counter-culture's hero, had by then dismounted, and you can hear him get off his stallion with 'Sign On The Cross.'

Dylan had been justifiably recognized by his peers as achieving what only truly important artists do when, in 1965, he defined anew the very art he practiced. That he might now be doing this again in 1967, that he might again be redefining his art, as illustrated here in Basement Tapes songs such as 'Sign On The Cross,' would escape his followers in the aftermath of his abdication, his subsequent silence, and the later (purposeful) debacle with *Self-Portrait.*

Those who heard the *Great White Wonder* bootleg songs from Big Pink would possibly have been the first Dylan fans to understand the changes he went through as an artist and as a person in Woodstock in 1967. Eight years later, those who purchased the 1975 two-LP *Basement Tapes* official release would certainly have been able to piece back together the changes Dylan went through in Woodstock.

But back in the day, no one but four Canadians, their Chicago manager, and a few intimates knew that Dylan was yet again redefining himself and his art, the third major change in five years. This would become clearer with the passing of time, but the faithful, so unaware of 'Sign On The Cross' and the rest in 1967, wondered where their hero went.

Up to this point, the Basement Tapes have been a fun, bacchanalian session that, had they stopped the day before 'Sign On The Cross' was recorded, would have been of interest to Dylan's usual cast of devotees, tape traders, and academic interpreters. Had the sessions stopped then, only 'I Can't Come In With A Broken Heart,' 'Tiny Montgomery,' and 'One For The Road' would have been considered unreleased Dylan classic originals. And while the sessions would have been hailed as full of interesting cover versions and full of interesting interpretations of old folk ballads, they would have been placed no higher on the shelf than that. Which would have been fine. Dylan's tape traders would have had more to trade and the earth would have continued to spin on its proper axis.

With 'Sign On The Cross' something changed. Many of the previous selections on the reel that yielded such a devotional song as this were drunken revelries recorded in an atmosphere of green smoke. 'Sign On The Cross' must have been recorded very, very late as a sad sobriety set in or perhaps some time at the next session before they got too out there.

Even though the guys are enjoying themselves here (Dylan fights off a smile or two from creeping into his voice toward the end) this is serious stuff. Dylan's muse, aroused by the camaraderie of playing all the cover versions and their semi-improvised romps through his originals, has reappeared, its pilot light ignited and now burning brightly.

'Sign On The Cross' is also the first song-length sighting of Dylan's direct and unmistakable attraction to the power of pure Christianity, as witnessed a decade and a year hence and seen periodically since. True, Dylan has referenced Christianity before in his originals, both in his choice of covers and as songwriting metaphor ('Gospel Plow,' 'With God On Our Side,' 'When The Ship Comes In,' 'Highway 61 Revisited,' and so on). But with 'Sign On The Cross' he is dealing one-on-one with The Greatest Story Ever Told. He is publicly beginning his quest for Salvation and musically announcing, musically beginning the debate that ultimately will tell him if his arms are too short to box with God.

It is also with 'Sign On The Cross' that the Basement Tapes get elevated into legend. A dozen obvious Dylan classics follow it on the many reels before the sessions conclude. Not all of them were released, either. Which is why for so many years the entire lengthy sessions have been considered the Great Lost Dylan Album and not *Bob Dylan's Blues,* the New York version of *Blood On The Tracks,* or the original song line-up of *Oh Mercy.*

Joel Bernstein confirms that in his years working for Dylan he witnessed a lot of unreleased songs come and go but no session he witnessed had the remarkably high quality of songs or the crucial ingredient of marvelously sympathetic playing by Dylan's backing band as the music recorded by Garth Hudson in 1967 in Woodstock.

The boldest hat-trick of Dylan's career is considered *Bringing It All Back Home, Highway 61 Revisited,* and *Blonde On Blonde,* but with 'Sign On The Cross,' 'I'm Not There (1956),' et al, the point could be made that the boldest hat-trick of his career is *Blonde On Blonde*, the Basement Tapes, and *John Wesley Harding.* All dynamite, each dynamic in its own way, each wildly different from the other, and yet each a complete artistic success.

It is indeed difficult to believe that this was cut on the same day as 'The All American Boy.' Surely something must have happened overnight in the Woodstock twilight that caused the next day's recordings to contain a certain magic. To continue to dramatize a point that ultimately can only be heard (yes, writing about music is like dancing about architecture), 'Sign On The Cross' may be the very song where The Hawks audibly complete their mutation into The Band. R&B has been seeping away a little for some time; "country funk," as Ronnie Hawkins called their new style, has been creeping in more and more.

Dylan sings and plays piano sensitively. He has apparently shown the musicians the chord structure beforehand but the song is not over-rehearsed (at 2:55 you can hear Dylan announce that a new section of the song is coming). Danko plays understated bass and sings a harmony part that matches Hudson's organ swells beautifully.

Hudson plays it straight faced as if backing the preacher on the week-day-afternoon gospel call-in shows heard on R&B radio down South for a quick hour before the programming shifted back to Jackie Wilson and James Brown for the rest of the working day.

Robertson's guitar work is everything that could be hoped for, a total revelation, and possibly something with which Michael Bloomfield would have struggled. A circle of uncluttered notes enhances Dylan's vocal in the grandest tradition of Curtis Mayfield, Sister Rosetta Tharpe in her quieter moments, and the great Don Paul Moore. At no time does the guitar do anything to draw attention away from the vocalist, although it draws attention to the song continually. The greatest achievement comes from the drumming of Richard Manuel. His kick is soft but steady, his hi-hat work sparse but on time, and he wisely leaves the snare out of it, using his loosely-tuned tom toms to give the song an almost African, modal feel. His percussive work here is the glue for the whole performance.

Manuel is also singing a soft, low harmony to Danko's higher part. Drumming while singing on key is a challenge that few in rock'n'roll take on easily. Dylan's vocal, until his audible smile at 7:01, is pure Luke the Drifter, and if this is a piss-take Dylan is a Dutchman.

Admittedly, some Dylanologists allude to this performance as an ironic prank, but it seems way more likely to be the first attempt at 'Tryin' To Get To Heaven,' 'Blind Willie McTell,' 'Every Grain Of Sand,' 'Not Dark Yet,' or any Dylan song where the meaning of existence is under consideration.

Author Paul Williams accurately writes: "'Sign On The Cross' is built like a symphony, with four separate movements. The first is deliberate and elegant, Dylan singing with sublime slowness while Robbie Robertson plays gorgeous grace notes all around him.

"The second movement starts with an inspired bridge … rousing and passionate, transitioning into a restatement of the musical theme from the first movement.

"The third movement is spoken/sung monologue – Dylan's vocal performance on this is nothing short of genius, and the improvised music is dazzling in its complexity and accuracy.

"Another great segue takes us to the concluding movement, which starts with echoes of the bridge but immediately moves onto new structural ground … while successfully incorporating everything that's happened so far."[5]

The song and the performance sound like Lenny Bruce finding religion. Each suggests 'The Old Rugged Cross' musically, and one cries out at the injustice of a world where Mahalia Jackson never covered this song.

The only disappointment in the entire affair is Dylan's re-editing of the words for his *Lyrics* book. With a title and the "key to the kingdom" from the New Testament and Dylan's "days are numbered" (shades of

'When The Ship Comes In') from the Old Testament, one would think that if ever any words were sacred then these were they.

Several Basement Tapes songs have their lyrics re-written for *Lyrics*, but most are relatively inconsequential compared to 'Sign On The Cross.' As performed, Dylan sings: "Later on you might find a door you might want to enter, but of course the door might be closed," another New Testament reference. Alas, Lyrics has: "Because the bird is here and you might want to enter it, but, of course, the door might be closed." It is a silly and shameful re-editing of the song's true words. But as stated before in these very pages, the Lord is not the only one who works in mysterious ways.

### SANTA FE
2:05
**Dylan** vocal, acoustic guitar, **Danko** bass, **Hudson** piano, **Manuel** drums, **Robertson** electric guitar.

• This was released 24 years after the fact by Sony on *The Bootleg Series Volumes 1–3 (Rare & Unreleased) 1961-1991*. Which raises some questions, as that first installment of Dylan's *Bootleg Series* claimed that Levon Helm plays on this. But where and how?

The annotator of that release was the late John Bauldie, a gentleman, a learned man, and a Dylan expert with damn few peers and no betters. Bauldie would have known Levon Helm was not in Woodstock when this track was recorded. Manuel is on drums, and doing well there, but the drumming is not in Helm's style. Hudson moves over to the piano and there is no organ heard. One could suppose Helm is on drums and Manuel is on piano and Hudson is up having a coffee in the Big Pink kitchen, but as this is mono it is probably early on and, although unlikely, it is possible that 'Santa Fe' is from the Red Room sessions. Helm had yet to arrive.

The song is catchy but slight, and on the original black-market releases there is drop-out on both channels at 1:24. After 'Sign On The Cross' this is quite a come-down, but how could it be any other way? And how did this slight if charming little ditty make the grade for official release while 'Sign On The Cross' did not?

## DON'T YA TELL HENRY
2:25

**Dylan** vocal, acoustic guitar, **Danko** horn, **Hudson** organ, organ bass pedals, **Manuel** drums, backing vocal, **Robertson** electric guitar.

• Fades in and the guys are well into their cups here. Bartender, cut these guys off, OK? They've had enough.

Another version of this has surfaced, lasting 2:33, but it is only a slightly longer version of the same take and not an alternative version.

Robertson plays his best Hubert Sumlin licks at the breaks but in all the gaiety you have to listen for them. Hudson plays the straight man again, or seems to; his humor is in the musical references he plays and hence not so overt.

Robertson reports: "There is no trombone on any [Basement Tapes] tracks ever. It is a baritone horn or euphonium. This is Garth on keyboards, Richard on the drums, and Rick on baritone horn. Dylan is singing." [6] But John Simon heard the same track and reckons it is a trombone that Danko is playing.

It's not the version on the *Basement Tapes* two-LP set, where Levon Helm sings. More on that story later.

"Sounds good," Dylan announces at 1:39. He's joking. Americans do understand irony.

## BOURBON STREET
2:24

**Dylan** vocal, acoustic guitar, **Danko** horn, **Hudson** organ, **Manuel** piano, **Robertson** drums.

• Recorded at the same session as 'Don't Ya Tell Henry' where it seems the bartender served them after all. This could have been the down-on-your-luck tale to beat all tales but the participants are too tiddly to tell it.

This and the previous four are mono sounding yet they are cleanly recorded so maybe they are from Big Pink. Hudson was only beginning to come to grips with the equipment back at Dylan's house and it is impossible to imagine Sara Dylan allowing such shenanigans to occur around her young children. Or herself.

At 1:48 and 1:55 an otherworldly sound suggests Hudson on some odd keyboard. Robertson plays drums here and Manuel is playing the piano. Robertson admits to being, at best, the third greatest drummer in The Hawks/Band, but Danko bravely told Barney Hoskyns that he too tried to pound the skins and was forced to admit he was their fourth best drummer. Robertson played drums on some Basement Tapes cuts when Manuel was on piano and when guitar was not necessary.

This fades in poorly and ends with drop-out. Which is kind of appropriate. Did Dylan get behind the wheel of his car and drive home to Byrdcliffe after this session? Oh God.

'Bourbon Street' was probably recorded in July 1967. Dylan's Columbia contract had long since expired and Grossman was in negotiations with Mort Nasatir of MGM Records. The rumor spread in the record industry that Dylan had actually signed with them. It was feasible, because the MGM deal was fantastic: a seven-figure advance and a 12 percent royalty rate. But not all of the MGM board were in favor and the deal was never consummated.

MGM's dithering allowed Clive Davis at Columbia to move forward. Davis had written Dylan's original Columbia contract when he was one of their leading attorneys. Now he was running the show. Davis was a man so sure of himself that a few years later his detractors claimed he thought the CD was named after him. He recognized Dylan not only as a popular bestselling recording star but as a prestige artist who brought other acts to the label in order to be near The Spokesperson For A Generation. Eventually, Clive Davis got what he wanted.

In August, Columbia announced they had re-signed Dylan. The terms drawn up by Davis gave Dylan a 20 percent royalty rate on his new albums, as opposed to the old 4 percent rate, and an increased royalty rate on his back catalog, a six-figure advance, and artistic control over his material and image.

Dylan still owed his label 14 songs from his original contract. From here on in, things became less bacchanalian and slightly more businesslike at Big Pink. Grossman must have said something at this point. A strong contract had just been signed, new product was needed, and they had to show Columbia that the well was not dry. Songs like 'Bourbon Street' and 'Don't Ya Tell Henry' were fine as material, but to play Davis and his staff such recorded demos as they were would only spook the horses.

(Some Dylan fanatics claim that the 14-song Basement Tapes acetate from late '67 was intended to service that 14-song debt to Columbia Records. But the jury is out here, particularly in light of Dylan detective Clinton Heylin pointing out that by the time the 14-song demo was compiled by Grossman's office, Dylan had re-signed to the label. Columbia, while legally owed 14 songs from the original contract, would put no real pressure on Dylan to deliver those songs as they now knew he was again their contracted prestige artist. He was back on Columbia and wasn't under the gun to do anything specific or immediately time-sensitive but be happy, be on Columbia, and give them some hits.)

A break was called on the 'daily' sessions when Anna Lea Dylan was born July 11, 1967. This happy event naturally necessitated a break in the sessions since it takes a time for family life to settle down. Dylan's parents visited not long thereafter. Abe and Beatty Zimmerman flew in to see their newest grandchild and stayed for two to three weeks. Understandably, this too slowed the work rate. Slowed, but did not stop it. Even though the players took a break of some length.

From now on the sessions would concentrate on Dylan's originals, which were seemingly crafted to wow the faithful – be they fans in the street or label honchos in three-piece suits. The hits just kept on a-comin'. He and his Canadian friends were on a roll.

**MILLION DOLLAR BASH** (take one)
2:34
**Dylan** vocal, acoustic guitar, harmonica, **Danko** bass, harmony vocal, **Hudson** organ, **Manuel** piano, harmony vocal.
• It is August 1967, probably the third week. Back to work after the Zimmermans fly home to Hibbing.
Starting with some trademark wheezing harmonica, this suffers from

poor tape quality, so it may well be a case of Hudson using one of his pre-owned Shamrock tape reels. Where is Robertson?

Like Presley's earliest singles on Sun, the lack of a drummer does not prevent the assembled from swinging on this nonsense song like the experienced players they are. In the way a great singer can sing the phone book and make it sound good, these dancehall desperadoes, should they be caught sober enough, can really groove. Glenn Miller would have been proud. (That's a compliment.) Danko's bass is largely responsible for this: it swings like something found on a playground. Musically, the others are playing off him and not off Dylan's acoustic rhythm.

Two seconds after the song ends, Dylan laughs and says: "Ah, it's not on?" Hudson then says: "Do a little, Rick," and Danko plays some bass so Hudson can get a level. Then he asks Manuel to sing into his mike and Manuel comes up with some priceless Ruben & The Jets doo-wop.

An important point: Hudson has us back in wide-channel stereo, and so we shall remain.

**YEA! HEAVY AND A BOTTLE OF BREAD** (take one)
1:48
**Dylan** vocal, acoustic guitar, **Danko** bass, harmony vocal, **Hudson** organ, **Manuel** piano, harmony vocal.
• Some very Lewis Carroll lyrics in this first pass at a Basement Tapes song that would be widely bootlegged after appearing on the demos and acetates Albert Grossman sent out. Dylan clears his throat at the beginning of this with enough drama to suggest a small furry animal was in his esophagus.

**MILLION DOLLAR BASH** (take two)
2:31
Same line-up as take one.
• For all the hubbub about Robertson putting songs on the official 1975 release of *The Basement Tapes* that were not cut in the basement or even in Woodstock, it is interesting to note that he happily placed songs on that two-LP set upon which he was audibly not present. This proves that Robertson has a real degree of modesty, for which he is rarely credited.

Hudson got a good sound on this one. Reissue engineer Rob Fraboni had little to do save decide whether to eliminate Hudson's chair-squeaking at the end.

This is one of the many songs about sensual exuberance from a man who was so intent on raising a large happy family that he and his missus gave the impression they didn't own a TV.

**YEA! HEAVY AND A BOTTLE OF BREAD** (take two)
2:11
Same line-up as take one.
• Manuel's low harmony vocal is more audible on the black-market recordings than on the 1975 release, and it is striking how sincere, how warm, and how beautiful a voice he had. Danko's backing vocal is on the opposite channel and somewhat less audible. This may be due to a bootlegger cutting one channel a bit hotter than the other; it is hard to believe Hudson would let one backing vocal part be louder than another in such a way.

**I'M NOT THERE (1956)**
5:07
**Dylan** vocal, acoustic guitar, **Danko** bass, **Hudson** organ, **Manuel** piano.
• Joel Bernstein remembers Hudson later as skeptical about the continued hoo-ha around the Basement Tapes. Band producer John Simon says: "The Basement Tapes are rough. They are cherished because they have Bob Dylan on 'em, but they are not any different from any other rough tape anybody else would make in their basement, in their living room, in their garage." [7] (He should hear the 1982 Long Ryders demos before he makes that distinction again.)

When Robertson, a shrewd judge of musical merit just like Hudson or Simon, was played this track recently, his only comment was: "Just another track from the basement." (Interestingly, Robertson referred to it as 'I'm Not There, I'm Gone,' which was the song title Hudson wrote on the tape box.)

The song was copyrighted in 1970, so someone on Dylan's team was

objective enough to recognize the beauty of this, the second great unreleased masterpiece of the recording sessions collectively referred to as The Basement Tapes. References to "the kingdom high above her" and the free-association lyrics of Dylan's verse make this the sister song to 'Sign On The Cross.'

At 3:30, Manuel's piano comes in quietly but with an aching pure beauty, his right hand gently skirting the notes like moonlight on the icy scarred surface of a frozen Catskills pond. At 4:04, Manuel murmurs an approving "ummm" and in that nanosecond of commentary you know exactly what he means.

When the 1975 *Basement Tapes* album was compiled, engineer Rob Fraboni knew how great 'I'm Not There (1956)' and 'Sign On The Cross' really were. "Yeah," he says, "they are terrific, those two. But on some of the songs, like 'Sign On The Cross,' which is on one of the reels I made for myself of Basement Tapes out-takes we did not use, pieces of it were missing. Same with 'I'm Not There.' There were technical reasons those songs, great as they are, could not be issued. They were not complete takes. A lot of songs had bits missing or cut off too soon or whatever." [8]

The very start of 'I'm Not There (1956)' is certainly missing and the song ends awkwardly (a fade starting at 5:01 would have made a fine ending), which may be why it was not included on that official *Basement Tapes* release. But lesser works were included, and other songs were clearly doctored, so surely something could have been done to resurrect this moving performance?

Yes, Dylan has only sketched out his lyrics and not finished them, but he still adds verses and changes lines in live performance today with songs from *Blood On The Tracks*. So the question must be asked: when is Dylan really ever finished with a given song's lyrics? It is not for Dylanologists to say, only to point out this is great stuff and that there are singer-songwriters of no little reputation working today who would sell their tour-merchandise rights to come up with material this strong.

The late, great Dylan expert John Bauldie referred to this as "Dylan's saddest song" as well as "one of his greatest vocal performances," and in terms of the tone of Dylan's voice, the characterizations he projects, and his phrasing, Mr. Bauldie is quite on target. Hudson has commented that Dylan would become inspired or The Hawks would have a riff going and some chord changes, and that was all that was needed, that Dylan would come down into the basement and start singing along through nonsense lyrics, scat singing, or even la-la-las. What is heard here is only a step or two forward from that kind of thing, and yet the performance is still masterful. The fact that if the words were written down the listener would find them less than complete linear thoughts is no matter.

Yes, on paper the words are incomplete. When heard performed, when heard sung by Dylan, they seem monumental, until the listener zeroes in solely on the words and pushes their performance to the side. The effect is like an out-of-focus photo slowly coming into focus or like a blurred photograph of something you recognize as familiar but cannot place. It is not that the viewer cannot clearly see the action, it is that the action has not completely taken place yet. The film is still being shot, the camera is still rolling.

This may be an incomplete sketch of a song, but the aural experience it provides, the emotional ride that Dylan's singing allows the listener, is something to be cherished by Dylan's followers, be they haves or have nots (as he says on his radio show).

Intriguingly, alongside those Dylanologists who feel his voice is his single greatest artistic asset, there are those longtime followers who take this school of thought a step further and downplay his words altogether. They point to 'I'm Not There (1956),' rightfully acknowledging its haunted Edgar Allan Poe feel and the way Dylan achieves his vocal power and performance even with few clear-cut lyrical ideas. Very Dylanesque statements such as "I was born to love her, but she knows that the kingdom (Kingdom?) weighs so high above her" leap out, so the emotional impact of the song is not only due to the ensemble's musical performance or Dylan's vocals. Yes, some lines of 'I'm Not There' are quite strong, nonsensical though they may be. But what a performance and what a vocal.

Dylan's vocal and performance illustrate that he certainly knew what he was singing about and what emotional effect he was trying to achieve. Why he opted again for his *Dont Look Back* philosophy and never returned

to polish this masterpiece is anybody's guess. Perhaps he was anxious to move on to the other masterpieces he had up his sleeve ('This Wheel's On Fire,' 'I Shall Be Released,' 'Tears Of Rage,' and the rest).

Suffice to say the immediacy of Dylan's voice, the startling imagery, the viewpoint, and even the subject matter of his songs as well as the overall performance he accomplishes with such material are all interlinked in a way that the layperson or, perish the thought, the insightful critic will never fully understand. Or to put it another way, with relatively little on display but a) one specific lyrical thought, b) a small unobtrusive backing band, and c) a few simple chords, the Bard of Hibbing nonetheless came up with a classic.

A classic, yes. Dylan's cup runs over with emotional content, performance projection, and artistic clout. It cannot be fully explained, as the process of its creation can never be experienced by anyone other than its writer. Dylan can create in this semi-improvised way and he tells us of his experience/s as he sings it/them. He does so apparently effortlessly. In pop music terms this is the stuff of genius. But few serious observers of late 20th century popular music doubt that Dylan has such a gift, and if 'Sign On The Cross' and 'I'm Not There (1956)' are the barometer by which the critic must judge, then our boy has a very real gift.

The irony (the tragedy?) is that the master has made his own particular genius seem so effortless that not only has his art inspired many to socio-political action, but also it has sent out a sweet siren song to far too many potential poets and would-be Spokespersons For Their Own Generation. When these potential poets attempt their own versions of the charm and lyricism of 'I'm Not There' they come up far, far short. They'd likely have been better off attempting to split the atom.

## PLEASE MRS. HENRY
2:32
**Dylan** vocal, acoustic guitar, **Danko** bass, backing vocal, **Hudson** organ, **Manuel** piano, backing vocal.
• "I can slam like a drake," sings Dylan, a man not averse to rhyming "I can crawl like a snake" with a reference to a male duck when nothing else

comes to mind. Dylan's chair squeaks delightfully early on, and no doubt some camp followers will find great significance in this. Perhaps the fact that its high-pitched squeak is nearly in the key of the song will mean something particularly significant. Perhaps it is of some import that Dylan then sings "my stool's gonna squeak" at 1:54.

Might he have meant chair? Perhaps he is semi-improvising the lyrics here, as well, and a squeaky seat amuses him. At 2:09 Dylan starts giggling through the chorus, which is odd considering how somber the gang sounds here.

Much was made of the official 1975 release using some mono-sounding tracks, and indeed this black-market version is in a more widespread and obvious 'stereo' than it is on the official two-LP set. The backing vocals from Manuel and Danko are more readily heard here, and it is no longer surprising how professional a sound Hudson has captured.

**CRASH ON THE LEVEE (DOWN IN THE FLOOD)** (take one)
2:03
**Dylan** vocal, acoustic guitar, **Danko** bass, **Hudson** organ, **Manuel** piano.
• Someone please call Dominique and ask where Robbie is. The Guild Echorec puts a very noticeable reverb on Dylan's vocal here. They are sounding serious. The sloppiness that was evident on so many of the earlier fun but drunken-sounding sessions is missing and the vibe is more professional. Loose, not uptight like session players in L.A. or New York City, but more professional.

Hudson's keyboard work was always professional sounding; even when he's having fun, he's on the money. But now Danko in particular is getting on the case. Surely Dylan or Grossman has spoken frankly to the guys as you can hear a more serious, creative approach taking place. They are no longer winging it with covers or performing Dylan originals in a rough and tumble manner.

They are recording and keeping multiple takes for most of Dylan's originals, and it is apparent all hands are on deck and at their battle stations, particularly when compared to the shore-leave shenanigans heard beforehand. Without any shadow of a doubt they are getting down to serious business.

**CRASH ON THE LEVEE (DOWN IN THE FLOOD)** (take two)
2:01
Same line-up as take one.

• Only four musicians are present but they are getting a surprisingly full sound, particularly as Manuel's piano is so distant. This is what *John Wesley Harding* might have sounded like had Hudson been overdubbed as Dylan originally intended.

It is again noteworthy that Robertson is not present on this unvarnished performance and yet he chose this in 1975 for official release.

This is a good song for All-American acts like Flatt & Scruggs to cover – which they did on their *Changin' Times* LP alongside their versions of 'Mr. Tambourine Man,' 'Don't Think Twice It's Alright,' 'Blowin' In The Wind,' and 'It Ain't Me Babe.' On their *Nashville Airplane* album (released in late 1968 before *Nashville Skyline*) banjo virtuoso Earl Scruggs actually convinced guitarist–singer Lester Flatt that it would be a good idea to do bluegrass covers of 'Like A Rolling Stone,' 'Rainy Day Women #12 & 35,' 'I'll Be Your Baby Tonight,' and 'The Times They Are A-Changin'.'

Flatt reluctantly went along with the idea, adding electric bass and drums to the act, but was understandably upset when producer Bob Johnston, also Dylan's producer at the time, added harpsichord and Jordinaires-styled backing vocals to the mix. He later admitted he was uncomfortable singing 'Like A Rolling Stone' and 'Rainy Day Women #12 & 35.'

Flatt was so uncomfortable that it helped break up the duo in 1969, although he was soon out on the road with a new band, Lester Flatt & The Nashville Grass, which by 1972 featured a young Marty Stuart on mandolin. Three decades later, Stuart told writer Colin Escott he had questioned Flatt about recording so many Bob Dylan songs in the Flatt & Scruggs days. "I remember [Flatt] saying, 'Marty, I got nuthin' against Bob Die-lan. He just don't write our kind of music.'" [9]

The "meanest flood that anybody's seen" in this song was not Pennsylvania's 1889 Johnstown Flood, which so inspired country and western songwriters (and was the biggest American news story since the assassination of Abraham Lincoln). Nor was it the 1927 flooding of the Mississippi River, which so inspired the Delta bluesmen (and about which

Charley Patton wrote 'High Water Everywhere' Parts 1 and 2). In fact, it was the worldwide flood detailed in the book of Genesis. That was the meanest flood anybody's ever seen, and Noah could have told Dylan all about it. In a way, he did.

### LO AND BEHOLD! (take one)
2:48
**Dylan** vocal, acoustic guitar, **Danko** bass, backing vocal, **Hudson** organ, **Manuel** piano, backing vocal.
• Dylan has fought back the urge to laugh many times before on these sessions, but at 1:51 here he loses the fight and laughs through the chorus before going back to a straight man's vocal persona, until at 2:25 he realizes he is "going back to Pittsburgh again" after having already visited the hometown of Andy Warhol. This wonderful first take features one of the key phrases of the Old Testament prophets in the King James version of the Bible: lo and behold!

### LO AND BEHOLD! (take two)
2:43
Same line-up as take one.
• Manuel brings his piano in at the top on this take and it helps move things along. He sings with greater confidence on the choruses, too, though he comes in a tad late on the first one. The chorus backing vocals from Manuel and Danko weave up and down behind Dylan's lead, an approach The Band would soon perfect with John Simon's help on songs like 'The Weight,' to the point where it became one of their trademark sounds.

Marianne Faithfull somehow fixated on this one when Mick Jagger, her partner at the time, got his 14-song acetate in very late '67. "I took it as if the apocalypse was coming," she told John Harris. "I couldn't stop playing it ... I was quite scared. I just felt it was like the end of the world coming. That sense of doom. It's not in all the songs, some of them are very funny. But the side that I liked was the more doomy one. There's a lot of stuff about water and ... something coming. 'This Wheel's On Fire,' 'Lo And Behold!' ... that one was crucial. It was one of the first times that

Dylan started talking almost in sort of ancient tongues. I always felt that the place where the great horrors were going to come from was America. And when I listened to these things I felt that he knew that too."[10]

That's a bit hard to take. Faithfull had already recorded 'Blowin' In The Wind' and knew Dylan personally (the Minnesotan was quite smitten with young Marianne; witness their hotel-room chemistry in *Dont Look Back*). But as Dylan's American counter-culture followers would soon learn, he was not anti-American: not politically (he has stated admiration for both Bobby Kennedy and Barry Goldwater); not culturally (witness the huge Stars & Stripes at the May '66 Paris gig and his telling John Lennon in *Eat The Document*'s limo ride about the glories of Texas and baseball); and not musically (the two Bengali Bauls on the cover of *John Wesley Harding* were as close to world music as Dylan ever went).

Bob Dylan was a free-thinking bohemian from middle America. With a helluva talent and a sizeable burden. He was obviously not the product of a Parisian garret or a London art college. He was the product of the Iron Range, baseball, Woody Guthrie, and Jack Kerouac. Nonetheless, it was Faithfull championing the acetate to Jagger that helped steer the Stones towards *Beggar's Banquet* and out of psychedelia, so full marks for that, girl!

Jagger gave a belated acknowledgement with the jacket of *Get Yer Ya Ya's Out!*. Note the mule to the left of the leaping Charlie Watts. It has cosmetic jewelry and a pair of binoculars hanging from its head, as per the lyrics of the fourth verse of 'Visions Of Johanna.' No wonder the normally taciturn Watts is smiling.

**YOU AIN'T GOIN' NOWHERE** (take one)
2:43
**Dylan** vocal, acoustic 12-string guitar, **Danko** bass, backing vocal,
**Hudson** organ, **Manuel** backing vocal, **Robertson** electric guitar.
• For ten songs, Robbie Robertson has gone AWOL, but he is heard on this one.

Sadly, Dylan sums this up all too well in one of his haphazard improvised verses: "Look here, you bunch of basement noise."

Alas, a fine if slightly tentative track is marred by lyrics not even Dylan can get away with. "Now look here, dear soup, you'd best feed the cats / The cats need feeding and you're the one to do it / Get your hat, feed the cats / You ain't going nowhere."

This, it must be said, is not an auspicious start to any song, no matter if the lyrics are by Dylan, Noel Coward, Ira Gershwin, Shakespeare, or Spike Jones.

It gets even worse: "Just pick up that oil cloth, cram it in the corn / I don't care if your name is Michael / You're gonna need some boards / Get your lunch, you foreign bib." Ye Gods.

As Robbie Robertson says, they weren't expecting anyone to ever hear this stuff. No kidding?

And they probably weren't expecting so many people to care so deeply when they finally did get the chance to hear these songs.

Dylan's improvised lyrics show some strain and reveal a pair of themes that he latches onto time and time again during this part of the sessions focused on his new material: nothing/naught and gonna/going. Many songs contain both. Think of 'Nothing Was Delivered,' 'Too Much Of Nothing,' 'I'm Not There.'

Also: "There was nothing more to tell, you know that we shall meet again if your memory serves you well" ('This Wheel's On Fire'); "Crash on the levee, water's gonna overflow" ('Crash On The Levee'); "When Quinn The Eskimo gets here, everybody's gonna jump and shout" ('Quinn The Eskimo'); "But I ain't gonna hear it said no more" ('Open The Door, Homer'); "Every boy and girl's gonna get their bang, cause Tiny Montgomery's gonna shake that thing" ('Tiny Montgomery'). And, yes, 'You Ain't Goin' Nowhere,' which has both the nothing/naught reference as well as the gonna/going one.

Even the mysterious, much-sought-after, unreleased Basement Tapes cut 'Minstrel Boy' reads: "Who's gonna throw that minstrel boy a coin?" Discuss.

## TOO MUCH OF NOTHING (take one)
2:59

**Dylan** vocal, acoustic 12-string guitar, **Danko** bass, backing vocal, **Hudson** organ, **Manuel** piano, falsetto backing vocal, **Robertson** electric guitar.

• This became the first basement song to be covered when Peter Paul & Mary hit the charts with it in November 1967, meaning Grossman, their manager too, gave them a copy in the summer, probably by mid August at the latest. This is also understandable because Hudson recorded the Basement Tapes sessions with some of their equipment.

The song is somewhat stillborn, without a lot of melody and rhythm. They would develop it later, but the world still awaits an official release of that take. It has to be said they sound a bit bored here, but they are somber as they are learning. A relatively monaural sound, with not a lot of audible separation.

Another Old Testament phrase is used here. Several times in the writings of unknown Bible scribes there are variations of Dylan's "it's all been written in the book." Beatty Zimmerman and Al Aronowitz were among those who remembered that a large Bible had pride of place in Dylan's *Hi Lo Ha* home. During Abe and Beatty's visit to see their new grandchild, Anna Lea, the much loved Mrs. Zimmerman commented how her son Bob was always jumping up to go over to the Bible and re-read this or that passage. Some of The Good Book obviously stuck with him.

For the official two-LP release of this take, drums were overdubbed in early 1975. The curious thing about the overdubbed drums was that the performance sounds nothing like Levon Helm's rhythmically developed, loosey-goosey style and only a bit like Manuel's functional but funky drumming. What is played on the '75 set sounds exactly like the style of drumming that Ringo Starr used in the late-period Beatles, with the skins loosened on the kit and a low-register, almost tom tom-sounding thump to the snare. Helm used loosened skins, yes, but the drums overdubbed on 'Too Much Of Nothing' at Shangri-La (see chapter 15) sound very *Abbey Road–Let It Be*. Those overdubbed drums sound not only like a different drummer but unlike any drum kit The Band would use.

## THIS WHEEL'S ON FIRE
(Bob Dylan, Rick Danko)
3:53
**Dylan** vocal, acoustic 12-string guitar, **Danko** bass, backing vocal,
**Hudson** organ, **Manuel** piano, **Robertson** drums.
• The phrase "this wheel's on fire" sounds like the Old Testament but isn't

– a nice twist from a writer who frequently references The Good Book.

The version on the official '75 *Basement Tapes* Columbia release has an acoustic guitar overdub from Robertson that, quite frankly, enhances the song's intro and outro.

On the first chorus on the official version, Manuel is the only one who starts to sing the opening "This... ." He and another vocalist were over-dubbed in early '75. (Again, see chapter 15.)

On the black-market take, Manuel's piano is almost ladylike, with several sweet right-hand splashes in the upper register. On the released version, eight years later, he blocks chords in a formal manner, reeking of testosterone and proper timekeeping. His overdubbed piano part is so in time it dramatizes how loose Robertson's drumming was back in '67 (although Robertson's drumming, when heard in the context of the unadorned original, sounds perfectly acceptable as it is not fighting the tempo of any other instrument but is perfectly at ease tapping alongside his fellow Hawks).

Full marks for Danko's bass playing too: he locks in perfectly with Robertson's happy-go-lucky drumming for an accomplished series of basslines.

On this Big Pink take, less is more. Dylan lets the song do the work for him; he rides it vocally instead of pushing it forward with emphatic singing. Danko has a great backing vocal at the chorus that is heard clearly, but on the official version it is somewhat obscured by Manuel's added vocal part.

This take fades more slowly and allows you to hear the musicians as they drift away.

Dylan co-wrote it with Danko, who said later: "I was amazed about eight or maybe ten artists recorded the song."[11] He needn't be.

## YOU AIN'T GOIN' NOWHERE (take two) *
2:41
**Dylan** vocal, acoustic 12-string guitar, **Danko** bass, backing vocal,
**Hudson** organ, **Manuel** piano, **Robertson** drums.
• Can Robbie Robertson really be getting that good on the drums? The piano is Manuel, the organ unmistakably Hudson, there is no guitar,

and Helm has yet to return. Yet Robertson does play some piano, so the possibility exists he is on the 88s and Manuel is on the drums.

The official '75 release of this has a Robertson electric lead-guitar part subtly added.

Or does it? Engineer Rob Fraboni says not, but he may have been elsewhere when the overdub was made. Robertson's guitar is inaudible on this original, and if it is not an overdub on the two-LP set, this means Helm is (inexplicably) back on drums. Could Levon Helm be responsible for the awkward fill at 2:22? No way, no way. The drummer's sidestick at the chorus is good, yes, but then if Helm is drumming here, why is Robertson's guitar totally, totally inaudible? It would seem this sidestick is from whoever is drumming, Robertson or not, and that Robertson did indeed overdub some lead guitar in 1975.

The lyrics have been tightened up considerably since take one, although they still fail any linear sense test. But at least they are not a series of improvised absurdities. And if they are still absurd, they sound wonderful. "Genghis Kahn, he could not keep / All his kings supplied with sleep / But we'll climb that hill, no matter how steep." Great stuff, and with the guys putting a bit of distance between themselves and the jazz cigarettes, there are substantial musical dividends.

This track swings. Hudson's organ tone and technique are by now so ingrained in the overall sound and feel of these tracks that he's become the Dylan–Band equivalent to McGuinn's 12-string in The Byrds, John Sebastian's swirling autoharp in The Lovin' Spoonful, or Tommy Hall's electric jug in The 13th Floor Elevators. You cannot imagine those songs without those elements; you cannot imagine a Dylan vocal existing from this era without Hudson's dignified but in-the-groove organ parts behind him, coloring Bob's vocal characterizations and musically echoing his thoughts.

### I SHALL BE RELEASED
3:55
**Dylan** vocal, acoustic 12-string guitar, **Danko** bass, backing vocal, **Hudson** organ, **Manuel** piano, falsetto backing vocal, **Robertson** electric guitar.
• In a fair and equitable society where all are judged on their merits and

their hearts, without the interference of worldly goods or fame, it will be either this or the gorgeous reading Manuel gives on *Music From Big Pink* that will be remembered as the definitive version for all eternity and not the overly pious, sanctimonious versions sung at the end of charity concerts by any number of rock superstars, including, on occasion, some of the very fellows heard on this first version.

It is alleged that Robertson did not put this prisoner's lament or 'The Mighty Quinn' on the official '75 release as he and Dylan thought the public already knew them well enough from their cover versions. Dylan sings this like the Leadbelly gospel number it is. Its many covers (over 160 at the time of this writing) are testament not only to the song's quality but also to its emotional power. It remains the most covered song from the Basement Tapes and while never a hit single is nevertheless arguably the most famous composition from the session.

This was finally released by Sony in 1991 on *The Bootleg Series Volumes 1–3 (Rare & Unreleased) 1961-1991.*

**TOO MUCH OF NOTHING** (take two)
2:48
**Dylan** vocal, acoustic 12-string guitar, **Danko** bass, backing vocal,
**Hudson** organ, **Manuel** piano, backing vocal, **Robertson** electric guitar.
• Much was made of Robertson picking the first take of this for official release, but this take two is hiss-laden, has a stumbling intro with Dylan unsure of when to come in, and ever-steady Danko hits a slurred bum note at 0:57 and again at 1:27 and yet again at 2:08. The bass performance is well beneath Danko's usual standard, which suggests Dylan had changed the song around before recording. Danko is also out of tune on the last note of the song. So while this take does have more melody and a better part from Hudson, a professional like Robertson is going to spot the errors and, considering everything, pick the earlier take. The real point is that it is shameful that this song wasn't further developed. If there are further seven-inch reels of Basement Tapes sessions left to be uncovered then surely there is another version of this.

**TEARS OF RAGE** (take one)
(Bob Dylan, Richard Manuel)
3:53
**Dylan** vocal, acoustic 12-string guitar, **Danko** bass, backing vocal,
**Hudson** organ, **Manuel** piano, backing vocal, **Robertson** electric guitar.
• "Listen," commands Dylan at the top. And they do. Listen they should, as Dylan sings so poignantly he sounds like a Stax–Volt session singer demoing for Otis or Johnny Taylor.

Danko is having trouble singing his soft harmony vocal while playing bass at the song's midpoint, and Manuel misses a chord at 3:40. Hudson has switched the recorder's channel inputs around: that is, the microphones are going into different channels now, so the sonic line-up has changed. This could suggest they have moved operations to Danko's house and this is the first song from there, but Helm is not heard on the track and Danko did not move out until Helm's return. Also, the same chair squeaks and they probably would not have moved the same old chairs to Danko's – and if they had, why take one that squeaks when you know you will be recording? No sir, we are still at Big Pink, although it is September and summer is gone in Ulster County.

Another break occurred when The Hawks went to New York City in September 1967 to record some demos on their own. (They were not The Band yet, not officially, even though their sound had left The Hawks' amphetamine R&B nighttime for the sunny country-funk with which they created their own legend.) The New York demos were an experiment, and done so that Grossman had something a little more slick to play for potential record labels than their basement recordings.

Dylan's producer Bob Johnston had come to Woodstock to speak to his most mercurial act about recording another album and discovered to his amazement that in an era of heavily-produced rock LPs where not one but two kitchen sinks were usually thrown in the final mix, Dylan wanted to cut an acoustic, stripped-down album with little production.

Dylan took time out to deal with Johnston while The Hawks, under Grossman's watchful eye, went off to the N.Y.C. studio. Without Helm back in the fold yet, The Hawks recorded on September 5, 1967 at Columbia Studios, in Studio E. There they cut 'Ruben Remus,' an early version of 'Chest Fever,' the first version of 'Yazoo Street Scandal,' an ensemble version of 'Orange Juice Blues (Blues For Breakfast),' and 'Ferdinand The Imposter.'

Robertson once said, "I didn't want to write Bob Dylan poems, not because I didn't like them, just because it wasn't my job," [12] but 'Ferdinand The Imposter' is awfully representative of the influence of The Hawks' boss, with its "to see the burning of the soup/down at Lucy's chicken coop" lyrics.

No one rated these N.Y.C. demos. Helm wrote in his autobiography that Grossman "took it upon himself to get the boys a record deal. They cut a demo, which I've never even heard. Robbie said it was terrible anyway."[13] Which confirms that Helm was not in Woodstock in September and therefore was not on any of the material recorded up to that point.

There is an odd sidebar to the story of the N.Y.C. demos. Producer John Simon, who had arrived in Woodstock to work on the footage of *You Are What You Eat* at Dylan's house alongside Howard Alk, is among those who remember that one Band demo session was skippered by Motown's Mickey Stevenson.

"I was brought in a bit later to work with them," says Simon, "and they're looking towards their first release [*Music From Big Pink*]. They had already recorded with a Motown producer but it had not worked out too well."[14] Robertson told academic and CD-booklet essayist Rob Bowman that they knew Stevenson and while on the Dylan tour (they played Detroit's Cobo Arena on October 24, 1965) had visited Motown to see him but that he did not produce these N.Y.C. sessions.

Mickey Stevenson would be a hard man to forget. Born William Stevenson, he was head of A&R for Berry Gordy's Motown during the mid 1960s when artists such as The Supremes, The Four Tops, Marvin Gaye, The Temptations, and Martha & The Vandellas enjoyed hit after hit. Stevenson assembled the company's legendary in-house studio band from a collection of then-obscure nightclub musicians, who soon became known as The Funk Brothers. They included such remarkable talents as bassist James Jamerson, guitarists Robert White and Joe Messina, and the tragic junkie drummer Benny Benjamin.

Stevenson wrote, co-wrote, and produced many hits for Motown, including 'Dancing In The Street,' 'Pride And Joy,' 'Ask The Lonely,' 'Mickey's Monkey,' 'It Takes Two,' 'What Becomes Of The Brokenhearted,' and 'Uptight (Everything's Alright).' He and his wife Kim Weston left Motown in 1967 for MGM, where she was signed as a recording artist and he was given one million dollars to put right the floundering subsidiary label Venture.

Since Stevenson was by summer 1967 associated with MGM, he was no doubt in league with MGM's Mort Nasatir in his attempts to get Dylan signed to their label. Nasatir has always maintained he sent a recording crew to Woodstock to record Dylan and The Hawks performing some new tunes. Stevenson was most likely there then. What a Motown man would have made of Dylan's absurdist lyrics and a five-piece band with no drummer can only be imagined. When contacted, Stevenson – in the middle of writing his Motown memoirs – remembered The Hawks but said that he cannot remember if he worked with them in a studio.

Anyway, all this could account for the confusion as to who produced the New York City demo sessions for The Hawks. There is also a rumor that while in New York that September to do the demos, the group, billed as The Crackers, the name with which they eventually signed to Capitol, opened for Allen Ginsberg at Carnegie Hall. Robertson: "What? We didn't play anywhere with Allen Ginsberg. I don't *think*. Hmmm, I don't remember that."[15]

Robertson told Rob Bowman: "On those [N.Y.C.] sessions, Albert Grossman was in charge and it didn't really work at all. When we went in and did those things, I thought, 'This doesn't sound at all like what I've got in my mind.' ... We just went in and slammed these things down, and Albert just kind of gave the engineer a little bit of input on it. The results, I thought, were very questionable."[16]

For this book, Robertson explains that at least they learned from this unhappy episode. "Yes, we had an experience in the studio and didn't like it. It just did not have the character. It sounded like a dry recording. That studio: it wasn't impressive, so we had to figure out what to do with these tools to make it do and sound like what we wanted. And John Simon was extremely helpful in that." [17]

This break in the action at Big Pink picks up with 'Tears Of Rage,' which sounds like the first song cut after Hudson got back from the big city and used a few new techniques he'd picked up. He's re-jiggled things and, as ever, is learning while on the job. Whatever Grossman did or did not do during the demo session in New York the previous week, Hudson would have learned something from it. Hindsight is always 20/20, but these Hawks – who always maintained, even on the Dylan world tour, that some day they would be their own masters – must have known that their big chance, their own time, was coming soon. And it was.

**TEARS OF RAGE** (take two)
(Bob Dylan, Richard Manuel)
2:26
**Dylan** vocal, acoustic 12-string guitar, **Danko** bass, backing vocal,
**Hudson** organ, **Manuel** piano, backing vocal, **Robertson** electric guitar.
• Dylan starts strumming impatiently and rapidly: he wants to get going. The groove almost shifts into waltz time here, but for an ensemble who have so effortlessly followed his improvisations for weeks and weeks, they sound tentative and unsure of themselves. They sing this way, too, and it all breaks down when Dylan moves from the mike and Hudson hits stop.

**TEARS OF RAGE** (take three)
(Bob Dylan, Richard Manuel)
4:08
Same line-up as take two.
• Jackpot. This is the template for the majestic *Music From Big Pink* opening cut, a version of this song so beautiful that Robertson pleaded with his bandmates to have it start the album, even though it had a slow tempo and it was something of a rule that up-tempo songs almost always started rock albums.

The song's author had yet again been reading the big Bible back at home

on the stand at Byrdcliffe. The line "and life is brief" is a recurring message in Psalms and Isaiah in the Old Testament. Further, "We pointed out the way to go / And scratched your name in sand" is a transparent reference to Christ's defense of the adulterous woman, a woman who was about to be stoned to death.

Christ bent over and wrote on the sandy ground with His finger, then rose and said: "Whichever one of you has committed no sin may throw the first stone." He wrote in the sand a second time, and when He stood up this time He found himself alone with the accused woman and asked: "Where are they, woman? Is there no one left to condemn you?"

Dylan was questioning existence and examining his own life in 1967. When he looked back on his whirlwind existence so far and looked back upon the Carnaby Street dandy he had once been, he would have appreciated this biblical tale of self-examination and crowd behavior. There would always be those who would readily condemn an easy public target such as Dylan might represent, but who among them would throw the first deadly stone?

The mix on the official '75 release of this is different, with Dylan's vocal quite upfront and the Guild Echorec reverb present and accounted for, as are Hudson's organ fills. The intuitive dance of guitar and organ behind Dylan's vocal that so embellished 'Sign On The Cross' is evident here again. Dylan may have played with other talented guitarists (Bloomfield, Knopfler) and keyboard players (Griffin, Kooper), but never did he time and again lock emotionally into such sensitive every-note-counts playing as he did when he worked with Robertson and Hudson.

This is Curtis Mayfield territory, with a gospel feel and a vocal from the former Spokesperson For A Generation that reveals him in exactly that persona, whether Dylan admitted it then or now or not ever.

His message is clear: forget the kids-are-all-right attitude; Mom and Dad are the ones who are all right, the family is all right – and so much so that no broken heart hurts more than the broken heart of a distraught parent. Dylan was learning all about parents and parenthood in these Woodstock days and would have more learning to do. Here he testifies to that notion.

Even the slurred hesitancy of his singing at 2:08 and the fluffed bass note from Danko at 2:31 add to the overall charm and help create the warmth of the moment. The music they collectively made in the four minutes and eight seconds after Hudson ran the tape is as representative of community, ageless truths, and the unbreakable bonds of family as anything in The Band's canon – or, for that matter, in anyone else's canon. Gorgeous, simply gorgeous.

### QUINN THE ESKIMO (THE MIGHTY QUINN) (take one)
1:58
**Dylan** vocal, acoustic 12-string guitar, **Danko** bass, backing vocal,
**Hudson** organ, **Manuel** piano, backing vocal.
"Waiting on you," an impatient Dylan says to one of his compatriots at the start of this first take of a song that would be a big hit for Manfred Mann. Ultimately a relatively inconsequential Dylan number, and particularly so in light of the compositional company around it here, this is for fun. Robertson speaks of some songs being for fun and some more serious. "There's all this basement tape music going on," he told Rob Bowman. "Some of it is a goof, some of it is serious. There is a difference in these things. ... Some of these fall into the 'Yea! Heavy And A Bottle Of Bread' category and some of them fall into the 'I Shall Be Released' category. 'Tears Of Rage' was not a goofy basement song. It was a beautiful song." [18] This is, to quote a man who should know, a goofy song.

### QUINN THE ESKIMO (THE MIGHTY QUINN) (take two)
2:12
**Dylan** vocal, acoustic 12-string guitar, **Danko** bass, backing vocal,
**Hudson** organ, **Manuel** piano, backing vocal, **Robertson** electric guitar.
• The feel of the song has changed considerably since the first take. They've worked hard to give the song some gravitas, which is difficult to do with such a childlike lyric. Was this a nonsense song sung to the Dylan youngsters, charmingly silly entertainment from a proud papa? Sounds like it. Dylan later told Cameron Crowe: "Quinn The Eskimo ... I don't

know. … I don't know what it was all about. I guess it was some kind of nursery rhyme." [19] Robertson is heard on guitar here but his playing is low-key and unobtrusive until the end, when at 2:04 he plays a James Burton pedal-steel-styled bend that underpins the gospel three-part harmony of Dylan, Danko, and Manuel. This take was released in 1985 on *Biograph* some 18 years after the fact.

### OPEN THE DOOR, HOMER (take one)
2:40
**Dylan** vocal, acoustic 12-string guitar, **Danko** bass, backing vocal,
**Hudson** organ, **Manuel** piano, backing vocal, **Robertson** electric guitar.
• This has a refrain from Count Basie's Number 1 smash of 1947, 'Open The Door, Richard' (and check out the version by Louis Jordan & His Tympany Five, which got to Number 6 that same year: it's all thriller and no filler too). That song itself was based on a 1919 vaudeville skit by Harlem comic John Mason, so this is a nonsense song based on a nonsense song. It was not the first time that Dylan had gotten a song out of playing another song. Danko always claimed Dylan changed the name in the title to Homer so folks would not think it a reference to Richard Manuel. This version was strong enough to release in '75, a fine first take.

### OPEN THE DOOR, HOMER (take two)
0:54
**Dylan** vocal, acoustic 12-string guitar, **Danko** bass, backing vocal,
**Hudson** organ, **Manuel** piano, **Robertson** electric guitar.
• A very country sound has to be expected at times with this mob. "You know, Rick would maybe be included there," says Robertson, "in the country music part of things. Richard is from Stratford, Ontario, the home of the Shakespearean Festival there. Not that it is any big cosmopolitan area but it was a small city. Garth was from London, Ontario, and these small cities had their bits of sophistication – and Rick was from a farm. Levon was from a farm too, so both of those guys knew a little more about real country music than the rest of us.

"I just remembered some great old songs, because my experience was at the Six Nations Indian reservation, where a lot of Indians there played country music. Yeah, they played it and they lived out in the country, and that is what you heard on the radio, country music. It is just kind of a North American thing or somethin'. That's were I heard old songs by artists like Webb Pierce or Lefty Frizzell. That's where 'Long Black Veil' came from on *Music From Big Pink*." [20]

**OPEN THE DOOR, HOMER** (take three)
3:11
Same line-up as take two.
● Robertson's guitar is getting more C&W. He is periodically dampening the strings with the palm of his right hand, and this in combination with a bit of reverb on his amp is giving him a chicken-pickin' sound he either had not mastered or at least refrained from using earlier in the sessions. Now he is periodically playing some nifty pedal-steel licks, which are perfect for this kind of song.

Hudson as usual is right on the money and his playing and tone here should remind all fans of how Eric Garth Hudson gained a lot of his keyboard technique and style playing memorial services in his uncle's funeral parlor back in Ontario. You hear that sound and feel here on take three.

It is an apropos sound for the moment that Dylan sings: "And remember when you're out there trying to heal the sick / That you must always first forgive them." Although the importance of healing the sick, bringing eyesight to the blind, curing leprosy, and making the lame whole occurs in several places in the Bible, both in the Old Testament as well as the New, Dylan must have been reading the book of Matthew, chapters four and five, which deal with such deeds as a sign of powerful prophecy and a sign of God's love.

In Matthew, Jesus travels all over Galilee preaching The Good News and healing people of every kind of disease and sickness. But there are those that doubt Him, who've heard it said before, and who ain't gonna hear it said no more.

**NOTHING WAS DELIVERED** (take one)
4:15
**Dylan** vocal, acoustic 12-string guitar, **Danko** bass, backing vocal,
**Hudson** organ, **Manuel** piano, backing vocal, **Robertson** electric guitar.
• A really good recording. Hudson is on top of his engineering now, and it is noticeable how songs are no longer cut off at the end and that the Ampex tape recorder is not started late any more.

The feel and the vibe coming from the basement is that these are serious Dylan songs making the latest statement in an already noteworthy career. Making this music is a serious business, as these songs will represent a revenue stream required now that The Artist Formerly Known As Bob is off the road. They are so obviously not covers cut for fun; they are so obviously not piss-takes. The musicians involved are, to use an overused contemporary phrase, going for it.

Curiously, the poor-quality tape used by Hudson allows some bleed-through of whatever signal was recorded on the tape beforehand. Frequently the faint sounds of a radio broadcast are heard, while on other occasions the bleed-through sounds like an earlier Dylan–Band song long since discarded.

This is a very Fats Domino version of yet another Dylan all-time tune. In fact, this sounds like the Fat Man doing Dylan. Which is a good thing. It sounds like the byproduct of playing 'Blueberry Hill' a bit up-tempo, of a song growing out of that. What a marvelous, slow ballad this would make for a post-Katrina New Orleans; even the title would fit the sad civic predicament of the true capital city of the Caribbean.

Manuel has taken to heart whatever stern speech Grossman gave him. His drunken life-of-the-party persona is no longer on keyboards. As for Danko, he is sober yet swinging as well. The intoxicated muso seen dueting in the film *Festival Express* alongside an equally smashed Janis Joplin is long gone and his Caucasian James Jamerson alter ego is right in its place.

"Nothing is better / Nothing is best / Take care of yourself and get plenty of rest" may well be the ultimate rural American advice to a neighbor. Manuel and Danko heard it, sang it, and must have agreed it sounded like a good idea. It would be Dylan's mantra for the next six and a half years, until the call of the road could not be denied.

**NOTHING WAS DELIVERED** (take two)
3:35
**Dylan** vocal, acoustic 12-string guitar, **Danko** bass, backing vocal,
**Hudson** piano, **Manuel** drums, **Robertson** electric guitar.

• "Ready?" asks a bemused Dylan, possibly curious about Manuel sitting
on the drum-stool again. There is a reason that Manuel was called an
excellent rhythm pianist, like there was a reason John Lennon was a fine
rhythm guitarist. It is a mistake to take him off the ivories and put him
on the drums for this take. This is getting back to the boozy swing of the
Red Room and this is not going to work out for anyone.

The feel of the song is now too sloppy, although it is apparent where
The Byrds got their inspiration from when they cut it: the chorus heard
here provided The Byrds with their creative starting-off point.

But at what cost? Robertson reverts to the R&B guitar work and the tone
that Guitar Slim used on countless bluesy ballads. His playing never
detracts for a nanosecond from the vocal but always effortlessly
references it musically.

Alas, this is not a good version, and even Dylan's old time
preacher testifying in the middle cannot save it. "Take three," announces
Hudson wearily at the end.

"Bob used to write all of his songs on a typewriter. I dunno if
anybody ever knew that," says Robertson.

"You know, you picture someone sitting down to write a song and
they have their instrument and their music stand and everything. He wrote
all those songs on a typewriter. He was just writing away! Dada, dada, dada,
dada dada PING. Dada, dada, dada, dada dada PING." Robertson imitates a
man shouting over his shoulder: "Hey, here's another one!" And then, says
Robertson, Dylan would put in another piece of paper and write some more.[21]

**GOIN' TO ACAPULCO**
5:25
**Dylan** vocal, **Danko** bass, backing vocal, **Hudson** organ, **Manuel** drums,
backing vocal, **Robertson** electric guitar.

• When this song appeared on 1975's official Columbia release it

announced to the world that there was more to the Basement Tapes than the *Great White Wonder* and its black-market cousins had let on. As can best be determined, this was recorded after The Hawks returned from the failed Columbia Studios sessions in New York City yet before Woody Guthrie died on October 3.

It's a musical relation of 'Tears Of Rage.' The lyric line "the stars ain't falling down" is taken from The New Testament, an apocalyptic vision where " the stars fell out of the sky to earth, like unripe figs falling from a tree when a strong wind shakes it" in the Book of Revelation.

Robertson's guitar is up in the mix on the original tapes, and the absence of piano and the simple but in-time drumming tells us Manuel is on the skins. Slightly distorted, maybe due to over-enthusiasm on the part of a bootlegger who cannot read a VU meter.

The song's protagonist is off to Acapulco to see his Rose Marie who pleases him romantically and sexually. Like the young cowboy in Marty Robbins's immortal 'El Paso' on his way back to Rosa's Cantina to see his wicked Felina, the attraction could be fatal – but what is love but the soul's dance with a certain kind of (emotional) death?

There are those who think that the passage about the broken well that occurs from 3:56 to 4:20 is a masturbation metaphor. But there are also those who think maybe the well didn't work in the literal sense, who suggest its pump don't work 'cos some vandals took the handles.

**GONNA GET YOU NOW**
1:26
**Dylan** vocal, acoustic guitar, **Danko** bass, backing vocal, **Hudson** organ, **Manuel** piano, **Robertson** drums.
• John Simon believes this is Manuel on drums, but that is only possible if the pianist is Robertson or Simon (who was in Woodstock in October '67 to work with Howard Alk on *You Are What You Eat*). It sounds like Manuel on piano and Robertson's happy-go-lucky timekeeping. Dylan is softly strumming his acoustic; you can barely hear it. Robertson says this is from Big Pink and that the move to Danko's new pad off Wittenberg Road has not yet been made.

Not much of a song and a bit of a throwback to the early Red Room sessions in its bawdy intentions. Recorded at the same time as 'Goin' To Acapulco,' after the N.Y.C. demo session but before the death of Woody Guthrie.

## FLIGHT OF THE BUMBLE BEE
2:07

**Dylan** vocal, **Danko** bass, **Manuel** piano, **Robertson** electric guitar.

• No Russian classically-trained composer could claim responsibility for this. Another 'song within another song,' and here the ensemble entirely wings it after being amused by Manuel playing a bit of 'Flight Of The Bumble Bee' at the top. It sounds like the earlier piss-takes done at the Red Room. Hudson must have asked them to give him something to measure the meters so they could record in a bit. This is what he got.

## CONFIDENTIAL
(Dorinda Morgan)
1:32

**Dylan** vocal, **Danko** drums, **Hudson** organ, **Manuel** piano.

• This must be Danko on drums. Robertson's drumming was never this foolhardy or amateurish, and Robertson and Hudson never sounded intoxicated when playing, while Dylan, Danko, and Manuel certainly did on occasion. There is no bass, either, so it points to Danko. Why has Dylan stopped playing an instrument?

'Confidential' was covered by The Fleetwoods but their well-sung version missed the charts, though Sonny Knight, real name Joseph C. Smith, took the original to Number 17 in 1956.

In the jumble of Basement Tape seven-inch reels, there is a case for this and 'Flight Of The Bumble Bee' coming from much earlier in the year (no Helm, that bawdy feel again, a rough recording) and that they got chronologically mixed up when Hudson re-used some of the tapes on which he'd recorded earlier songs. This would also explain that faint musical signal bleeding through on some tapes. If the recording heads on the Ampex were worn, it is possible some earlier signal would stay on the magnetic tape.

**ODDS AND ENDS** (take one)
1:48
**Dylan** vocal, **Danko** bass, backing vocal, **Hudson** organ, **Manuel** drums, **Robertson** electric guitar.
• Manuel counts this one in, a tune later described by Helm as "a great rock'n'roll song." [22] Robertson's Telecaster has some real Hawks R&B bite to it on this number.

Only Manuel's fills give away his status as an intermediate drummer, but the boy is learning. Fast. If Dylan is playing his acoustic guitar he is playing it awfully quietly.

**ODDS AND ENDS** (take two)
1:46
Same line-up as take one.
• Nonsense, but worthwhile nonsense, and good enough to kick off the official Basement Tapes album when it finally came out in '75. In all fairness, this kind of song represents no challenge to the men once collectively known as The Hawks. They'd been playing this kind of silly but fun R&B-cum-rock'n'roll with one mind for years.

**GET YOUR ROCKS OFF**
3:45
**Dylan** vocal, acoustic 12-string guitar, **Danko** bass, backing vocal,
**Hudson** organ, **Manuel** piano, backing vocal, **Robertson** electric guitar.
• They blessed us with a mid-tempo re-write of 'Blueberry Hill' and now here's a slow-tempo version of the same Fats Domino signature song. Manuel uses the Voice Of Conscience microphone once again. Dylan cracks up at 2:12 – and remember, Dylan was a fellow who had attended comedy films alongside Bob Neuwirth where the two of them would practice not laughing out loud and not cracking a smile. So if Bob thinks this song is funny, it must be funny. And it sounds like Manuel is what is making him laugh. Is that Tiny Tim whooping it up in the background at 2:22? Could be: Dylan invited him to dinner at Byrdcliffe several times during the year.

### CLOTHES LINE SAGA (ANSWER TO ODE)
3:21

**Dylan** vocal, acoustic guitar, **Danko** bass, **Hudson** organ, **Manuel** piano, **Robertson** guitar.

• When Clinton Heylin saw Neil Young's Basement Tapes reel, he noticed this song was written down on the box as 'Answer To Ode.' Doing some calculations with Joel Bernstein, they quickly figured out this was a parody of Bobbie Gentry's 'Ode To Billie Joe,' a Number 1 hit in the States in late August 1967. Dylan could not have missed the song had he turned on his radio in August or September, so a parody recorded in October is right on schedule.

(He'd done his share of parodies before: the early song 'Acne' was one; 'I'm Your Teenage Prayer' and 'The All American Boy' from this same year are two others.)

In the Gentry song, the tragic suicide of a local boy is discussed calmly and dispassionately by a Southern family around their dinner table, the boy's ghastly death of little more emotional interest than a change in the weather. Billie Joe MacAllister has jumped off the Tallahatchie Bridge, throwing something off it before he did so. And all this particular family can think about is "pass the biscuits, please."

It was the catchiest, most unforgettable song of a memorable summer, but 'Ode To Billie Joe' quickly got tiresome. Dylan must have thought it was ripe for parody, and he aims, pulls the trigger, and hits the bullseye on this one. He starts off and gets 20 seconds in with no one joining him (shades of 'Bob Dylan's 115th Dream') before asking Hudson: "Is it on? Oh, it is. OK, let's start all over again." From that point on it is the same as the official release.

Dylan's song is as much mundane daily activity as the Gentry original. That is the point. However, at 1:41 a neighbor passes by with some extraordinary news that is anything but mundane. The Vice-President has gone mad. As the neighbor doesn't say Vice-President of anything in particular this would mean the Vice-President, the second most powerful man in the country.

The veep at the time of 'Ode To Billie Joe' was Hubert Humphrey of

Minnesota, once a young, courageous Mayor of Minneapolis who did so much to combat the pronounced anti-Semitism and bigotry in the city. He was a liberal and founder of both the Minnesota Democratic-Farmer-Labor Party and Americans for Democratic Action. He gave one of the best American political speeches ever when at the 1948 Democratic National Convention he took the platform and wildly offended the conservative Southern Democrats, who were pro-States Rights and pro-segregation. Dylan, a fellow Minnesota man and fellow civil rights enthusiast, would have been proud of this particular Humphrey, the one he had read about while growing up back in Hibbing.

In his address to the that convention in '48, Humphrey said: "My friends, to those who say that we are rushing this issue of civil rights, I say to them we are 172 years too late! To those who say, this civil rights program is an infringement on states' rights, I say this: the time has arrived in America for the Democratic Party to get out of the shadow of states' rights and walk forthrightly into the bright sunshine of human rights!"

A pro-civil rights plank was narrowly adopted, although as a result of the Convention's vote the entire Mississippi and half the Alabama delegation walked out of the hall. Many Southern Democrats were so enraged that they formed the Dixiecrat party and nominated their own presidential candidate, the arch-racist Strom Thurmond.

In short, Humphrey was a heroic figure to those in the civil rights movement. However, in 1964, President Lyndon Johnson offered Humphrey the Vice-Presidency at that year's Democratic National Convention, on the caveat of a) supporting his Vietnam War policy and b) not causing any more undue civil rights hassles with the Southern Democrats (who would soon defect to the Republican Party in droves). Shockingly, Humphrey agreed.

At the convention, Humphrey helped prevent the recently organized Mississippi Freedom Democratic Party from taking their seats in the hall and being legally recognized. (The M.F.D.P. was created by black and white Mississippians with the assistance of Dylan's old friends from the Student Nonviolent Coordinating Committee.) Instead, an all-white delegation from the state's racist Democratic Party would be seated. That the pro-civil rights Humphrey would not support the integrated, pro-civil rights M.F.D.P. over a bunch of old white racists shocked American liberals. It was no doubt especially painful for a fellow Minnesotan like Bob Dylan, who if nothing else politically was identifiably pro-voting rights and pro-civil rights.

It is inconceivable that Dylan is not singing of Hubert Humphrey going mad in 'Clothes Line Saga.' The dispassionate tenor of his voice only exaggerates the parody of the song and hides the bitter disappointment of an artist who once memorably wrote: "How can a man turn his head and pretend that he just doesn't see?"

'Clothes Line Saga,' like 'Ode To Billie Joe,' is a chapter of life from those who see but nonetheless turn, turn, turn away.

**APPLE SUCKLING TREE** (take one)
2:36
**Dylan** vocal, piano, **Danko** bass, backing vocal, **Hudson** organ, **Manuel** tambourine, backing vocal, **Robertson** kick drum, snare.
• Another nonsense song, but another good nonsense song. And it swings. Whoever is playing kick and snare here sounds like he is having such fun. Robertson has been given credit for drums on this, but it might be Manuel. Robertson remembers drumming in the basement, true, and his guitar is absent from the track, but Dylan's more primitive piano style is heard here. No way is this Manuel on the ivories. So it is either Manuel on the drums and Robertson on the tambourine or the other way around.

"Yeah, that's true," Robertson agrees. "I did some engineering, if you will, and I played drums on a few songs. I think 'Apple Suckling Tree' was one. The engineering part of it was just a matter of turning a machine on, getting a microphone, and putting it in front of whatever it was supposed to record." He pauses to laugh. "Garth did most of that stuff."

**APPLE SUCKLING TREE** (take two)
2:36
Same line-up as take one.
• The hard-hit fills at 1:37, 1:52 and 2:13 sound like Robertson; Manuel's time would have been a bit better. When will Levon Helm come save

them percussively? (Answer: soon.) Good God, listen to Hudson's fill at 2:25 to 2:32. Unworldly! Be it Helm, Robertson, or Manuel on the drums, they are swinging like the greatest garage band on earth and it is a joy to hear.

This was the last song the Dylan–Band line up cut at Big Pink. Helm remembers working in the basement, but that would be on Hawks songs as Dylan was off to Nashville about the time Helm returned. Plus Helm and Danko were soon to move to Wittenberg Road. As were these very sessions.

Recently, five more takes of this Dylan-sung song have surfaced. In chronological order, their timings are: 2:00, 0:54, 0:45, 2:31, and 2:45. They are nothing more or less than the usual suspects rehearsing the song, which in this case meant take two was released on the official *Basement Tapes* LPs in 1975.

September was now turning into October 1967. Dylan was booked by Bob Johnston for a recording session on October 17 in Nashville, his first for the *John Wesley Harding* album, and none of The Hawks were coming along.

The Hawks had been recording off and on in Woodstock on their own, no longer waiting for Dylan, for Helm's return, nor for divine inspiration to arrive. They recorded impromptu sessions in the living room upstairs at Big Pink as well as more formal sessions downstairs in the basement. They would have to come up with some goods soon if they were going to go out on their own.

The sessions at Big Pink with Dylan were winding down after months and months. But another break in the work suddenly arrived, although there was some warning it was coming. On October 3, Woody Guthrie died.

**MILLION DOLLAR BASH**

# 11. Another Best Friend, Somehow

*The move to Wittenberg Road*

Woodrow Wilson Guthrie was hospitalized at Greystone Park Psychiatric Hospital in a ten-acre park near the town of Parsippany in north central New Jersey from 1956, when he was only 44, until 1961. He was then moved to Brooklyn State Hospital for a further five years before ending out his days at Creedmoor Psychiatric Center in Queens.

Due to his failing health during those final years Guthrie was unable to enjoy first-hand the renewed interest in his songs and in his prose that the 1960s folk revival brought him. But he knew from his visitors and from reading the press that he had not been forgotten.

He died on October 3, 1967 from Huntington's chorea, a degenerative disease marked by progressive mental deterioration. Guthrie's ashes were scattered into the waves off Coney Island, New York, not far from his final and much loved family home on Mermaid Avenue.

Bob Dylan had fallen in love back in Minnesota with Woody Guthrie's music and his autobiography, *Bound For Glory*. Through Guthrie he discovered many other authentic folk voices and grew not only to admire artists such as Guthrie acolyte Ramblin' Jack Elliott but also to know them as friends. Dylan first met Elliott when both went to see Guthrie on the same day.

The young Dylan had first visited Guthrie in January 1961, shortly after Dylan first arrived in New York City. He traveled out to Greystone to meet his hero. Much is made now of Dylan's early stance and repertoire being influenced by Guthrie (and Elliott). But the true depth of feeling that young Dylan had for Guthrie was displayed publicly on Friday April 12, 1963 at New York City's Town Hall when for his encore Dylan read his poem *Last Thoughts On Woody Guthrie*. He had never before and has never since read a poem onstage. The one he read that night was as full of Guthrie's spirit as it was possible for a young and still awestruck singer-songwriter to write.

At the end of 1967, Dylan could not be expected to continue to attend sessions in the Big Pink basement with an important new LP starting in mid October in Nashville and in light of the death of Woody Guthrie, one

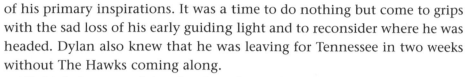

of his primary inspirations. It was a time to do nothing but come to grips with the sad loss of his early guiding light and to reconsider where he was headed. Dylan also knew that he was leaving for Tennessee in two weeks without The Hawks coming along.

All this helps to explain why the *John Wesley Harding* sessions are so full of the reflective spirit of the Bible-referencing Dylan so evident in the Big Pink basement. It also helps explain why those Nashville sessions would contain such strong narrative songs full of colorful characters. There is none of the bacchanalian sense of life as one big goblet of red wine that for a time was such a strong theme in the music made at Big Pink. Dylan knew that was a side of life he was leaving and, while he might return to it at some point, this was not a time to cast away stones (as the book of Ecclesiastes stated) but a time to gather stones together. His Canadian friends had the big-goblet-of-red-wine approach down cold anyway, and in Nashville he would not need their assistance.

In a way, The Hawks didn't need Dylan. They were growing musically and gaining confidence in their new country-funk sound. And their line-up was about to be augmented by two allies who would help them define their sound further: Levon Helm, an old friend coming home, and John Simon, a new friend upon whom they would come to rely for a great deal in the next few years.

After Columbia passed on The Hawks' unsuccessful N.Y.C. demos, recorded September 5, 1967 with Helm still absent, Grossman flew to Los Angeles around the third week of September and tried to interest Mo Ostin of Warner Bros. in Dylan's talented friends. According to reports, Ostin was out of town, so Grossman moved on to Stanley Gortikov at Capitol, who immediately heard potential in the tapes. It was this meeting with the eager Gortikov that prompted the Canadians to think about getting Helm back into the line-up.

Rick Danko volunteered to make the call. He remembered later: "I said we'd be getting a couple of hundred thousand dollars we wanted to share. ... He said, 'I'll be on the next plane.'"[1] In his autobiography, Helm said that he flew to Woodstock from Memphis with his friend Kirby Pennick after Danko had told him they'd signed to Capitol Records. In fact, they did not sign until February 1, 1968, but Grossman was at least in negotiations with Gortikov at the time. Did Danko exaggerate to get Helm interested again? Or does Helm not quite remember?

Danko would not have called his comrade after only one meeting with Capitol, no matter how promising. There is further evidence that it was definitely October when Helm flew to New York City to be picked up by Richard Manuel and Rick Danko for the drive north to Woodstock. John Simon went to Woodstock in October to work alongside Howard Alk, editing the *You Are What You Eat* footage, and he distinctly recalls meeting Robertson and the others. "I came up to talk to Robbie about doing The Band thing. This was the day after Levon had arrived from working in the oil rigs. I don't know the exact dates, but Levon was with us and brought his friend Kirby Pennick – they'd both been on the oil rigs and were both now at Big Pink. That's where Levon was now living.

"Howard and I had holed up together in a house in Woodstock working on *You Are What You Eat* and one night, on Howard's birthday, this ungodly noise came from outside," Simon continues. "It was the guys in The Band. They had costumes on and they were playing funny instruments. They were serenading Howard for his birthday. That was the first time I met The Band. And Levon was certainly there." [2] Howard Alk's birthday was October 25, and Simon had been working with Alk for a while by then. This means Helm arrived in Woodstock to rejoin his comrades at some point during the first three weeks of the month, probably the second week.

Dylan was soon off by train to Columbia Music Row Studios in Nashville for his October 17 *John Wesley Harding* session. He would return there for sessions on November 6 and 29 – and that would be all it would take for him to finish the album for his belated return to the marketplace. The LP was released December 27, 1967 with little fanfare from his label (as per Bob's instructions).

John Simon was now becoming part of The Hawks' team. (They were still Hawks and not yet called The Band.) This was Alk's idea. Simon had gone to Woodstock to work with Alk, not to work with Dylan's backing group. Alk had heard an album that Simon had produced for Columbia, *The Medium Is The Message*, based on Marshall McLuhan's famous book. "It was a very Dada-ish recording, not too musical, just nuts," says Simon. "The only thing that we'd really heard of from The Band, as they hadn't really done anything yet aside from their backing of Dylan, was a tape they put together in the basement, which, if my memory serves me well, was called *Even If It's A Pig, Part Two*. That was the name of the tape."

That tape was crazy, too, says Simon, and Alk figured that the producer of the off-the-wall *Medium Is The Message* album might well hit it off with the guys who made *Even If It's A Pig*. "Which we did," says Simon, "but for other reasons. Albert Grossman actually made the deal with Capitol Records after we started working together. I don't know where Albert got the seed money to start recording, but he made the deal after we got the first four or five Band songs."[3]

Those first four or five songs were not cut until January 10, in New York City's A&R studio. There was much work for them to do beforehand while they were still in Woodstock. The Basement Tapes sessions with Dylan were winding down, even though they were moving to a new location. Simon was soon working with Robertson & Co. when Dylan was with his family or in Nashville recording *John Wesley Harding*. He was sometimes around when Dylan and his musical cohorts worked on the final batch of Basement Tapes material, such as 'Gonna Get You Now' at Big Pink.

When Levon Helm arrived he rather comically put his bags into Rick Danko's spacious bedroom in Big Pink and took over the room. Danko had to find a new place to snooze unless he wanted a bearded roommate. Big Pink was becoming more than a little crowded, especially if women were on the scene, and so Helm and Danko moved to a home on nearby Wittenberg Road (N.Y. State Road 45) that Danko had stumbled across just southwest of

Grossman's Bearsville homestead. Hudson and Manuel moved out as well, to a crib off Ohayo Mountain Road.

These new homes were only five miles from Big Pink and put everyone within less than three miles of each other, a short drive on those back country roads of the day. They all saw each other almost every day: there were plans to make, footballs to throw, beers to drink, and women to be discussed. Little had changed in that regard. (However, the Basement Tapes recording sessions were not done on a literally daily basis, despite what has been written since.)

Peter Paul & Mary's equipment was set up in the new Danko–Helm home at Wittenberg Road and recording began again. To keep our view of the times in focus it helps to remember something Dylan said. In a *Rolling Stone* interview published in late 1969, he was asked about the true purpose of the Basement Tapes songs and if they were demos for himself. He replied: "No, they weren't demos for myself, they were demos of the songs. I was being PUSHED again … into coming up with some songs. You know how those things go."[4] (Those capital letters appeared in the original interview.)

The new Dylan songs were published by Dwarf Music, the publishing company he formed with Grossman in January 1966. (Dwarf would also publish the early material written by The Band.) Dylan was indeed pushed into recording some new songs. From his point of view, he was keen not to work so hard as before and wanted time off. Consider how he dropped the novel, *Tarantula*, consider his off/on editing of *Eat The Document* with no deadline to worry about, the cancellation of all his concerts, his refusal to confirm any formal recording studio dates for Columbia in 1967, and the fact that his growing family increasingly needed his attention. Yes, he sought time off or, at least, the time to work at his own pace and not at the world's pace.

Grossman, meanwhile, would be acquiring yet more grey hairs as the clock ticked. The manager knew that revenue was slowing at the same time as costs continued to mount for a four-piece band on retainer and

the other sundry expenses of stardom and its successes. Getting Dylan to record some jokey songs for fun and to pass the time was one thing, a first step. Yet by late summer 1967, the Big Pink basement sessions were sounding more and more serious.

And how could they not? Grossman had expenses too. He owned property here and there and he was making deals for his expanding businesses. He needed to keep the income flowing from his biggest and most prestigious act. Grossman owned 50 percent of Dwarf Music – a fact that Dylan didn't realize until August 1968. He only found out then when his employee Naomi Saltzman at her Gramercy Park office in New York City told him he couldn't change the Dwarf name to honor the recent birth of Samuel Abram Dylan. Grossman would have to agree, as half-owner of the company.

A disappointed Dylan claimed later that he'd signed the original papers based upon Grossman's word that it was OK to do so – and that was what he had always done in the 1960s. Besides putting the rooster in charge of the hen house, the young Dylan's continual deference to his manager speaks volumes not only of his trust (or naiveté) when it came to business but his absolute need for a father figure.

This also explains why Grossman sought to have these 1967 sessions produce some top-flight new Dylan material, and why he then so rapidly had that material shopped out to popular acts of the day.

As early as August 1967, ten new Dylan songs were dubbed to mono by order of the Grossman office, and in October a 14-song demo tape was copyrighted and its songs registered with Dwarf. While Grossman ordered the demos of Basement Tapes songs to be made, to generate publishing income through cover versions, it was most likely Garth Hudson who would have known which takes were best to make into acetates after possible consultation with Dylan. (Some artists who covered these very songs distinctly remember being played acetates; others firmly recall receiving a reel tape from the publishers when they requested Dylan material to record.)

The 14 songs on this first collection of demos were:

'Million Dollar Bash'
'Yea! Heavy And A Bottle Of Bread'
'Please Mrs. Henry'
'Crash On The Levee (Down In The Flood)'
'Lo And Behold!'
'Tiny Montgomery'
'This Wheel's On Fire'
'You Ain't Goin' Nowhere'
'I Shall Be Released'
'Too Much Of Nothing'
'Tears Of Rage'
'Quinn The Eskimo (The Mighty Quinn)'
'Open The Door, Homer'
'Nothing Was Delivered'

The easiest way for Grossman to get a Basement Tapes song covered immediately was to have one of his other acts cover one. That's exactly what happened. Frequent *Billboard* Hot 100 residents Peter Paul & Mary had a cover of 'Too Much Of Nothing' in the charts in December while the Basement Tapes sessions were still continuing.

Later, Ian & Sylvia, another act managed by Grossman, recorded 'Tears Of Rage,' 'Quinn The Eskimo,' and 'This Wheel's On Fire.' This Canadian duo would have had access to the new material before the 14-song demo was assembled. As Dylan had covered some Ian & Sylvia songs at the sessions, the duo would surely have been high on the list of acts, managed by Grossman or not, to get an acetate or reel tape from Dwarf.

Dylan's dissatisfaction with Grossman and his co-ownership of Dwarf Music also explains why the Basement Tapes were of so little interest to Dylan for so long (and perhaps still are). When Dylan found out that Grossman got 50 percent of Dwarf Music's income he was furious.

Relations between Dylan and Grossman, which were already strained, never recovered.

For Dylan to publish these songs and then get them covered would give Grossman a much bigger slice of the Dylan publishing pie than the artist thought was warranted. To record them himself would give Grossman even more income as he was a Grossman act who paid his manager a percentage. By the time of the Woody Guthrie Memorial Concert on January 20, 1968 at Carnegie Hall, this artist and his manager were no longer speaking to one another. As their relationship worsened, it only helped to keep the Basement Tapes a bootleg-only release for years.

(The Dylan–Grossman managerial contract would expire at the end of 1969. Dylan formed a new publishing company, Big Sky, in 1968. Grossman owned a part of this, but a much smaller slice than the 50 percent that so irritated his artist. Also, Dylan had legal control over any material published by Big Sky. Songs would continue to be registered to Dwarf Music in the first half of 1968, but these were primarily early Dylan compositions and Basement Tapes material. New compositions would go to Big Sky.)

It was not long before the ten song and subsequent fourteen-song demo sets began to have an impact. By October 1967 copies in London were repeatedly played, discussed, and absorbed by the good and great of the British pop world. The November 4 issue of *Melody Maker* gave a preview of seven of the new Dylan songs. Although the paper listed the titles inaccurately, memorably referring to two of the better tunes as 'I Shall Be Relieved' and 'If Your Memory Serves You Well,' they were more on the mark than many bootleggers down the years, who seem to enjoy mis-hearing key lines and then naming the song after the mis-heard lyric. No one in Britain and certainly no one at *Melody Maker* had a clue who the backing musicians were. The assumption was that they must be Nashville cats.

At The Pheasantry in London's Kings Road, where Eric Clapton had an apartment, one of the residents, David Litvinoff, played the Cream guitarist seven of the songs. Clapton's life changed forever. By the time summer '68 rolled around, he had been listening to the Basement Tapes and to an early copy of *Music From Big Pink* for months. They only confirmed for him that Cream was playing dinosaur music and that he and his two bandmates were yesterday's men. He decided to disband his very popular band.

Playing the recordings for Chris Welch of *Melody Maker*, Clapton said: "They were recorded in the basement with friends at Woodstock. There is some really great music coming out of America. ... I've got another tape here of Bob Dylan's band. I think this music will influence a lot of people. Everybody I have played it to has flipped."[5] Clapton is so taken by The Band that, before Cream flew home from their last concert tour of the States, he journeyed to Woodstock to meet them.

Many years later, Clapton said more at a Rock & Roll Hall Of Fame ceremony where he was inducting The Band. "I want to talk about what it was like to be a musician, a serious musician, who couldn't be in The Band. That was tough; that was hard," said Clapton. "I remember being on tour with Cream in '67 and we thought we were the bee's knees. ... I wanted to be in The Band. I went to Woodstock to actually ask to be in The Band, but I didn't have the guts to say it. I didn't have the nerve. ... I just sorta sat there and watched these guys work.

"I spent the rest of my career, or until *The Last Waltz*, anyway, trying to imitate what they had," Clapton continued. "And it was an impossible dream, really, because where I came from and where they came from were completely different worlds. But it was something to do with the principle that I got from what they did, which was integrity. Integrity, and a standard of craft which really didn't bow down to any kind of commerciality. I really identified with that and I adored it."[6]

Yet the sessions in Woodstock were not yet completed. Clapton and his London movers and shakers would be able to hear more later on from the basement and elsewhere. Changes were afoot in Woodstock, but the players all adapted.

Rick Danko and Robbie Robertson helped Garth Hudson set up the equipment at the Wittenberg Road home that Danko had rented, and soon the gang were at it again.

# MILLION DOLLAR BASH

## 12. Giving Back All Of What You Owe

*Recordings at Wittenberg Road*

Albert Grossman's need for first-class product was on everyone's mind, whether they admitted it or acted like they knew it or not. While no one knew what Dylan was thinking at any particular time, anyone could guess what a manager would be thinking at such a time.

Grossman did his best to keep things moving forward but Levon Helm's return in October 1967 was the musical and professional shot in the arm. The drums were no longer an afterthought or something they had completely forgotten about. The boys in the basement could really rock it again.

When Helm, Danko, Manuel, and Hudson moved out of Big Pink there was no way the sessions could continue in the basement there: the guys lived elsewhere. Helm and Danko were near Wittenberg on the road toward Bearsville, Manuel and Hudson not far off Ohayo Mountain Road. The rhythm section somehow won the toss of the coin and the Wittenberg Road pad became the new recording location.

Again, what follows here is my view of each of the songs recorded at Wittenberg Road. The listings have the title followed by the composer, specified if not Bob Dylan, then the length of the recording, who played which instruments, and what it sounds like.

## WILDWOOD FLOWER

(A.P. Carter)

2:18

**Bob Dylan** vocal, autoharp, **Rick Danko** bass, **Levon Helm** drums, **Richard Manuel** harmonica.

• "It's rolling," Garth Hudson says to Richard Manuel, and they begin. This is one of the greatest and most famous Carter Family songs ever, and the one song that virtuoso country guitarist and Nashville session wiz Norman Blake said every picker had to learn to play well before they could call themselves a guitarist.

The world will never know which parts of the song Alvin Pleasant Delaney Carter wrote and which he learned from the Clinch Mountain neighbors upon whose doors he knocked looking for material – material that he would then polish and hone with guitarists Sara and Maybelle.

A.P. played some fiddle, but not well, as he suffered from the shakes and was essentially a songwriter. He didn't sing much, either. Wife Sara played autoharp, too.

Robbie Robertson confirms that Dylan is the autoharpist here and that Manuel is on harmonica.

There is right-channel drop-out at 1:07, which lasts until 1:26. As the harmonica is played at the exact same time as the drums, this means Helm is back on the skins as Manuel could not play this precise harmonica melody and the in-time drums simultaneously. And these drums are played in such good time, so it cannot be Robertson on the stool. Yes, 'tis Helm, up from Memphis finally. The simple drum pattern he plays is explained by comments in his autobiography. "I was uptight about playing [drums] because I'd been away from it for so long," wrote Helm, "but soon they had me working so hard. There wasn't anything else to do." [1]

This was surely recorded after October 3, a sudden return to folk music inspired by the death of Woody Guthrie. Ironically, when it was time for Guthrie to write his powerful lyrics he often borrowed many of the same traditional melodies that The Carter Family used.

## SEE THAT MY GRAVE IS KEPT CLEAN
(Blind Lemon Jefferson)
3:33
**Dylan** vocal, autoharp, **Danko** bass, **Helm** drums, **Manuel** harmonica.
• Also covered by The Grateful Dead (twice), Canned Heat, Dylan's old guitarist Mike Bloomfield, The Dream Syndicate, Diamanda Galas, the unforgettable Meindert Talma & The Negroes, and L.A.'s shambolic 1980s also-ran punk suburbanites Thelonious Monster.

Dylan recorded this on his very first album but what is remarkable here is not that he revisits the song but that he is singing it with his *Nashville Skyline* crooner's voice, more than a year before the rest of the world knew he could sing that way. Dylan had sung in this very voice in Minnesota as a teenager, in his Purple Onion pizza joint gigs in St. Paul, before he fell head over heels in love with Woody Guthrie and began to mimic the

Oklahoma man's entire approach to music. The crooning was a vocal style that Dylan had discarded until now. And it was a vocal style he would use on 'Lay Lady Lay' to such commercial acceptance that the single hit Number 7 in 1969. How odd to hear that same soft country croon here.

Helm is on drums and, while he is a bit rusty after all that work on the Gulf Of Mexico oil rigs, he is in time – something that occasionally defeated The Band's other drummers.

## COMIN' ROUND THE MOUNTAIN
(Traditional)
1:36
**Dylan** vocal, autoharp, **Danko** bass, **Helm** drums, backing vocal,
**Robbie Robertson** acoustic guitar.
• Listen to the backing vocal starting at 0:59, the bit about killing the old red rooster. That is Levon Helm singing. And the drums are starting to swing a bit. This isn't Manuel's heavier drumming or Robertson's endearing rhythms; this is definitely Helm back in the warm arms of his musical family. Bizarrely, Dylan's vocal sounds just like Leon Redbone.

The song is based on death, which alongside unrequited love has proved to be folk music's most enduring subject, for centuries, no matter whose culture is being examined.

Also known as 'She'll Be Coming Round The Mountain,' this folk chestnut was somehow turned into a harmless children's song around 100 years ago but is based on an old African-American spiritual called 'When The Chariot Comes,' a clear metaphor for the redemptive power of death and the reward of an afterlife in heaven.

In 1927, the song was first published in Carl Sandburg's *The American Songbag,* although it had been sung for years during the late 19th century by railroad work gangs in the U.S. plains states. Folklorists debate whether those laborers were singing about the coming of a train on the tracks they were building or (clandestinely) singing about the coming of a labor union to organize them, while they continued to work right in front of the watchful eyes of their bosses. It was a labor union inspired and possibly organized by activist women such as Mother Jones, hence the female pronoun in the song's title. Or maybe they just liked singing about death while they worked. Certainly Dylan did.

**INSTRUMENTAL JAM**
2:02
**Danko** bass, **Helm** drums, **Manuel** harmonica, **Robertson** electric guitar.
• Forty years later, a laughing Robbie Robertson calls this 'Untitled No. 67.' It's a typical three-chord R&B workout sounding not unlike 'Captain Soul' by The Byrds on their *Fifth Dimension* album a year earlier. Robertson confirms that Helm is on drums and that Hudson was busy engineering during this take, which suggests the previous three traditional folk songs and this track have Hudson getting up to speed with equipment now set up in a different place. An autumnal chill is in the air, October leaves are falling, and Helm's presence and Dylan's absence – he's occasionally away to record in Nashville – are inspiring the guys to try a few things on their own.

**NOTHING WAS DELIVERED** (take three)
0:30
**Dylan** vocal, acoustic guitar, **Danko** bass, backing vocal, **Helm** drums, **Manuel** piano, **Robertson** electric guitar.
• Wittenberg Road sessions continue apace with the drums set up, although Helm plays this one too quickly. It's almost as if you can hear Dylan signal Hudson to shut off the tape recorder – and let's sort this one out. The shame is that this snippet suggests how much better some of the earlier material would have been had Helm been around to give the songs another color and some extra punch when needed.

**SILENT WEEKEND**
3:00
**Dylan** vocal, acoustic guitar, **Danko** bass, harmony vocal, **Helm** drums, **Garth Hudson** organ, **Manuel** piano, **Robertson** electric guitar.
• No wonder Danko is Dylan's most frequent harmony vocalist: his voice

matches and enhances Dylan's without getting in the way or being thrown by Bob's most quirky phrasing.

This is rockabilly, and Ronnie Hawkins would have been able to suggest so much with these lyrics that it's a shame they didn't send a reel to him straight away. "Man alive, I'm burning up on my brain," Dylan sings in his best mid-1960s drawl.

"Harmony!" Dylan requests at 0:15. The opening guitar part is frighteningly like 'Get Back.' Drop-out at both channels at 2:41 for a second.

Helm's drum part is developed and accomplished and right up his alley. The track is tight, too, and about as tight as any of the Basement Tapes get. Yet the chorus begs out for a Helm vocal harmony and there is none.

### ALL YOU HAVE TO DO IS DREAM (take one)
3:59

**Dylan** vocal, **Danko** bass, backing vocal, **Helm** drums, **Hudson** organ, **Manuel** piano, backing vocal, **Robertson** electric guitar.

• Like the last track, this is one of the rare songs from Woodstock recorded by the full line-up of The Band with Dylan singing. Or is it? As there is no acoustic guitar heard, the possibility exists that this is Dylan on piano and Manuel on drums. The song could be the last thing attempted before Helm returned. As it is, Dylan croons it like Bing Crosby and it seems to be one of the few songs from these sessions that would have logically fit on *John Wesley Harding*, since it is easy to hear this as one of the Pete Drake-dominated country tracks that end that LP.

### ALL YOU HAVE TO DO IS DREAM (take two)
3:37

Same line-up as take one.

• They pick up the tempo and it sounds a bit mo' betta: less Bing Crosby and more like a Red Room warm-up. After the song ends, they pick it up again as the tape is rolling.

It's a song based on Robertson's guitar groove and, if a bit inconsequential, nonetheless interesting to hear. Who did they think

would cover this one? Perhaps no one, as it never made the acetate stage like so many of Dylan's other 1967 songs.

Thus ends the Dylan-sung songs from Woodstock in 1967. As regards Dylan vocal performances on tape, only three things remain: unreleased material such as 'Wild Wolf,' 'Chilly Winds,' and 'Minstrel Boy;' snippets of songs like the seven-second 'Big Dog' and 'Won't You Please Come Home' (both of which sound like rejects left on the seven-inch reels when Hudson didn't fully erase them); and fragments of Dylan strumming this chord or that or fooling with his harmonica. The difference in Dylan's harmonica doodling and Manuel's is night and day: Dylan blows in a more open, folky style than the Little Walter-sounding tones that Manuel gets when he picks up what Southern bluesmen call the Mississippi saxophone.

Which leaves us with The Hawks as they mutate into The Band. (In consideration of the reader's sanity I have seldom referred to them as The Crackers, which is how they announced themselves to the Carnegie Hall stagehands the night of the Woody Guthrie Memorial Concert and as they were to Capitol Records on the February 1, 1968 contract, or The Honkies, as they were briefly at Capitol Records until Capitol's Stanley Gortikov got wind of its true meaning.)

No one has ever made reference to The Hawks recording their own material in the Red Room yet they certainly did some recording in the basement at Big Pink and continued at Wittenberg Road as late as January 1968. Robertson includes these sessions as Basement Tapes because, he explains, "The Basement Tapes refers to ... a process, a homemade process. ... What it really means is homemade." [2]

With that in mind, it's time to examine The Hawks/Band tracks that have survived since they were recorded in and around Woodstock in 1967.

MILLION DOLLAR
BASH

## 13. Go Down, Miss Moses

*The Hawks/Band-only recordings*

A tipsy Rick Danko had announced to Dylan on the World Tour in early '66 that he and his mates didn't see themselves as anyone's backup band forever, that one day they would strike out on their own. One of the reasons Levon Helm quit the Dylan shows was because he was frustrated. Helm was the nominal leader of the act when they stopped backing one wild, opinionated musician, and after a frustrating but promising time on their own they were backing yet another wild musician who, in his own Beat poetic way, had an equally strong outlook.

Guitarist Robbie Robertson was not called The Duke by Ronnie Hawkins for nothing. He was famous for coolly observing what Dylan did in a given situation and was greatly influenced by what he learned from Albert Grossman. He saw a door opening.

Danko was almost as frustrated as Helm at their continuing status as a backing group. They were talented, restless, ambitious men. They knew that Dylan was going to Nashville without them for sessions for what turned out to be the *John Wesley Harding* LP, on October 17 and on November 6 and 29, and this would have focused their minds, professionally speaking. There was no guarantee Dylan would ever use them again. The retainer from Dylan could end at any time.

These Hawks had known that Dylan would not be there with them forever. Even back in New York City, before the move to Woodstock in February '67, they had been recording demos on their own using temporary quarters such as Barry Feinstein's Manhattan photography studio. Richard Manuel's sweet unfinished ballad 'Beautiful Thing,' eventually released on the 2005 boxed set *The Band: A Musical History*, was recorded at Feinstein's studio in the fall of 1966 and is the earliest example of them thinking ahead, post-Levon & The Hawks, while still on the Dylan payroll.

Also on that boxed set are Manuel's funky R&B workout 'Words And Numbers' (the backing track of which is found on a number of Basement Tapes black-market releases), Robertson's Impressions-inspired 'You Don't Come Through,' plus an early two-keyboards version of 'Caledonia Mission' cut while the Big Pink residents were waiting for Dominique to

let husband Robbie out of his household chores one morning, and 'Will The Circle Be Unbroken,' an all-too-rare stab at mountain music that sounds as if it was recorded upstairs in the living room at Big Pink during one of the many informal jams held there.

The 2005 boxed set has the stereo version of 'Odds And Ends' with Dylan singing, which had appeared 30 years previously on the official *Basement Tapes* 2-LP release, as well as 'Ruben Remus,' 'Katie's Been Gone,' 'Ain't No More Cane On The Brazos,' 'Don't Ya Tell Henry,' and 'Bessie Smith.' Also on the '05 set is an alternative take of 'Yazoo Street Scandal' (from the January 10 N.Y.C. Band sessions with John Simon) as well as alternative takes of 'Orange Juice Blues (Blues For Breakfast)' and 'Long Distance Operator' from Band sessions at L.A.'s Gold Star Studios in February '68.

That *Musical History* version of 'Orange Juice Blues' had appeared on The Band's first boxed set, 1994's *Across The Great Divide*, and is not the same version found on the official *Basement Tapes* double LP. A version of Robertson's Dylanesque 'Ferdinand The Imposter,' previously released as an extra track on the CD reissue of *Music From Big Pink*, was included on *Musical History* too. (The origins of some of these songs in the Big Pink basement is a matter of dispute and is discussed in chapter 15, which deals in more detail with the official release of the *Basement Tapes* set in 1975.)

There are two great differences between the material that The Hawks cut in Woodstock in 1967 with Dylan and the material they cut there on their own when Dylan was occupied elsewhere. The most obvious is that Dylan's absence usually leads to an even more serious and professional approach to recording. One might think that when the cat's away the mice will play, but the opposite is true. Without Dylan around, they know they can do some work that represents themselves, and so the four Canadians (and later Helm) frequently buckle down to some real work, leaving amusing larks such as 'Even If It's A Pig' far, far behind.

The second difference is that Dylan's absence completely changes the idea of recording so-called Basement Tapes. With Dylan, the tenor of the sessions is what Robertson has described time and time again and which he explained again to Japanese TV. "We made the Basement Tapes with a freedom unknown to man," he said, "because while we were doing the Basement Tapes we thought nobody will ever hear this, so it doesn't matter what we do." [1]

The Hawks' own sessions were cut in the exact knowledge that they were working on material that they most certainly *did* want people to hear. They wanted Grossman to be impressed, they wanted A&R men to be impressed, and they wanted the tapes they were cutting on their own to be professional enough that when they played them to people in a position of power it would allow the group to take the next step forward in their career. They were leaving The Hawks behind and evolving slowly but surely into The Band.

This was reflected in their music, as it slowed down and took on country overtones, and in their appearance, as their hair grew more unkempt and facial hair was left unattended.

Knowing the approximate time that Levon Helm arrived in Woodstock and having a fair sketch of the early history of The Band, the astute listener can go through the available reels of Band music recorded in Woodstock while Dylan was unavailable (off with his folks, with his producer Bob Johnston, or away in Nashville cutting *John Wesley Harding*) and come up with a surprisingly strong track listing.

Had these Band Basement Tapes been released as they were, they surely would have made a splash, not unlike the splash that the more polished *Music From Big Pink* made a few months later, after John Simon taught them to treat each part of the song as having a separate feel and vibe and to mind their arrangements more.

Nonetheless, this early Band material is stirring stuff. Many an Americana act today would kill to have material as effortlessly authentic, as down-home believable yet musically accessible as 'Ruben Remus' or 'Yazoo Street Scandal.'

And let's remember those are two songs that The Band at first left on the cutting room floor. Such was the strength and amount of material available to them. Their methodology was similar to the way they'd worked when Dylan was singing the songs earlier in the summer. That summer was a time when the pop world had flowers in their hair and San Francisco was the place to be – while The Hawks, soon to be The Band, were in Rick Danko's own words "drinking coffee and hanging out in the basement …" (laughter) "… in the middle of one hundred acres in New York state."[2]

Once again, what follows is my view of each of the songs, this time the ones that The Band recorded on their own. From here, I think it is more realistic to refer to these musicians as The Band. Although they were not officially using the name yet, the music they made was clearly that of The Band, with The Hawks' raucous amphetamine R&B a thing of the past. As usual, I've given the title followed by the composer, then the length of the recording, who played which instruments, and what it sounded like.

**BEAUTIFUL THING**
(Richard Manuel)
1:41
**Rick Danko** bass, **Richard Manuel** vocal, electric piano.
• This song was first recorded at Barry Feinstein's N.Y.C. photography studio, but at least two versions slipped onto Garth Hudson's Woodstock reels, though they too may have been cut at Feinstein's. The song was pitched to Eric Clapton when he was recording his *No Reason To Cry* album in 1976 at Shangri-La, The Band's Malibu studio, and it became the lead-off track on that album.

Richard Manuel said in 1971: "Robbie and I write together or separately… Our music has come from a variety of influences, really. I think it's just the most comfortable type of music for our collection of people. We're not trying to out-rock anybody or to outdo them. We let it be as natural as we can."

Two points. First, there was a time when these Canadians most certainly did try to "out-rock anybody." Second, Clapton spent years recording Band-influenced solo albums and, looking back, The Band musician whom Slowhand's efforts sounded most like was clearly Manuel and not guitarist Robertson nor white-negro Helm.

## YOU SAY YOU LOVE ME

(Robbie Robertson)

2:41

**Danko** bass, backing vocal, **Garth Hudson** organ, **Manuel** vocal, piano, **Robbie Robertson** electric guitar, backing vocal.

• In reality an earlier take of 'You Don't Come Through' (see later entry). Some gremlin switched the titles around on the seven-inch tape box. No tambourine yet, and very stark, with both keyboardists playing a very simple chord pattern. But still a beautiful song.

## CALEDONIA MISSION

(Robbie Robertson)

2:29

**Danko** vocal, **Hudson** Clavinet, **Manuel** piano.

• A faster version than on *Music From Big Pink*. This is a prime example, Exhibit A, of The Band's emerging sound, even though only three of them are here and only two instruments are heard. Their unique blend of Stanley Brothers mountain music and Impressions urbane R&B is starting to take on a life of its own. It is beginning to manifest itself as something new and unheard of, yet obviously rooted in the near past. It must have been a frightfully exciting time for these men.

## EVEN IF IT'S A PIG, PART TWO

(Rick Danko, Garth Hudson, Richard Manuel)

2:50

**Danko** euphonium, vocal, **Hudson** baritone saxophone, vocal,
**Manuel** tambourine, vocal.

• This is what they would come up with while waiting for Robertson or Dylan to show up. As John Simon says: "If It's A Pig, Part Two was the name of the tape. Now that tape was crazy too. Garth sang – it was nuts. 'Even If It's A Pig' is off the wall." [3]

And indeed it is. Various versions abound, presumably including 'Even If It's A Pig, Part One.' This song appears on multiple black-market

releases in abbreviated form and the bootleggers have done it no favors with their pointless editing and separating of different portions of the work as if it were different songs. Hudson's spoken-word bits are frequently left on their own as if from a different source entirely, serving only to dilute what is a challenging Dadaist work.

Maybe it's Hudson on euphonium and Danko on another horn? Trombone has been suggested. Robertson today confirms that this is certainly Hudson, Manuel, and Danko but doesn't remember a trombone being played at Big Pink. As the frequent ringmaster of this particular rock'n'roll circus, Robertson should know. But it is worth pointing out that later on Danko did play trombone on such memorable Band tracks as 'Across The Great Divide' and 'Unfaithful Servant.'

(And it is worth pointing out here that, although Danko's violin seems missing from the recordings made in Woodstock during this happy year of reinvention and discovery, he played fiddle during most of the upstairs informal jams at Big Pink, as well as playing violin, or fiddle if you will, on both 'Chest Fever' and the later 'Daniel & The Sacred Harp.')

There is no way to describe this. Like Brian Wilson's *Smile*-era out-take 'George Fell Into His French Horn,' like The Beatles' 'What's The New Mary Jane?' (which Lennon wanted as an A-side to a Fab Four single), and like any of The Mothers Of Invention's various versions of 'Help, I'm A Rock,' this is the sound of the inmates taking over the asylum. It has nothing to do with The Band's eventual sound at all and even less to do with The Hawks' pounding R&B, although they were still Hawks at the time this was placed on tape. Ye Gods.

**RUBEN REMUS**
(Robbie Robertson, Richard Manuel)
2:54
**Danko** bass, **Manuel** piano, **Robertson** electric guitar.
• The three Rs work their way through RR. How fascinating to hear them routine this song so enthusiastically and how remarkably it can swing with only three guys playing sparsely, with such restraint yet still with

passion, and no percussion. John Simon fans note that these three musicians are already giving each of the song's different parts a different feel so that it adds up to a more colored listening experience. Robertson, once king of the hot Hubert Sumlin style of guitar, is now firmly playing Curtis Mayfield cool.

There is a 3:09 version of this, which is not the officially released version but it does have the whole Band performing on it. It has a different ending and features higher-pitched Danko backing vocals, missing on the take used for the 1975 two-LP set.

## KATIE'S BEEN GONE
(Robbie Robertson, Richard Manuel)
2:39
**Danko** bass, backing vocal, **Hudson** organ, **Manuel** vocal, piano, **Robertson** electric guitar.
• Engineer Rob Fraboni and Robbie Robertson agree that this is an early version from Big Pink. The version on the official 1975 release has drums on it and sounds suspiciously like this particular take with just such a percussive overdub added.

Think of this: Robertson–Manuel was the songwriting credit for this sweet lament as well as 'Ruben Remus,' 'When You Awake,' 'Whispering Pines,' 'Jawbone,' 'Sleeping,' and 'Just Another Whistle Stop.' That is a formidable songwriting partnership. Had it continued, this partnership had the potential to be a rustic Lennon–McCartney, a great rock-music songwriting duo like Leiber–Stoller, Jagger–Richards, or Strummer–Jones. But they ended before they really got started. (Sigh.)

Robertson recognized Manuel's loss of interest in The Band at the time. "These things are completely mysterious," he says today. "You know, people have come out who have written one book. People have done one thing once really well and were never able to retrace footsteps and get back to the same place. I'm not sure, I cannot answer for Richard, but somehow he got discouraged in his attempts at writing. And I used to try to do stuff with him, and we did do 'Whispering Pines,' a really lovely experience. I tried to keep him going but it just didn't work, he just didn't have the ambition to [write] any more."[4]

## YAZOO STREET SCANDAL (version one)
(Robbie Robertson)
4:02
**Danko** bass, vocal, **Manuel** drums, **Robertson** electric guitar.
• This has to be from before Helm's return, although the drumming is pretty clever, which would suggest Helm is the one pounding those skins. The song is not in Danko's key and no melody instruments are present save Robertson's guitar (and he only plays a few chords). They are learning this, but it is bizarre to hear it in such a sparse fashion with Danko singing it in a key way too high for him.

## FERDINAND THE IMPOSTER
(Robbie Robertson)
3:54
**Danko** bass, vocal, backing vocal, **Hudson** organ, **Manuel** drums,
backing vocal, **Robertson** electric guitar.
• The version of this on the 2005 Band *Musical History* set has piano and drums, so there is audible evidence of that version being cut when Helm was back and John Simon had the guys working on *Music From Big Pink*. This unreleased version from 1967 is a completely different take and has no piano. The drums are more elemental, so it's Manuel having a bash. Hudson's Lowrey organ is prominent and distinctive, as per usual, but the tempo is slower and Danko has a more tentative delivery in his lead vocal. The entire thing is a bit stiff, a tad formal.

This, then, is the September '67 version cut under Grossman's tutelage in N.Y.C., the recordings that Helm never even heard because Robertson told him it was not what they wanted to sound like at all. If this was a cut from Woodstock the guys would have been swingin'. They were loose as a tipsy goose in Woodstock, but in a Manhattan recording studio with a clock ticking and a famous manager overseeing the entire project – a project that could help determine their collective future – they would no doubt tighten up (and not in the positive Archie Bell way). Robertson is correct: this is not so hot; they would do much better with it when John Simon arrived. That it found its way onto Hudson's many archival reels from Woodstock is curious but understandable. After all, Hudson was an archivist whose only rock-group rival is the obsessed Bill Wyman.

## WILL THE CIRCLE BE UNBROKEN
(A.P. Carter)
0:55
**Danko** vocal, **Hudson** organ, **Manuel** vocal, foot kicking the floor, **Robertson** acoustic guitar.
• This is from upstairs at Big Pink at one of the informal jams, jams that occurred even more often when Helm returned. In Danko's words: "I had a king-size bed in my bedroom and I remember [Helm] walked in and moved into my bedroom, and a few days later I got another house." (Laughter). "Levon, Richard, and Garth became the house residents. I got another house."[5]

## WORDS AND NUMBERS
(Richard Manuel)
4:09
**Danko** bass, **Levon Helm** drums, **Hudson** organ, **Manuel** vocal, piano, **Robertson** electric guitar
• Also referred to as 'Don't Drink The Water' on some tapes – but surely the mix up in titles was the work of a wise guy at Rubber Dubber.

A stinging R&B mid-tempo number from Manuel with Helm returned and his drums showing exactly what he could have added had he been in town all along.

It would be easy to mistake Manuel for the most promising songwriter in The Band at this stage. Up to their magnificent second album he at least – at the very least – held his own with the more prolific Robertson. It's a shame that alcohol so obviously played a part in Manuel losing his muse,

a tragedy that quite possibly would not have been allowed to happen in later, more psychologically aware years. Should as talented and as sensitive a musician today become addicted to alcohol, no doubt treatment would be prescribed immediately. In the late 1960s, very few on the pop-music scene knew, or seemed willing to admit, where this behavior would ultimately lead.

As it was, the loss of Manuel as a songwriting force would definitely hurt The Band and limit their scope somewhat. It limited their lyrical outlook to Robbie Robertson's artistic vision; it limited the act's three talented yet quite different lead vocalists to singing the thoughts of only one writer. (In 1978's *The Last Waltz*, supposedly a look back at The Band's classic repertoire, not one song is a Manuel composition or co-authored composition.)

That Robertson was able to shoulder the songwriting burden for as long as he did is also remarkable. That Danko, who showed such promise co-writing 'This Wheel's On Fire' and 'Bessie Smith' as well as the later 'Life Is A Carnival,' never pursued his own songwriting more seriously is almost as tragic as Manuel letting his muse slip away into the night.

But in the bright dawn of Woodstock '67 it would have been difficult for any of the participants in the Big Pink sessions to have believed that long shadows would one day creep forward and a very dark night would fall.

**YOU DON'T COME THROUGH**
(Robbie Robertson)
2:03
**Danko** bass, harmony vocal, **Helm** harmony vocal, tambourine **Manuel** vocal, **Robertson** electric guitar, backing vocal?.
• An Impressions impression from the Curtis Mayfield-obsessed Robertson, and a good one as well. When Robertson admits to sitting Dylan down and telling his boss how Dylan's long songs are losing him and how acts such as The Impressions have far fewer words "but are slaying me," he confesses to being a brave man.

"When I first met [Dylan]," says Robertson, "I played him a ballad from The Impressions' *Keep On Pushing* album, 'I've Been Trying,' written by Curtis Mayfield. I said [to Dylan], 'They're not saying anything much and this is killing me, and you're rambling on for an hour and you're losing me. I mean, I think you're losing the spirit.'" [6]

Not only was Robertson frankly if politely telling Dylan that there might be something amiss with stellar material such as 'Visions Of Johanna' or 'Sad-Eyed Lady Of The Lowlands,' but his comments did, to some extent, help get Dylan to shift his material to a more simplistic, rural feel. Which would make Robertson quite a target for the fans of the 1966 model of Bob Dylan. But then Robertson did take his share of risks back in the day.

Robertson, Danko, and Helm spoke openly and honestly to Dylan, and such frankness was no doubt infrequent when the Pop Messiah held a conversation with employees.

**ORANGE JUICE BLUES (BLUES FOR BREAKFAST)** (version one)
(Richard Manuel)
3:29
**Danko** bass, **Manuel** vocal, piano.
• A demo and a good one: many have claimed that this track was overdubbed for the official 1975 release. Engineer Rob Fraboni points out that they cut full-band versions of it in '67, although there is some dispute about whether those ensemble versions were done in the basement at Big Pink or not. Like 'Ruben Remus' there are several versions of this, including a more up-tempo take that doesn't suit Manuel's voice at all.

**ORANGE JUICE BLUES (BLUES FOR BREAKFAST)** (version two)
(Richard Manuel)
3:14
**Danko** bass, **Helm** drums, **Hudson** organ, **Manuel** piano, **Robertson** electric guitar.
• The backing track only for the version found on the official release.

It swings. Go boys, go! There has to be a reason that this turns up as part of The Hawks' Woodstock archival reels. Obviously it is an early Manuel composition that his comrades thought good enough to explore, because they returned to it several times. However, while charming on its own, it would not have fit in with *Music From Big Pink* as it was something all too apparently from their past: an up-tempo, bluesy number The Hawks might have played in the second set at Lucy's Orbit Lounge in rural Ontario in 1964 – and those days were over. They were The Band now.

**YAZOO STREET SCANDAL** (version two)
(Robbie Robertson)
3:20
**Danko** bass, **Helm** mandolin, vocal, **Hudson** organ, **Manuel** drums, **Robertson** electric guitar.
• Helm gives a fine vocal and Manuel plays his finest drums to date on this version, but it's very late '67 in Woodstock. It sounds like the version found on the official '75 release, with only the ending shorter, so perhaps there was an edit.

The only question is why Helm's mandolin is always sacrificed in the mix. It is almost entirely inaudible on the reel here but Helm gets mandolin credit when this track is mentioned elsewhere. Robertson's guitar is played through a Leslie speaker cabinet or at least something that gives it a swirling effect, which he had in common with George Harrison's playing around this time, and it makes his picking sound like something Hudson would orchestrate.

**LONG DISTANCE OPERATOR**
(Bob Dylan)
4:10
**Danko** bass, **Helm** drums, **Hudson** organ, **Manuel** vocal, harmonica, **Robertson** electric guitar, **John Simon** piano.
• The Hawks first played this with Dylan at the Berkeley Community Center in California on December 4, 1965 (a performance attended by a

young Greil Marcus). The unedited take lasts 4:32 yet it is not from Woodstock 1967 at all. It was recorded February 21, 1968 at Gold Star in Los Angeles during sessions for *Music From Big Pink*, although they had played it as a warm-up number with Dylan during the basement sessions at Big Pink the previous summer. A 3:38 edit of this appears on the official *Basement Tapes* release, with a verse about a call from Louisiana omitted.

### ORGAN RIFFS
1:28
**Danko** bass, **Helm** drums, **Hudson** organ, **Manuel** piano, **Robertson** electric guitar.
• A gem of a germ of a tune never completed. When played to Robbie Robertson recently a light bulb appeared over his head as a smile appeared on his face. "It's a song I wrote, and I believe it was called 'Poughkeepsie Or Bust.'" [7]So, another tune with merit tossed to the side, another that any rock group would surely have killed to have. The Band were starting to pump with all cylinders and only the strongest of their offspring survived.

### BLUES INSTRUMENTAL
3:31
**Danko** bass, **Helm** drums, **Hudson** organ, **Manuel** piano, **Robertson** electric guitar.
• This is the sound of men at work. And what they are working on is Manuel's 'Words And Numbers.' The groove is there in a major way with Helm back. Around the 2:00 mark Hudson locks into Helm and this devilry allows Robertson to play some odd buzz-saw guitar that no one, repeat no one, was doing at the time. His tone, his musical ideas, and his attack suggest Jeff Beck's contemporary work but on a higher emotional plane. Beck and the rest were still playing R&B through the new psychedelic filter. Robertson's playing here is positively cubist, and it is possibly the only Band track one can imagine Hendrix playing on and yet still fitting in.

Robertson remembers working on the writing of this with Manuel at some point and says that 'Just Another Tomato In The Glass' was a possible title at one point, as was – wait for it – 'Don't Drink The Water.' That was some coffee Danko and Dylan had those boys drinking, yes sir.

## INSTRUMENTAL BLUES
1:52
**Danko** bass, **Helm** drums, **Manuel** harmonica, **Robertson** electric guitar.
• Exactly what it says on the tin, although the title can easily be mistaken for the above number. This is a plodding 12-bar blues that can only be a warm-up. Hudson isn't on it; he must have asked them to play something while he checked the VU meters.

## SPOKEN WORD / INSTRUMENTAL
1:21
**Danko** bass, **Hudson** horn, **Manuel** piano.
• More of 'Even If It's A Pig.' Hudson speaks some professorial instruction about "some forms of American music." This is Hudson, Danko, and Manuel on horns, bass and piano acting like the avant-garde musicians and aesthetic elitists that Danko and Manuel most certainly were not. Hudson may not always have been avant-garde and a scholar of music, but he became both as his interests expanded, and he helped give such terms a good name.

Sometimes this is listed as 'Ginsberg Reads Poetry Over Music.' While Allen Ginsberg did visit Woodstock to take books to the recuperating post-accident Dylan, this track is the spoken part of 'Even If It's A Pig, Part Two.' Dylan's Beat-poet pal was nowhere to be heard.

## BLUE MOON
(Richard Rodgers, Lorenz Hart)
2:00
**Danko** bass, **Hudson** saxophone, **Manuel** piano.
• Danko, Hudson, and Manuel ham it up like a lounge act as part of the

'Even If It's A Pig, Part Two' craziness. Which raises the question: where is 'Even If It's A Pig, Part One'?

## GLORIA IN EXCELSIS DEO / BANANA BOAT (DAY-O)

(Traditional / William Attaway, Irving Burgie)

(3:55)

**Danko** bass, guitar, **Hudson** saxophone, **Manuel** piano.

• More of 'Even If It's A Pig, Part Two' with the same line-up, but Danko is also heard fooling about on a guitar as if it were a balalaika. It is startling how Hudson's spoken voice sounds like American comedian George Carlin.

After messing about with 'Gloria In Excelsis Deo' they mess about on a traditional Trinidadian calypso folk song. It had already appeared as a recording by others when songwriters William Attaway and Irving Burgie wrote new lyrics and Harry Belafonte turned 'Banana Boat (Day-O)' into a substantial hit in 1957. Folk group The Tarriers wrote lyrics for their competing version, 'The Banana Boat Song,' which was also a big hit, and it was covered by Shirley Bassey for a British hit. The Tarriers, who had actor Alan Arkin in their line-up, claimed it was a Jamaican folk song and not from Trinidad, but that's what we know it as today.

'Gloria In Excelsis Deo' is a Greek melody from the 2nd century that only reached the western European Christian Church some 200 years later. Which makes this amusing doodle the oldest known song ever covered by the young men who later became The Band.

## GARTH HUDSON PIANO SOLO

(Garth Hudson)

2:11

**Hudson** piano.

• The great man warming up, working on polishing a song, playing an old piano-roll favorite from years gone by, or checking the tape machine. Who is to say? We are not worthy. The inventive and imaginative title given it by whoever compiled the black-market release of these recordings is indeed indicative of what is heard, but what exactly is it that Hudson is

working on? With keyboard chops like his, it is possible this is the sound of him warming up for a day's work in the studio. (Listed on some collections simply as 'Piano Solo.')

**INSTRUMENTAL**

0:38

**Danko** bass, **Robertson** electric guitar.

• Robertson puts down on tape some Hubert Sumlin licks. Listed on some underground releases as 'Guitar Doodling.'

**INSTRUMENTAL**

0:41

**Danko** bass, **Robertson** electric guitar.

• Robertson and Danko play a beautiful progression once, no doubt to get it down on tape before they forget it. This sounds like the introduction to a soft ballad from the first Velvet Underground album. A shoe-gazing British band could write a terrific ballad out of this short segment.

**INSTRUMENTAL**

5:40

**Danko** bass, **Helm** drums, **Hudson** organ, **Manuel** piano, **Robertson** electric guitar.

• Another 12-bar blues–funk workout. At this length, they were probably planning a greater use for this than a mere recording of them warming-up. Otherwise Hudson would have erased it, because it took up almost six minutes of their precious tape.

**IF I LOSE**

(Charlie Poole, Norman Woodlieff, arr. Ralph Stanley)

2:23

**Danko** bass, backing vocal, **Helm** vocal, drums, **Hudson** piano, **Manuel** piano, Robertson acoustic guitar.

• A Stanley Brothers rewrite of Charlie Poole's 'If I Lose, I Don't Care' from

July 1927. Poole was the North Carolinian whose life in early country music mirrors Robert Johnson's in Delta blues: both were inventive players, both impressive songwriters, both hard livin' men, both dead way too early. Poole drank himself to death at 39, a Hank Williams demise years before Hank was well known. At one time, a Charlie Poole 78rpm recording was said to be owned by every sixth family down South who possessed a Victrola record player.

Poole is remembered for this and many other songs that 1960s rock bands popularized: 'Old And Only In The Way,' 'Don't Let Your Deal Go Down,' 'White House Blues,' and 'Good Bye Sweet Liza Jane' among them. 'Sweet Liza Jane' was the grandmother song to Ronnie Hawkins & The Hawks' own 'Go Go Liza Jane' from September 1965.

Helm was the bluegrass fan in The Band and The Stanley Brothers are one act of the Bluegrass Holy Trinity (the others are Bill Monroe & The Bluegrass Boys and Flatt & Scruggs). Rick Danko was a big country fan too, and it would have taken little to get these two country boys to start twangin' away on this or that upstairs at Big Pink or later at the house Danko rented on Wittenberg Road.

This is a rarity among Band songs because it features two pianos: Hudson playing the honky tonk piano panned slightly right and Manuel blocking the chords right behind Helm's vocal in the mix. Helm's mandolin would have been perfect for a song like this but it is not present.

Recorded in the run up to the formal *Big Pink* sessions, this logically found its way onto the reels of ace collector and archivist Hudson.

This marks the end of the road for the unofficial underground discography of what is now referred to as The Basement Tapes, for the recordings made by Bob Dylan, Rick Danko, Levon Helm, Garth Hudson, Richard Manuel, and Robbie Robertson (with some valuable assistance from John Simon beginning late '67 when he started working with The Band).

Songs have crept onto unofficial Basement Tape releases that have nothing to do with Woodstock in 1967. These include the Tiny Tim cuts from *You Are What You Eat* and 'Bacon Fat,' a Hawks R&B workout from

Toronto in 1964. In reality, the Basement Tapes are a collection of recordings from at least three different locations (and maybe four, if perhaps something included among them was recorded during one of the informal acoustic jams upstairs at Big Pink). Those sessions possibly stretched into 1968, ending some time after Dylan completed recording *John Wesley Harding* on November 29, 1967 in Nashville but before John Simon started The Band's formal recording sessions for their ground-breaking first album, *Music From Big Pink*, on January 10, 1968 at A&R's seventh-floor studio in New York City. (Just to add to the confusion, they were then in the middle of a brief period when they called themselves The Crackers. Thankfully the monicker didn't last.)

The Basement Tapes are also noteworthy as the place and time where the listener can hear the powerful R&B of The Hawks, a fine though hardly unique blues band on the barroom/ballroom circuit, as they mutate into The Band, a democratic and creative unit like no other in rock'n'roll.

Today the Basement Tapes are comparable to such iconoclastic releases as Harry Smith's *Anthology Of American Folk Music* or the *Fireside Book Of Folk Songs*. The Fireside volume was a very popular piano songbook with 147 old ballads, railroad work songs, sea shanties, cowboy songs, hymns, patriotic Civil War songs, Southern spirituals, and Christmas carols. Published in 1947, it reintroduced post-war consumerist America to its recent past. In many ways, the Basement Tapes would do something quite similar for the 1960s rock & roll audience, those psychedelic fans who had forgotten where the music of their long-haired heroic Homers had originated.

Yet the show was not over in Woodstock. Garth Hudson continued to work, even when the others were not around. He produced an unforgettable album, *The Bengali Bauls ... At Big Pink*, which would be released in November 1970 on Buddah (BDS 5050).

The Bengali Bauls were from India and were culturally important iconoclastic heroes to many people back in their native land. But to the rock'n'roll audience, however, they are noted not for any particular achievement in world music nor for their Hudson-produced album. They are most famous in the West because two of their number – Luxman Das and his brother Purna Das – are seen standing to the right and left of Dylan on the front of the jacket of his *John Wesley Harding* album.

(The *JWH* jacket photo, taken in the rear of Albert Grossman's house in Woodstock, remains a distinct departure from the rococo rock-album cover art of the time. Standing behind Dylan and the two Bengali Bauls is a local stonemason, Charlie Joy, in the shot simply because he was working on Grossman's property that day. The white cowboy hat at the bottom of the photo belongs to a neighbor, who is cropped out of most of the pictures from the session, shot by Columbia Records staff photographer John Berg. Whether the neighbor is crouched down wearing the hat or the hat is sitting on a chair or a tree stump isn't known.)

There were five Bengali Bauls, and Hudson, a man who loved world music before the rest of the world even called it that, recorded them in the basement of Big Pink on the very equipment that he used to tape 'This Wheel's On Fire,' 'Sign On The Cross,' and the rest.

Purna Das performed on khamack and kartal (plucked drum and cymbals); brother Luxman also on khamack; Hare Krishna Das on dotara (fretless lute); Sudhananda Das on harmonium and kartal; and Jiban Das underpinned the whole ensemble on tabla (drum). Everyone sang except Jiban Das. In fact, Purna and Luxman Das still record today with Jiban Das.

It could be said that Purna Das and his father, the singer and poet Guru Shri Nabani Das Baul, are Bengali answers to Pete Seeger. Purna Das has twice been awarded the title Baul Samrat (meaning King or Emperor of the Bauls) by the President of India, in 1967 and 1999, and is therefore formally known as Samrat Purna Das Baul.

The Bengali Bauls have been described frequently in the rock'n'roll press as itinerant street musicians, but this belittles them. They reject worldly goods, yes, they roam the Bengali countryside, yes. But they are not unworldly and downtrodden musical vagabonds. Far from it. With a singing style alleged by their devotees to date back 30 centuries, these men are completely aware of the complex, rich tradition that they maintain and bring to the rest of the world.

For all Dylan's multiple guises, his music stays rooted in North America. World music identifiably crossed his path only when Purna and Luxman Das stood next to him on that album jacket. (Purna Das maintains they rehearsed once with Dylan in Woodstock and even taped the rehearsal.) The Bauls travel, singing at villages, temples, local fairs, street corners, religious shrines, and music festivals, wearing their multicolored robes while playing music that has roots deep in the soil of tradition. Comparing the expense and planning of Dylan's more recent Never Ending Tour to wandering minstrels continually performing in the sub-continent is indeed a stretch, but nonetheless there is a connection there.

Further, The Bengali Bauls frequently sing about love and the worthiness of the downtrodden and have many songs that deflate the status of the privileged, the arrogant, and their society's wealthy. North America has a famous singer who frequently does the same thing in his songs. That North American singer once wrote of Jimmie Rodgers: "His voice gives hope to the vanquished and humility to the mighty."[8] He could have been writing about The Bengali Bauls. Or himself.

The Bengali Bauls ended up in Woodstock in September '67 after a series of interconnected circumstances. Allen Ginsberg met them when he was living in India in 1962 and '63. He first met Nabani Das, who introduced him to Baul music. Upon returning home, Ginsberg told Albert Grossman about the Bauls' music and Grossman was intrigued. (The front cover of the Bengali Bauls ... At Big Pink LP has a photograph of Nabani Das, Purna, and Luxman's father which Grossman had on his office wall for over a year before Garth Hudson ever met, much less recorded, the Bauls.)

In early 1967, Grossman and his wife Sally traveled to India where they befriended the Bauls after Nabani Das and his sons played a lengthy concert for them in their hotel room in Calcutta. The Grossmans soon arranged for them to come to the U.S.A., with Grossman their host and their business manager. Landing in San Francisco, The Bengal Bauls performed several West Coast dates with rock groups, arranged by Grossman, including a support to The Byrds at The Fillmore West.

Upon their arrival in Woodstock in December 1967, the five Bengali

Bauls were billeted in an apartment in a converted barn on property that Grossman owned in Woodstock. Hudson was already involved with Indian music and was immediately taken with the Bauls. Almost as smitten were Levon Helm and Rick Danko, who found Purna Das's high voice beguiling – and they asked Purna if he could sing in English a little bit so they could better follow his songs.

The Bauls and The Hawks bonded. During introductions, one startled Hawk asked Hare Krishna Das if he was *the* Hare Krishna. (He was informed that it is a common name back home, like Mohammed in the Middle East.) They got high together, played checkers together, and swapped questions back and forth, although the language barrier sometimes did not allow for a complete answer.

Robbie Robertson remembers them well. "The Band were really gearing up to go into the studio, so we needed to get back to business on everything," he says. "The Bengali Bauls were just around. We used to see them and they would come to Big Pink all the time. I don't know if we ever got around to trying out some messing-around things with them. Usually what happened is that we would play and they would simply stand there and dig it, appreciating it for all it was worth. And when the Bauls played we stood there with our mouths open."

Robertson says he remembers Western musicians playing with people from other places at the time but that he wasn't interested in 'raga rock.' "So I don't even know if we felt it was the right thing to do to record with The Bengali Bauls. Maybe in a different time or situation it would have come to that." [9]

Jazz saxophonist and flutist Charles Lloyd was visiting The Band one evening before Christmas and he, Danko, and Helm wanted to jam. The Bauls were over for some checkers. Hudson, probably the best qualified to jam with the Bauls, took everyone down to the basement. The Bauls sat on sofa cushions and prepared. They sat in a circle, not unlike The Band, so that they could see themselves play and not merely hear themselves. Within a very short time the three Western musicians admitted that they were driving on the wrong street and got up. That moment may be on the

*Bengali Bauls ... At Big Pink* album, as just a minute or so into the first track, 'Alone, I Have Caught A Fish,' there is the sound of the musicians growing quieter and voices speaking in two different languages. Hudson asks, "Are you ready?" and after a brief indecipherable discussion, Sudhananda Das kicks it off and the Bauls resume. Joining Hudson at the controls, Danko, Helm, and Lloyd watched the Bauls play for several hours.

Hudson recorded 'Alone, I Have Caught A Fish,' 'Praise My Beautiful Birthland,' 'With What Flower Shall I Worship Your Feet?,' 'My Boatman Friend,' and 'Say Hari, Mynah Bird.' At the end of 'Say Hari, Mynah Bird' both Hudson and Danko can be heard complimenting the Bauls on their performance. The performances that day certainly stuck with Hudson, a musician always open to the sounds of other cultures. At the 2002 movie premier of the re-cut *The Last Waltz*, Hudson showed up with two of The Bengali Bauls.

Thus ends all the known recordings from Big Pink, the Basement Tapes sessions, and Hudson's tape archives. Rumor persists that there is more, much more. There may well be, for as we are about to discover, the Basement Tapes story does not end with the release of *Bengali Bauls ... At Big Pink.*

**MILLION DOLLAR**
**BASH**

# 14. That Million Dollar Bash

*The cover versions*

In the early months of 1968, many people in the record industry displayed their hip credentials by playing intimates and the impressionable their prized copy of the 14-song Dylan acetate. These were the publisher's demos that Albert Grossman's office was sending around to popular rock acts, foreign music publishers, friends of Dylan's, and any notables who might help get these mysterious songs covered.

The first Basement Tapes song out of the box was 'Too Much Of Nothing' by Peter Paul & Mary, which entered the *Billboard* Top 40 just before Christmas 1967. "I never did know what the chorus meant," laughs Peter Yarrow. "'Say hello to Valerie, say hello to Vivian.' But it didn't matter, because the verses were so colorful."

By this time Peter Paul & Mary were doing a little experimenting, says Yarrow. They were moving beyond vocals and guitars, making LPs such as *Album 1700* and *Late Again* with 'Leaving On A Jet Plane,' 'I Dig Rock'n'Roll Music,' and 'Too Much Of Nothing.' He describes this as the beginning of the second wave of the trio's career. "It was really a good shot in the arm for us. The whole musical choice of idioms was up for grabs."

Presumably Albert Grossman, as manager of both Bob Dylan and Peter Paul & Mary and as owner of a chunk of Dylan's publishing, coerced PP&M into covering a Basement Tapes tune? "Never, never," Yarrow replies forcefully. "It would be the farthest thing from his mind. He was supremely tasteful. Not just tasteful: he had a real sense of quality, and that really was the most important thing he had. That is why he was so feared, because if he thought something was not authentic, then, generally, he was right. And if it was good – a good project with a genuinely gifted person behind it – then Albert would usually see that value and get the project through to the light of day. You learned to rely intuitively on his ears. Albert protected his artists from that institutionalized form of business called the music business."[1]

Soon, the new Dylan demos became available at hip record stores in Los Angeles on seven-inch tape reels (although these tapes were not nearly so widely distributed as the later underground LPs, which began to appear in

summer 1969). New underground FM radio stations on the West Coast catering to the longhaired anti-war rock audience acquired these Dylan tapes and boldly played selections on the airwaves. And more musicians began to discover the demos and cover the material. The Byrds had been one of the most popular and influential rock groups in 1965 and '66, and of course made a Number 1 smash cover of Dylan's 'Mr. Tambourine Man.' But by 1968 the band was slipping in popularity, even though their music retained and even sharpened its cutting edge.

CBS vice president Clive Davis had written a letter to Byrds manager Eddie Tickner dated March 13, 1967 after the release of the group's groundbreaking psychedelic excursion *Younger Than Yesterday*. "It's evident that 'My Back Pages' is really in The Byrds' bag and stands out," wrote Davis. "Obviously, no one wants to interfere with their originality and creativity but the group will have a long, long future if they continue to work with simple folk tunes." [2]

This corporate idea does not refer to 'Wildwood Flower' or 'She'll Be Coming Round The Mountain.' No, the CBS veep is politely telling The Byrds to continue to record Dylan tunes. Which they did not do on their next album, *The Notorious Byrd Brothers*, but did rather masterfully on the one after that, *Sweetheart Of The Rodeo*.

"What folks call The Basement Tapes were sent to me way back when," remembers Byrds bassist Chris Hillman. "I was living in Topanga Canyon and I got sent the tapes – I think a reel tape – around late 1967 sometime. Possibly very early 1968, but I believe late 1967. I don't remember where they came from, but we were no longer managed by Jim Dickson or Eddie Tickner, we were managed by Larry Spector then. Yet Dickson was the one who had the connection to Dylan, so how this material was sent to me I do not know. They did not go to Roger [McGuinn], they were sent to me."

Hillman says his copy had 'You Ain't Goin' Nowhere,' 'This Wheel's On Fire,' 'The Mighty Quinn,' 'Down In The Flood,' and some others he can't remember. It sounds as if he was sent the 14-song demo. "I remember thinking this is a whole album's worth of good material by Dylan. All of them were good songs. All of them. But I sorta just passed this material on to Roger, saying: 'Check this out, I don't know what to do with it, but you are our singer so you have a listen.'"

The Byrds subsequently recorded 'Nothing Was Delivered' and 'You Ain't Goin' Nowhere' in March 1968 for their album *Sweetheart Of The Rodeo*. "Roger and I picked them," says Hillman. "Those two songs were probably two of the very best songs on *Sweetheart*. But I have to say it is not my favorite Byrds album. We weren't ready for a straight country album in some ways. My lead vocals were not there yet. But on the other hand there was Gram Parsons and two of his greatest songs, in 'Hickory Wind' and 'One Hundred Years From Now.' And the two cool Dylan songs we did helped make the album stand out." McGuinn saved 'This Wheel's On Fire' for the next Byrds LP, *Dr. Byrds & Mr. Hyde,* released in February 1969 after Hillman's departure.

"Those two songs of Bob's which we cut off the Basement Tapes struck a nerve with Roger and me," says Hillman. "To this day, to this very day, I do 'You Ain't Goin' Nowhere' onstage, and the moment I strike it up people recognize it. They recognize it almost to the extent they recognize 'Turn, Turn, Turn,' which is wild, because I consider 'Turn, Turn, Turn' to be the number one all-time Byrds signature song, even above 'Mr. Tambourine Man.' Yet I consider 'You Ain't Goin' Nowhere' to be the number two all-time Byrds signature song – especially if you base it on audience reaction. Good song. I imagine Bob wrote that laying up in bed nursing his broken bones after the motorcycle accident." [3]

The only Byrd to stay in the act's line-up from cradle to grave was 12-string guitarist Roger McGuinn. He recalls no grand design behind The Byrds recording Basement Tapes songs. "We always had a good relationship with Dylan's publishers," he says. "Columbia Records put the word out to keep us in mind if there were any strong Dylan songs we could get our hands on. Periodically, his material would show up, before others had heard it. We never and I never purposely went out and got these songs."

McGuinn believes it may have been Byrds producer Gary Usher or Chris Hillman who received the acetate or tape. "We heard the songs," says McGuinn, "and we were as thrilled as you might expect us to have been by this new material."

As far he recalls, the only songs they considered were 'You Ain't Goin' Nowhere' and 'Nothing Was Delivered,' and McGuinn felt that 'You Ain't Goin' Nowhere' was perfect for The Byrds at the time. "It was country-ish and had that Dylan mystique where you really couldn't figure out what he was talking about, yet the lyrics nevertheless drew you in. You could make your own conclusions as to what the song was about. I always thought it was about when Bob was laid up in Woodstock after the bike accident and sure wasn't going anywhere. 'Nothing Was Delivered' sounded then like a drug deal gone bad. It had a slightly dark or ominous tone to it. That song struck me as a good one as well. And I loved 'This Wheel's On Fire.'"

They always tried to change Dylan's arrangements, says McGuinn. It became a kind of tradition with him that had started with 'Mr. Tambourine Man.' "I took that from the 2/4-time demo we heard to 4/4, and 'All I Really Want To Do' I changed from 3/4 to 4/4, that sort of thing. It was almost an adventurous, fun game to do them in a new way."

McGuinn feels that part of the reason that *Sweetheart Of The Rodeo* was not accepted at first was down to the group's past history rather than them taking Dylan songs to country radio in 1968. The album consisted of material recorded before their audience had heard it live, he explains. "However, I do remember going to Ralph Emery and playing it on WSM. He played about 15 seconds of 'You Ain't Goin' Nowhere' and then said to me, 'What's it about?' I said, 'I don't know, it's a Dylan song.' Emery hated Dylan, and he looked at me and said, 'That Dylan … if he wore green socks the whole world would wear green socks.' So in that sense the hippie–Dylan association might have had something to do with that album's difficulties."

It's hard to imagine someone like Emery coming around to Dylan. Yet

McGuinn tells a good story about an appearance on Emery's TV chat show decades later. "When I was on, Emery would always bring up the song Gram [Parsons] and I wrote about him and his reaction to 'You Ain't Goin' Nowhere,' which was 'Drug Store Truck Drivin' Man.' Emery didn't know about the song for years until Waylon Jennings told him about it. Then I was on his TV show and he suddenly said to me, 'Waylon Jennings was on my show the other day and he told me about a song you wrote about me when you were in The Byrds, Roger. Could you tell me about that?' And I said, 'Ah, we were just kidding around, Ralph, you know? Can't ya take a joke?' So they not only embraced it, they became it. Look at the outlaw country movement and today's alt.country scene. It all emanated from there. Not that they ever gave us any credit, nor did we ask for it."

McGuinn reports that The Byrds did get reaction of a sort from Dylan. "Not in so many words, but you do get feedback with Dylan. With 'You Ain't Goin' Nowhere,' later on he released his version and put my name in it, because I inverted the words on 'pack up your money, pick up your tent' or whatever it was. I'm still not sure how I swapped something around, but I did get it wrong, and Dylan does not like his words to be messed with. So when he did his version, the correct way, he put my name behind the line quickly, to show me he heard me mess with his words." McGuinn stops and laughs at the memory. "So that's the feedback we got." [4]

The stature of the Basement Tapes was growing fast, not only in the underground but now anywhere a radio was played. Manfred Mann hit big with 'The Mighty Quinn' in January (U.K.) and March (U.S.A.) and then Julie Driscoll, Brian Auger & The Trinity scored in Britain with 'This Wheel's On Fire' in April.

Manfred Mann's guitarist was Tom McGuinness, and today his words tumble out enthusiastically with the happy memory of 1960s London audible in almost every phrase. "Of course, no one called them the Basement Tapes then," he says. "Albert Grossman brought them over to London and I suppose it was through B. Feldman's, who published a lot of Dylan's stuff, that we heard them. The Manfred Mann band got pitched a lot of things."

When the Basement Tapes hit London, the shockwave was felt first among the music publishers where the songs arrived. To be precise, in the Charing Cross Road offices of Dylan's U.K. publisher, Francis Day & Hunter. (FD&H bought B. Feldman & Co. in 1968, which explains why some British artists remember visiting Feldman to hear Basement Tapes demos. FD&H was in turn purchased by EMI Music Publishing in 1972.)

McGuinness says that the group's relationship with Dylan material began when he and bandleader Manfred Mann were watching television at his mother-in-law's house out in the country. Dylan performed a dozen songs in his last-ever solo acoustic concert, for BBC TV, on June 1, 1965 in London. Six songs were broadcast on June 19 and seven days later the final six songs were televised. (All BBC video tapes of these two shows were either erased or thrown away but a black-market CD of Dylan's audio performance with very clean sound showed up in Spain in summer 2007.) 'If You Gotta Go, Go Now' was among the songs broadcast on June 19.

"We watched him sing 'If You Gotta Go, Go Now' and we both looked at each other," recalls McGuinness. "We said: 'Great song, we could really do that.' That was on the weekend, and on the Monday morning our manager rang his publishers and we got a demo of it in no time at all. We recorded that. And even before that, we'd recorded 'With God On Our Side,' which was on our EP *The One In The Middle*. That made the singles charts, as you could back then. 'With God On Our Side' was a big, big number for us. Very dramatic." The Manfreds' cover of 'If You Gotta Go, Go Now' earned them a British Number 2 hit in September 1965.

When original Manfreds vocalist Paul Jones left the band and Mike D'Abo replaced him, almost the first thing they recorded was 'Just Like A Woman' after they were played the *Blonde On Blonde* tapes before the album came out. "Then the Dylan version of 'Just Like A Woman' came out in America," says McGuinness, "and I remember seeing this advert in *Billboard* which read, 'No one sings Dylan like Dylan.' And we could not disagree with this view, not in our heart of hearts." Their cover of 'Just Like A Woman' hit the British Top 10 in August '66.

Dylan's British publisher was aggressive in putting the Dylan material out and getting it recorded, says McGuinness. "Our manager got a call from Feldman's who said they had some interesting Dylan tapes and did we want to come in and hear them? Albert Grossman had brought them over from New York. I cannot remember exactly who went, but certainly I did and Manfred, and I think Mike D'Abo. We went to Feldman's to listen to this new Dylan music no one had heard.

"The funny thing is, we were walking down Wardour Street towards the publishers and there was this guy in front of us wearing a suit but with a grey ponytail. One of us remarked what an unusual sight that was. And of course it was Albert Grossman, who then turned into the same building that we were headed for."

McGuinness's recollection is that Grossman had acetates with him rather than tapes. "We listened to the songs – and remember, they were all done after Dylan's motorcycle crash. After about three songs, Manfred says: 'Albert, why does Dylan get this terrible singer to make his demos?' And there followed a breathless hush. Albert Grossman looks at him, like, 'Are you putting me on?' And then he says: 'That is Dylan.' 'Ah,' says Manfred, 'right.'" [5]

McGuinness says the group selected three songs from those they heard, certainly 'Mighty Quinn' and 'Please Mrs. Henry' and possibly 'You Ain't Goin' Nowhere.' They recorded the first two, although 'Mrs. Henry' was not released at the time and 'Quinn' sat around for months.

Bandleader Manfred Mann says that 'The Mighty Quinn' wasn't his first choice from the Basement Tapes for the group to cover. "I chose a song called 'Please Mrs. Henry' for us. And we recorded it. But listening back, I didn't feel it was that strong a song, and so we went on to record 'The Mighty Quinn.'"

Mann describes the method the group used to come up with arrangements for all outside material. "We always, always started by having no respect for the original recording at all. We never said gee, this is great – how do we do this sound again? We never said well, Dylan's

done it like this, so we've got to do it like that too. The way I arrange – and of course everyone pitched in – was I would play a song over and over myself until I got something which seemed to work. I would not refer back to the original all the time. I learned it and played it at the piano over and over again. That way, the strongest points of the song became evident and shone through."[6]

Manfreds guitarist Tom McGuinness too remembers how they made the arrangement for 'Quinn' standing around the piano at Mann's house. "Manfred is a very good arranger, very good at picking out a lick from the song and using it as an instrumental feature. We did that on 'The Mighty Quinn,' found that lick which we turned into the signature riff of our song, played memorably on flute by Klaus Voormann. Klaus played flute, bass, and some guitar, and Manfred's Mellotron is in there somewhere."

The song was not released immediately after recording it because there was a feeling from some people in the band that it wasn't right and that they had not recorded it properly. Singer Mike D'Abo met the head of Mercury Records, Lou Reizner, who told him the Manfreds really needed a hit in America. They had not had a Top 20 hit there since 'Sha La La' in late 1964. "Lou asked him if we had anything, and Michael said we had some demos. He put on 'Quinn' after a bit, and Lou Reizner said: 'That's a hit!' Michael expressed some of the doubts the band had about the song and Lou simply said: 'Listen to it again!'"

They did. They went back to the studio and added some overdubs, including tabla, and sped up the master tape by a half-step. "If Lou Reizner had not heard it, the song might well have sat next to 'Please Mrs. Henry' in the Manfred Mann vaults for the next 30 years or so," laughs McGuinness. Instead, it hit Number 1 in the U.K. and went Top 10 in the States.

Dylan has remarked on several occasions that Manfred Mann were among his favorites when it came to interpreters of his work. During his televised press conference at KQED in San Francisco on December 3, 1965 Dylan fielded a question by promoter Bill Graham. "Of all the people who record your compositions, who do you feel does the most justice to what you're trying to say?" Dylan answered: "I think Manfred Mann ... they've done about three or four. Each one of them has been right in context with what the song was all about." [7]

McGuinness remembers the quote with amusement, noting that Dylan can be "quite a mischievous person." He also notes that Dylan said he didn't know what 'Quinn' is about. "And then he said it might be about Anthony Quinn. But he said Smokey Robinson was his favorite poet, and then a year later said, 'Oh, I meant Rimbaud.'"

Certainly the Manfreds never had any direct reaction from Dylan – although McGuinness and singer Paul Jones did have a near miss in the 1980s. "We were changing planes in Paris. Paul and I were walking down the corridor in a daze and suddenly there was Dylan with an entourage going in the opposite direction. I nudged Paul and told him we should have said hello. I really wanted to shout after him: 'We made you a lot of money!' But he was 20 paces past us before I could speak." [8]

Since the Basement Tapes were pretty unusual lyrically – and as McGuinness noted, even Dylan himself has talked of not knowing what 'The Mighty Quinn' is about – it might seem odd that the song was such a big hit. Manfred Mann agrees. "I was always surprised when something became a big hit. We had a good reputation as a commercial group, but a Number 1 record in England then was a pretty big hit. Looking back on it and listening to 'The Mighty Quinn' today, I don't think it is that good a record, frankly, though it is a good song. But yes, I suppose I was surprised as there was a lot of good competition around at the time from other people who were very, very good. We never got any reaction from Bob Dylan about our hit with 'The Mighty Quinn.' And I have never met Bob Dylan, no." [9]

The Manfred Mann connection to 1967-period Dylan goes beyond covering Basement Tapes songs. The group also covered John Simon's song 'My Name Is Jack' from the Peter Yarrow movie *You Are What You Eat*, providing another Top 10 U.K. hit. This was the very film that Howard Alk and Simon were working on in Woodstock when Simon first met the men whom he would soon help to evolve into The Band. The Manfreds saw Yarrow's film at a private screening arranged by Feldman, came out shaking their heads in bemusement, but liked "that song." McGuinness later tried to have John Simon record his post-Manfreds band, McGuinness Flint.

Manfred Mann; McGuinness Flint; *You Are What You Eat* ... Stop right there! Tom McGuinness seems to have a strong claim to the title of Musician Most Connected To The Basement Tapes Who Wasn't Actually There. And yet his connection goes further still.

A friend at B. Feldman & Co., Ian Kimmett, would find Dylan recordings and copy them on to quarter-inch tape for McGuinness. He ended up with hours of rare Dylan, from the earliest demos right the way through. "We are talking about a hundred songs of Dylan's which I was given." The sound of fainting Dylan fanatics is now heard worldwide. "I'm afraid I don't have them now," McGuinness says. "I have no idea where they have gone, although I have a few things lying around. Some were admittedly only fragments, as he would go into the studio and demo a load of songs, sometimes playing only the first verse and chorus before going on to something else." [10]

All these unreleased Dylan demos gave McGuinness the idea for a group after McGuinness Flint disbanded that would be based on exactly such Dylan material. More specifically, it would be based upon Basement Tapes material that no one had heard. Others had already made albums centered on Dylan material, notably Joan Baez and The Hollies, but *Lo And Behold* by Coulson Dean McGuinness Flint was designed to spotlight lesser-known Dylan songs and as many Basement Tapes songs as possible.

The original LP was released in 1972 with a dozen songs. Seven were covered directly from Big Pink basement acetates: 'Lo And Behold!,' 'Open The Door, Homer,' 'Don't Ya Tell Henry,' 'Get Your Rocks Off,' 'Odds And Ends,' 'Tiny Montgomery,' and 'Sign On The Cross.' Five more obscure Dylan songs filled out the album, each astutely chosen by McGuinness with some help from his bandmates: 'Eternal Circle,' 'Let Me Die In My

Footsteps,' 'Lay Down Your Weary Tune,' 'The Death Of Emmett Till,' and 'I Wanna Be Your Lover.' This was the first time that many of these songs were commercially available. McGuinness's old chum Manfred Mann and Manfreds drummer Mike Hugg helped out on the project (although they were not in the band formally), as did several of the unheralded but heroic U.K. session players of the era.

McGuinness says the record is one of his favorites from his six decades of music making, and he has a right to hold his head up. The *Lo And Behold* album didn't sell very well – its single, 'Eternal Circle,' proved less than a smash on radio – but Coulson Dean McGuinness Flint were rewarded with great reviews in *Billboard, Rolling Stone,* and *Cash Box* in the U.S.A. and a particularly memorable one in Britain's *Disc* where Martin Lewis called it "a stunning one-off album destined to become a classic."

Back in 1968, with the Dylan publisher's demos doing the rounds and several covers already hitting the charts, the word was out among the counter-cultural inner elite about the origins of these songs. Soon, the general pop-music public was onto the story of the Basement Tapes too.

The June 22, 1968 issue of *Rolling Stone* magazine had a front-cover feature called 'The Missing Bob Dylan Album.' Written by editor Jann Wenner, it described the music heard on these demos and demanded that they be released. In short, a popular recording artist who had hardly been heard in the last two years had recorded some new material, some outstanding material. And understandably, given the print coverage and hit records, his fans were becoming curious.

In July, The Band released *Music From Big Pink*, a groundbreaking and influential album that featured their versions of 'I Shall Be Released,' 'This Wheel's On Fire,' and 'Tears Of Rage.' It was becoming known that these Band guys were Dylan's old backing group. A demand for this music was growing. But there was no way to satisfy that demand because the songs were not coming out through the artist's record company.

Meanwhile, more intrigued musicians lined up to hear the new Dylan songs. Joe Boyd is an American who went to London in the mid 1960s,

liked the place, and stayed. By the time he settled down in Britain he was already a veteran road manager of European tours by several American blues legends as well as an experienced record producer and, to use a term that would no doubt make him cringe, a scenester. He knew (or soon found) everyone who was worth knowing in the music scene of the time.

Shortly to become a guiding light in British folk-rock, he witnessed from a much closer viewpoint than many how the Basement Tapes affected the pop music culture of the day. He was busy making a name for himself with The Incredible String Band, Pink Floyd, and Fairport Convention, to say nothing of his launch at Christmas 1966 of London's hip epicenter, the UFO club on Tottenham Court Road.

Boyd recalls that the first Basement Tapes song he heard was an advance copy of 'The Mighty Quinn' by Manfred Mann, probably in the first weeks of 1968. "Rumor was that this was one of a new batch of Dylan songs. I was working with the Fairport Convention at the time, who were huge Dylan fans, and they started pestering me. 'Can't we get a copy?' and 'C'mon Joe, you got connections.' So I called up Feldman's and one thing led to another."

He remembers ending up in a tiny listening room the size of a closet at Feldman with the Fairports and a woman named Brenda Ralfini (who was married to Ian Ralfini, later head of Warner Bros. in the U.K.). "She put on this acetate, or perhaps it was a tape, I'm not sure which. There was all of the Fairport Convention and me, seven or so people practically sitting in each other's laps, hanging over each other, a very crowded situation. But nobody was willing to not be there. And Brenda played us 'Million Dollar Bash,' 'This Wheel's On Fire,' 'I Shall Be Released' … and we were just amazed. We knew Dylan was going to write something great during this period of recuperation – and by God he had! Each song was an unbelievable gem."

Boyd remembers a dollop of Grossman-style cloak and dagger around his audition of the Basement Tapes. Feldman would not give him a copy. They had just one copy, no more, and were not about to let it out of the building. "Grossman's rules were that you just don't give acetates to people, you don't cut another copy and let anyone simply walk out of the place. No: you negotiate a cover and you do whatever is practically necessary to allow this band to make their cover of a new Dylan song. But you don't allow someone to walk out with an acetate or tape of the whole collection of new songs."

Fairport probably made their selection of what to cover right there in the listening room. "We listened to all this material and I think we huddled right there and said, yes, we'll record 'Million Dollar Bash' on the new album we want to make. And somehow we managed to get out of her a tape, a reel-to-reel tape, of the songs we promised we would cover. And she would only give us two songs, tops, just two. So the group would then take the tape away and go learn it. I think we got another one out of her by playing back to her a mix of one or both of these first two Basement Tapes songs we recorded, to prove we had actually done something with the songs."

Fairport went on to record 'Million Dollar Bash,' as well as 'Percy's Song,' an out-take from *The Times They Are A-Changin'*, which Boyd thinks they heard in the same circumstances, and these appeared on their *Unhalfbricking* album of July 1969.

But the influence of the Basement Tapes was to have even greater consequences for Fairport Convention. Their change from an American-sounding band into a British-sounding unit, and one as profoundly influenced by the U.K.'s cultural past as Dylan and The Band were by the cultural past of the southern American states, was a change brought about by a very real tragedy. In May 1969 the van in which Fairport were returning from a gig veered off the M1 motorway and down an embankment. Everyone was injured and two of the van's occupants died, including the band's drummer, Martin Lamble.

The immediate reaction was that this marked the end of Fairport Convention. But the surviving group decided that a fresh start with a new sound and a new drummer was possible. Dave Mattacks joined on drums,

and Joe Boyd introduced them to folk fiddler Dave Swarbrick. The two new members joined vocalist Sandy Denny, guitarists Richard Thompson and Simon Nicol, and bassist Ashley Hutchings, and together they created their new sound: English folk-rock.

Boyd says that during the time when Fairport recorded their groundbreaking album *Liege And Lief* in late 1969, everyone in the group was obsessed with The Band's *Music From Big Pink*. "They played it, they talked about it, they talked about the drum sound, the vocal sound, the way the record sounded," Boyd recalls. "That moment, that context, that time in London was the moment of *Big Pink*. And we had already heard the Basement Tapes at Feldman's and gotten those precious tapes from them.

"But remember, Fairport had been an American folk-rock band playing that style of music, even though they were English. The new music they wanted to make had to be a reflection of their own cultural sensibilities. And knowing their sensibilities and their knowledge, they could never be The Band. So the next logical thing was to say: 'Hey, we're good, so we can do with our own culture what they did with American culture.'" [11]

Dylan's new material may have been triggering new cultural responses, but elsewhere there were thoughts of a more commercial nature. In his book *Bootleg*, author Clinton Heylin credits radio station KRLA in Pasadena in greater Los Angeles, California, as the first to broadcast *Great White Wonder*, the LP bootleg that included Basement Tapes material. Yet the genie was already out of the jar before KRLA was delivered a copy of that LP in summer '69. KSAN-FM in San Francisco, operated by the legendary Tom Donahue, played *Great White Wonder* that summer too, as did its Los Angeles sister station KMET, also run by Donahue.

Donahue had created America's first alternative radio programming in 1967 while at the Bay Area station KMPX-FM when he took over the 8:00pm-to-midnight shift. He played album cuts instead of singles, broadcast live music when the mood struck him, refused to air certain commercials, made public announcements of a political nature, and generally did what his audience would have wanted a hip DJ to do.

KMPX soon became the first full-time album-oriented FM radio station. It proved to be a groundbreaking idea. Other West Coast stations followed Donahue's lead and his new and revolutionary format spread across the country. After a strike against KMPX management, Donahue and most of the staff moved to KSAN-FM on May 21, 1968.

Donahue invented a free-form radio format that promoted spontaneity and anti-establishment views, and he was committed to a relatively anarchic approach to the airwaves. Without that, *Great White Wonder* would never have been played a first time. You need only look at what happened on the East Coast. The large New York City rock stations WPLJ and WABC were owned by corporate radio networks, to whom Tom Donahue was anathema. To play the *Great White Wonder* on these stations was to risk the sky falling in.

It was two L.A. longhairs who worked for a record distributor who had the idea that they could press up a couple thousand LPs with the new Dylan material. The record, released in July 1969, was dubbed the *Great White Wonder* by an employee at the underground paper *The Los Angeles Free Press.*

In fact, our L.A. longhairs compiled a rather confusing release – thereby setting the rather low standard for most of the bootlegs that followed. They pressed up a two-disc set that contained two full sides of very early solo Dylan recorded back in Minnesota in 1961, a side of miscellaneous studio out-takes that ended with some songs cut in the Big Pink basement, and a fourth side entirely devoted to the Big Pink publisher's demos. People bought the *Great White Wonder* for the Big Pink material – unlike the other Dylan music on the two-LP set, this was the material they'd seen described in *Rolling Stone* and heard on the underground airwaves. It was the most recent series of pronouncements from their hero and they were aching to hear what he had to say.

The whole thing snowballed. Other hip young record industry longhairs bootlegged *Great White Wonder*, releasing their own vinyl versions of it. In summer 1969, those in the know could readily purchase a copy of the

Dylan demos in LP form, a much easier item to find than the earlier seven-inch reel version. Even *The Wall Street Journal* printed an article on the phenomenon. Soon a European version of *Great White Wonder* appeared from a pressing made in Sweden.

"It was weird," says Robbie Robertson, "because I don't remember any bootleg records back then. It was the first, right?" It felt like someone was peeking over your shoulder, like a small invasion, he says.

"If we knew it was gonna be on the radio, we would have done it differently. We would have done it so it was properly put together. We would have thought of it in those production terms, like anything else you do hoping to get airplay on. Which is what *Music From Big Pink* is: the end product of a project where you were hoping it would get its fair share of airplay. That was a project which was put together properly – which the Basement Tapes were not." [12]

Band engineer Rob Fraboni agrees with Robertson's assessment that *Great White Wonder* was not put together properly. "I noticed that it played fast," he says. "Tunes in A minor were almost all the way to B-flat minor. That was because of sloppy copying. The machine they played their cut back on was running off speed." [13]

The legal department at CBS's Columbia Records swung into action against *Great White Wonder* and its offspring, but some problems arose which the record company did not foresee. The songs on *Great White Wonder* that Dylan sang into a Minnesota tape machine in December 1961 were mainly public domain material that Dylan had never copyrighted. It wasn't known if Dylan was even under contract to CBS when he recorded them. In fact he was, but he was a minor when he signed his first CBS contract and he had no guardian or parent sign with him, so the contract might not stand up in court. Further, his name and likeness did not appear on *Great White Wonder* and so a charge that his good name or likeness were illegally used could not be made.

The publisher's demos from Big Pink were most certainly part of *Great White Wonder*, but without firm evidence of their recording date it could have been argued in court that they were perhaps recorded in the period between Dylan's two CBS contracts and therefore not covered by either of them. The side of the record with Columbia studio recordings was of course illegal, and CBS attorneys should have jumped all over them. But that seems to have passed them by.

Joe Boyd considers the Basement Tapes and Dylan in 1967 as a remarkable mix of self-belief and creativity. "There was something fascinating and intimidating about the relentless confidence of Dylan at that time," he concludes. "Those guys, Dylan and The Band, sat up there in Woodstock and they felt no necessity to broadcast it. There was a feeling that you could be as cool as you want at the Scotch Of St. James or in Laurel Canyon or Greenwich Village, but up here in Woodstock, in this basement room, we are doing shit we know is the best. And we don't even care if you ever hear it.

   "They created a kind of white-hot firestorm of confidence, which was so intimidating to everyone else – and then you heard evidence of it in The Basement Tapes. Those tapes just reeked of attitude. It was as if they were saying: 'We *know* … and you don't.'" [14]

    That mix of confidence and arrogance about Dylan and The Hawks/ Band and their Basement Tapes recordings seldom lessened within this particular group of musicians. But there was a downside, the after-effects of fame, that came with mailbox money (as musicians call posted royalty checks) and, at least for some of the participants, an increasing involvement with drugs.

   Dylan left behind his most prolific songwriting year of 1967 only to enter into a half decade where he wrote less and less. In contrast, the legend of the Basement Tapes only grew, fuelled by the continuing sales of the various bootleg releases. And then it had quite a boost when The Band rejoined Dylan for the *Planet Waves* album and subsequent North American tour in 1974. The June 20, 1974 release of the tour's live album, *Before The Flood*, increased still further the growing interest in Dylan's

on–off connection to The Band.

Dylan's involvement with The Band had the same effect on his art in 1974 as it had in 1967. On both occasions he left them behind to start a new album that was full of strong new material, was largely acoustic, and had no Band involvement. This second time around it was *Blood On The Tracks*. In early 1975 it was being hailed as arguably the best album of Dylan's career.

The stage was set for a new look at The Basement Tapes. In Malibu, California, Robbie Robertson, Garth Hudson, and a couple of engineers were beginning to investigate the contents of the reels. Dylan had given his permission to open up the vaults and see what Garth and God had preserved. The Basement Tapes were about to see the light of day.

# MILLION DOLLAR
## BASH

# 15. Deep In Number And Heavy In Toil
*The official 1975 two-LP release*

When the University of California campus in Berkeley again erupted in anti-Vietnam war protests in 1969 and 1970, Xeroxed copies of the photo of a smiling Bob Dylan from the jacket of *Nashville Skyline* were passed out to gathering protesters as a subtle but effective reminder to keep their demonstrations peaceful.

Violent clashes between students and police or National Guardsmen were a constant prospect. Demonstrating students were shot to death at Kent State University in Ohio and Jackson State University in Mississippi in May 1970. Three South Carolina State University undergraduates had been fatally shot by policemen two years earlier. Keeping an anti-war demonstration entirely peaceful on an American college campus seemed a task worthy of God.

And so the God of many students was called upon in Berkeley, smiling at the camera and tipping his hat, a quiet but forceful suggestion to take it easy.

The man in that album picture had led a rebellion in lifestyle and attitude for much of the previous decade, whether purposefully or not. To many of America's youth, as well as their puzzled parents, he had signified what the media of the day referred to as the counter-culture.

When he hooked up with a Canadian group who had been performing R&B covers on an endless treadmill of bars and seedy saloons, this smiling fellow had turned pop music upside down, given it a good shake, and placed it back where he, and they, had found it. But when he set the music back, it was at an angle. Rock'n'roll music was now rock music. Now he was rock's biggest single iconic figure since Elvis. The world was his to take.

In a way, the man on the *Nashville Skyline* jacket began to reject everything: rock'n'roll music, the demands of the world around him, the adulation of the students gathered in Berkeley and on the other 400 or more American college campuses that protested the escalation of the Vietnam war.

Starting from a basement in early 1967, Bob Dylan and his Canadian musicians led a quiet musical rebellion against the youthful, cultural rebellion for which this Minnesota singer was the nominal figurehead.

Their anti-rebellion started with The Basement Tapes. Lengthy fire-breathing solos, rock'n'roll drive, opaque Beat-poetic lyrics – all this was jettisoned in favor of tight arrangements, rootsy pre-rock flavors, and opaque, semi-improvised lyrics based on who knows what.

As Robbie Robertson said later: "The way we played in the basement had nothing to do with the way we played with Bob on tour [and] it had nothing to do with the way we'd played as The Hawks or with Ronnie Hawkins. It was a whole new persona. ... Subtleties came into the music: it had this kind of timeless spirit. And when we would play on acoustic instruments, upstairs in the living room, there was a whole different balancing thing going on." [1]

"We were rebelling against the rebellion," said Robertson. "Whatever was happening. If everybody was going east, then we were going west, and we never once discussed it. ... It was an instinct to separate us from the pack." [2]

Richard Manuel said in 1971: "We didn't try to overplay everything; maybe it was just easier for people to hear. The time seemed to be right for softer music, although there was a lot of psychedelic rock going around."

Even more succinct was Levon Helm's comment. "Oh, we didn't want to have anything to do with that psychedelic stuff. We thought it was all bullshit." [3]

By January 1975 there were forces at work at Columbia Records seeking to release some form of the fruits of the '67 Basement Tapes from Woodstock. Dylan unexpectedly gave his OK, having come to some agreement with ex-manager Albert Grossman over these songs published by Dwarf Music, a company jointly owned by Dylan and Grossman. The Band were arguing that the release should count as an album under their Capitol contract. (It would not.)

Garth Hudson dug out and dusted off all his reels of tape. And some of the finest recording engineers were called upon to help Robertson and Hudson clean up and assemble the best possible and first ever official

Basement Tapes release. Rob Fraboni was the primary engineer on the project, working alongside Ed Anderson, Mark Aglietti, Richard Berwin (curiously uncredited on the 1975 set), and Nat Jeffrey.

Fraboni grew up in southern California in a family of musicians. Moving to New York City in 1971, he attended the Institute Of Audio Research and stumbled upon a good engineering job with Herb Abramson, a co-founder of Atlantic Records, at Abramson's A-1 Sound Studios on the ground floor of a hotel off Broadway and 72nd Street. There they recorded Johnny Nash, Dave 'Baby' Cortez, and Lloyd Price among others.

Fraboni moved to the Record Plant, working with engineers Roy Cicala, Shelly Yakus, Jack Douglas, and Jimmy Iovine. He found himself in the studio with Labelle, The Raspberries, and John Lennon before a move in 1972 to Village Recorders in Westwood, an affluent Los Angeles suburb. He soon became chief engineer, and the studio's reputation grew. Fraboni engineered the hit single 'Sail On Sailor' and then mixed half of *Holland* for The Beach Boys before starting work on *Goat's Head Soup* with The Rolling Stones. In short, this was a young man who was savvy and on his way up.

He remembers meeting Dylan at that time. "It was about 1972 or maybe late '71, for the Allen Ginsberg album which had the song 'See You In San Diego' ['Going To San Diego'] on it. Bob Dylan and John Lennon were both on that session." At Village Recorders, toward the end of 1973, Fraboni heard that Dylan was coming in to record what turned out to be *Planet Waves*. At first, he considered working instead on a record with Seals & Crofts, who had recently hit with 'Diamond Girl.' But then he discovered that The Band were coming along with Dylan. "That was it for me," he laughs. "There was nothing better than working with The Band, and so I booked myself on the session."

Fraboni recalls that Robertson came to the studio first and told him what was going on. "He was kind of manipulating things as much as he could and he was telling me the lay of the land from his point of view.

Then Dylan came, and I remember Robbie introducing me to him in the hallway at Village Recorders. Bob's handshake was like a dead fish: very funny. He turned out to be great. He had this little smile and a great sense of humor. He really does."

There was no nominal producer on *Planet Waves*. "Just Bob and Robbie and me," explains Fraboni, "and a few times it was just me and Bob. The day we had done the recording and assembled the master reels is the day we recorded 'Wedding Song.' Dylan was laying on his back in the studio with a felt-tipped pen and some paper and writing, and he said: 'Well, at some point I am gonna want to record this.' And God, he just got up, went out to the mikes, played it once – a song he had just written – and played it well. He only did the one take."

The Band and Dylan were living in the Malibu area, just up Pacific Coast Highway from Village Recorders. Rick Danko – clearly the one member of The Band who could have had a successful career in real estate – found yet another communal house-cum-potential-recording-studio and dragged his bandmates and Fraboni out to the Shangri-La ranch at 30065 Morning View Drive. Which they then agreed to purchase.

Danko told Fraboni and the others to come and check it out as he thought it would be a great place for a studio. "They'd often done that kind of recording-studio-as-home thing, what with Big Pink and recording the brown album in Sammy Davis Jr.'s pool house or guest house. They were into doing that," says Fraboni. He was hanging out a lot with The Band and they became friends. "I think I was the closest with Richard Manuel, and I was close to Danko and, in a way, to Levon. I guess to everybody except Robbie, who is the kind of guy who keeps everyone at arm's length anyway."

They started to work at Shangri-La on what became The Band's 1975 album *Northern Lights–Southern Cross*, with equipment at first rented and later bought from Village Recorders. "Dylan had no input at all into Shangri-La's set-up," says Fraboni, "and it is not correct to say he did. It really was only about The Band, although Bob would come up there and check things out." During 1975, The Band worked in Shangri-La as frequently as possible. The Basement Tapes were being prepared for a June release and they wanted the new *Northern Lights* album to be out for the Christmas market. Some Band members, Richard Manuel in particular, were sometimes in no shape to record, but Robertson pushed onward.

Hudson had all the Basement Tapes in a trunk at his place, says Fraboni. "I was the only engineer there. I went through the stuff with Robbie. Sometimes Rick Danko was there, but mostly Robbie. Bob was there just a little bit. There was ten hours of stuff. We went through everything, and I admit there were a lot of great things we could not put on the record because, for instance, the first ten or fifteen seconds would be missing or garbled. They were all on plastic seven-inch reels: there must have been 50 or 60 reels of Shamrock and all these rather off-brand tapes. Garth had engineered all of it."

Normally, reels of audio tape would have a short length of 'leader' tape on each end to keep them from unraveling and to protect the start and finish of the tape itself, but none of Hudson's tapes had that. Some of them were not in great shape. "We had to take good care of them," recalls Fraboni. "Garth did take good care of them, as good care of them as he could since these tapes were moved around a lot. They weren't falling apart, but there were a couple of reels where the oxide was falling off. Most of them were pretty much OK. *Most* of them."

Fraboni admits that if the Basement Tapes reissue project was undertaken today, technically there would be much more that he or any good engineer could do to clean up the tapes. Back then, he and Richard Berwin and the other engineers were limited by the technology of the day. The extent of the treatment of the tapes in 1975 was to run them through a single-ended noise reduction unit to reduce some of the noise, and through a compressor and an EQ to draw out as much clear, clean signal as possible.

"It was a little tedious," remembers Fraboni, "as we were limited in what we could do. You'd have to play the whole tape carefully to see if

there were going to be any technical or sonic surprises. You certainly couldn't do what you can do today with a state-of-the-art computer. You had to do it all in real-time and listen to everything carefully."

Fraboni says that the released 1975 *Basement Tapes* set sounds practically mono and is not as 'spatial' as some listeners used to modern sounds might expect a stereo record to be. Hudson certainly recorded the originals on 2-track, but that was not stereo as such. As we learned in chapter 8, Hudson's original tapes have instruments and vocals recorded on the left or on the right, with no 'common' information in the center of the stereo picture.

When the official *The Basement Tapes* set was released June 26, 1975, some listeners were disappointed that different takes were used compared to those heard on the 1969 vinyl bootleg *Great White Wonder* and its descendants. Also, some listeners were surprised that songs cut at the original sessions, such as 'Quinn The Eskimo' and 'I Shall Be Released,' which had become quite famous in subsequent covers, were not found on the Columbia set. The takes were selected by Robertson and Dylan, and Fraboni says Dylan wasn't in the studio that often. "Robbie Robertson was the driving force behind that record set," he says. It seems likely that the very fact that some tracks had become well-known may have counted against their appearance on the LP set.

Fraboni also recalls discussion of the problem of groove cramming. This is a phenomenon that could cause vinyl records to lose some high-end and low-end tones when too much music was put on one side of a disc. "A three-record *Basement Tapes* release was talked about at one point," he says, "but it was decided not to do that as the retail price might be too expensive. So the guys elected to do a two-LP set."

Three songs on the two-LP set were not from the Basement Tapes sessions at all, but were recorded in early 1975 at The Band's Shangri-La studio. That may have escaped the attention of Dylan, Fraboni suggests. "He didn't really come to the studio more than twice or so, and when he did it was really briefly, so I don't know how much he knew about the three new songs. He just probably thought these new songs were stuff from Big Pink's basement, as The Band did record some stuff there when Bob was late to rehearse or had left early or whatever." [4]

Fraboni continues: "We cut these new tracks and said that they were old, which they weren't. 'Ain't No More Cane' was one, 'Bessie Smith' was another, and 'Don't Ya Tell Henry.' I believe we did 'Going Back To Memphis' then too but didn't use it." A song called 'Back To Memphis' would appear on the reunited Robertson-less Band album *High On The Hog* in 1996, but Fraboni is probably referring here to the Chuck Berry song of the same title that The Band performed in the 1970s. 'Going Back To Memphis' is a bonus track on the 2001 *Moondog Matinee* CD reissue and this same version appears as 'Back To Memphis' on the fraudulent *Live At Watkins Glen* CD with audience applause overdubbed – both are the same Chuck Berry composition.

"I believe some of the extra songs on the *Big Pink* CD reissue in 2000 have some of these same so-called Basement Tapes songs on them," says Fraboni, referring to 'Yazoo Street Scandal,' 'Katie's Been Gone,' 'Long Distance Operator,' and 'Orange Juice Blues (Blues For Breakfast),' which augment the *Music From Big Pink* CD today.

Robbie Robertson admits the official release of the Basement Tapes had Band studio out-takes but maintains that at the time he, Hudson, and Dylan did not have access to all the Basement Tapes now known to be in existence. The idea, he says, was that if bootlegs were appearing of tenth-generation copies or worse, then why not do it officially and with the best sound possible? "We had access to some of the songs, and I don't know if we had everything. Some of these things came under the heading of 'homemade,' which meant a Basement Tape to us."

Robertson's definition of what constitutes a Basement Tapes recording is much broader than many others would allow. Rock critics regard the Basement Tapes as material recorded in Woodstock in 1967 by musicians trying out things for themselves: nothing more or less. Robertson feels the Basement Tapes are a process, a homemade feel, and that this

can include recording in just such a situation almost anywhere. His definition casts a wider net and allows for his inclusion on the official 1975 Basement Tapes release of recordings that had nothing to do with the Red Room, the Big Pink basement, or Danko's home on Wittenberg Road.

If the rock-critic version of what qualifies for Basement Tapes is held to be absolute, then the other five musicians involved in this music should be placed in the dock too, alongside Robertson, because there are no reported complaints from his Band-mates or from Dylan about what was included on the official set.

"Everything that is on the 1975 release is, I guess, what they'd call today out-takes or B-sides or something," says Robertson now. "That's what they were: just homemade stuff. Some of them probably were being made up lyrically on the spot. I don't have a copy of all of it. Some people I was working with to put together the *Musical History* Band [2005 boxed set] would say: 'There are different takes of that song, and hey, this song has a false start and then the whole song.' So I really haven't examined it too much. I never really knew what was on those reels. Greil Marcus told me about it, that there was this material still out there." [5]

With all this in mind, we should now take a listen to the recordings on the official '75 set and consider their origins, comparing them to the '67 Woodstock recordings. The first release was in 1975 on two vinyl LPs; I'm listening to the remastered CD reissue of 2000.

## ODDS AND ENDS
This track opens the official *Basement Tapes* album on Columbia and is exactly the same as take two from Woodstock. Hudson recorded it with great separation between the two tape tracks but this 'official' version has a collapsed mono feel with the vocal centered.

## ORANGE JUICE BLUES (BLUES FOR BREAKFAST)
There can be little doubt that what appears on the 1975 release is the version featuring only Manuel and Danko from some eight years earlier

but with Robertson's guitar, Helm's drums, and Hudson's wonderful horn work all overdubbed in '75. Fraboni doesn't remember this, but there were other engineers credited on the official release, so perhaps they engineered the session where the overdubs took place while Fraboni was given the greater task of recording the new versions of three old songs from scratch.

## MILLION DOLLAR BASH

This is audibly the same as take two from the Big Pink basement. No overdubs, but again there is greater 'stereo' separation on the underground releases compared to this official release, which is in collapsed mono. There is a possibility that another backing vocal has been added on the chorus but this could be either Fraboni bringing out all the sounds using EQ and compression in 1975 or proof of Joel Bernstein's theory (see chapter 8) that when Hudson's original tracks are set in perfect balance there is nothing audibly missing or distorted.

## YAZOO STREET SCANDAL

Thankfully no one picked the version with Danko's strained vocal, which was probably done at Woodstock or possibly from September 5, 1967 in New York City's Columbia Studio E, with Helm yet to return. A longer, slightly more sedate version of this from the *Music From Big Pink* sessions with John Simon now exists on the extended CD reissue of that album. That version is in full stereo; this *Basement Tapes* one is collapsed mono.

It sounds like The Band are playing live with no overdubs. Fraboni says it is from the Big Pink basement in 1967 and he is probably right, given Robertson's loose "homemade process" definition of what Basement Tapes means.

## GOIN' TO ACAPULCO

When Robertson included this on the official release at Danko's behest it alerted the world to the fact that more music was recorded in the basement at Big Pink than previously thought. The Hudson original is widely-spread 2-track; the official release is, again, mono-ish, and there are no overdubs.

### KATIE'S BEEN GONE
At Woodstock, this was recorded without Dylan and without drums. The versions heard on both the '75 set and the expanded CD reissue of *Music From Big Pink* are the same. Therefore, the version Robertson chose for the '75 set was either an out-take from *Music From Big Pink* or, more logically given his looser definition of Basement Tapes, the earlier take from '67 Woodstock with overdubs such as drums added in '75 at Shangri-La (and recorded with an engineer other than Fraboni).

### LO AND BEHOLD!
If an engineer knocked this down into mono, then he didn't have much work to do. The version that escaped from Hudson's archives is near mono anyway, although it isn't known if Hudson did the rejigging or Elliot Mazer did it for Albert Grossman in 1967-68 when the demo tape reels were compiled. Certainly Rob Fraboni, Richard Berwin, and the other engineers involved in polishing up the tapes did a splendid job here. It sounds much clearer than the original demo tape. No overdubs – this is pure Woodstock with no Shangri-La.

### BESSIE SMITH
This was the most far-fetched selection included on the official *Basement Tapes* release, even by Robertson's broad standards.

'Bessie Smith' is an excellent Danko–Robertson composition (recently sung by Norah Jones) and was around as a song if not as a recording since The Band's second album. It was either left off that album or not even recorded for it, perhaps because a Bessie character already appeared in 'Up On Cripple Creek.'

Rob Fraboni says this is one of three songs purposely recorded at

Shangri-La in early 1975 for the official two-LP set. But according to Rob Bowman in his notes for the expanded CD reissue of *Cahoots* in 2000: "Robbie is certain that ['Bessie Smith'] was recorded sometime between [the 1969 second LP] and *Stage Fright*."[6] Which prompts the obvious question: why did The Band not release it on 1970's *Stage Fright*, as it was better than some of the songs that did make that LP? Even better, why not put it on the original *Cahoots* LP of 1971? No one would be so foolish as to leave such a strong piece off that relatively weak LP. All that points to it surely having been recorded in 1975, as Fraboni says. But whatever its origins, clearly it has nothing at all to do with the Woodstock summer-of-love sessions.

The version on the *Cahoots* CD reissue is the same as that found on the official Basement Tapes album on Columbia. Neither is overdubbed after the fact; both are mono-ish.

### CLOTHES LINE SAGA

Apart from the false start of the original, the version on the '75 set is the same recording. Hudson's original as usual has the channels wide apart while the official release has the mono-ish sound imposed at the time in an attempt to boost clarity and authenticity.

There are no overdubs on the official release, but Hudson's playing on the original is enough to make you think he had three keyboards and six arms. Garth Hudson is arguably the most underrated talent in modern popular music.

### APPLE SUCKLING TREE

The same lovely original version is here on the official Columbia release, but Hudson's original wide-spread 'stereo' is once more lost in the rush to mono for two-LP set.

### PLEASE MRS. HENRY

Same again: original version but mono feel. No overdubs here, either.

### TEARS OF RAGE
No instrument overdubs, but the official version seems to have an extra backing vocalist (or two) on the chorus. A more spatial, widespread sound is heard here, with the two channels not as separated as on the original Hudson recording and Dylan's vocal dead in the middle.

### TOO MUCH OF NOTHING
For this '75 release, Helm's drums and Hudson's keyboard swirls were overdubbed at Shangri-La, with Robertson's guitar much louder, making this official release audibly different from the spare Woodstock original demo. Backing vocals have been added, another Danko harmony is in place, and Helm is heard singing on the chorus as well.

### YEA! HEAVY AND A BOTTLE OF BREAD
Robertson, Dylan, and Fraboni are in agreement here: this is indeed from the basement at Big Pink. Needless to say, it was in wide 'stereo' in its original Hudson incarnation but is in collapsed mono on this Columbia release of 1975.

### AIN'T NO MORE CANE
This is one of the three new songs that Rob Fraboni recorded at Shangri-La in '75 to give The Band more profile on this release. "I remember doing it when we did 'Bessie Smith' in '75," says Fraboni. "They are both great songs and both sound cool: we need to say that." [7]

Understandably, Dylan's fans wanted more than the 14 Basement Tapes songs they could have tracked down by the time Columbia got around to a proper release of the sessions. No doubt those fans were intrigued by the listing inside the original gatefold of titles they did not know, such as 'Goin' To Acapulco' or 'Clothes Line Saga.'

Yet surely those same fans could not have been too disappointed by the songs featuring Dylan's old backing band, a group of musicians who were now stars in their own right?

'Ain't No More Cane' may be included under false pretenses, but it is stirring stuff, full of "an old, old sense of mystery crossed with an intensity," as Greil Marcus wrote, "that indeed had not been heard in a long time."[8] How could this old bluesy work song taught to Levon Helm by his father not contain both mystery and intensity? It was distilled from and clearly marinated in such things.

Helm sang the first verse and played a simple mandolin part; Robertson sang the second verse and played acoustic guitar; Danko played bass and sang the third verse; Manuel sang the fourth verse and played drums. They all brought it back home together on the chorus, and Hudson underpinned the entire shebang with his accordion. (Credits in CD booklets and memoirs are wrong; this is the correct line-up instrumentally and musically.)

'Cane' does sparkle more than the actual basement songs and is eight years late to that particular party. And while a Dylan fan might understandably grumble that he wanted to hear another Bob song, a fan equally versed in and interested more generally in late 20th century American music would only smile and thank the Good Lord for the gift of this song.

All in, this is a fine example of what went on upstairs at Big Pink in the informal acoustic living-room sessions that the participants remember so warmly.

### CRASH ON THE LEVEE (DOWN IN THE FLOOD)
Back to a mono sound as opposed to the wide separation found on Hudson's original reel. It is noteworthy that Robertson includes selections like this when he isn't even on them. This remains pleasantly sparse with no after-the-fact overdubs.

### RUBEN REMUS
Early tapes of this from Woodstock exist with only Robertson, Danko, and Hudson working up the song; later tapes from Woodstock exist with

different backing vocals and different endings; a version was cut September 5, 1967 at Columbia Studio E in New York City before Helm returned; and 'Ruben Remus' was dragged out yet again at the John Simon-led early sessions for *Music From Big Pink*. Rob Fraboni is probably correct when he recalls this as the version that Simon got the guys to tape at the *Big Pink* sessions in early 1968. Robertson seems to feel the song is a bit of a goof, but it is much better than he would have folks believe and as effortlessly charming as 'Katie's Been Gone' or 'Ferdinand The Imposter,' two more out-takes from the same era.

**TINY MONTGOMERY**
The basement original lasts a bit longer as it does not have the fade of this cleaned-up 1975 release. On Hudson's reel-to-reel tape it's in widespread 'stereo' but, again, it is heard in mono on this Columbia collection. Dylan's acoustic guitar is always lost a bit in the shift to mono, but this is a proper mono and a proper performance from the day, with no 1975 overdubs.

**YOU AIN'T GOIN' NOWHERE**
Guitar overdubbed by Robertson and, as Phil Spector would like us to remain, we are back to mono here. Fraboni maintains that this is not an overdub but something that would have been audible if the *Great White Wonder* bootlegs (and the subsequent bootlegs of that bootleg) were mastered and manufactured properly. Though Dylan's vocals are moved to the middle for this official release, there is nonetheless a stereo spread, with the drums to the left and Robertson's new country & western guitar part to the right.

**DON'T YA TELL HENRY**
Only a Dylan obsessive would prefer the drunk-as-skunks version found on one of Hudson's 1967 reels to this hilariously bawdy remake from The Band sans Dylan, which Rob Fraboni recorded at Shangri-La eight years later.

True, the argument could be made that Robertson was way outside his brief in including this on the two-LP set, as this isn't from Woodstock or '67, has no Dylan on it, and was recorded in a fairly formal studio and not a basement or living room. But it is a song from the Basement Tapes era and it swings like a randy sailor on shore leave in a bisexual bar. So give Robbie a break.

Helm on mandolin and vocal, Danko on bass and backing vocal, Robertson on a stinging guitar part, Hudson on a fine honky-tonk piano, Manuel drumming like Helm's best pupil – and every damn one of them playing for their very lives.

### NOTHING WAS DELIVERED

One of Hudson's best engineered tracks, it appears on this official release much as it did originally. Other than Dylan's vocal moved to the centre, this is pretty much 'stereo' and one of the key performances to point to when someone asks about the dynamic and the true strength of the Dylan–Band partnership. It's still Dylan doing Fats Domino, however. Which is a good thing.

### OPEN THE DOOR, HOMER

What would Louis Jordan have thought of this? He was struggling when Dylan and his friends recorded this 'song within a song' in 1967 but had been a kingpin 30 years earlier when he recorded tunes like 'Open The Door, Richard.'

Like 'Nothing Was Delivered,' the Dylan vocal is centered, but there is a stereo effect with Hudson's organ panned right.

### LONG DISTANCE OPERATOR

This can be found on the reels in Hudson's Woodstock archives, but that doesn't necessarily mean it was cut there. Engineer Fraboni thinks this is from the *Music From Big Pink* sessions and Rob Bowman's notes with the CD reissue of that album claim it was recorded at Gold Star in Los

Angeles on February 21, 1968. Again, this would make it akin to 'Don't Ya Tell Henry' and 'Ain't No More Cane' here as it is not a Basement Tape by any stretch of the imagination – not even by Robertson's standards, for this could hardly be called homemade. The track was edited for the 1975 set, so it is shorter in length than the *Big Pink* reissue version, but it is the same song. If only Ronnie Hawkins were singing it, he'd have torn it up – and Bobby 'Blue' Bland would have done an even better job than that.

**THIS WHEEL'S ON FIRE**
Only an acoustic guitar overdub from Robertson at Shangri-La eight years after it was recorded differentiates this from the original 1967 version.

After the two-LP set was polished up at Shangri-La and the running order assembled, Robertson asked Fraboni to contact the best person in the country to master the record. They knew they needed the best of the best to help them preserve and present the limited sound range of *The Basement Tapes*. Fraboni says it was mastered up in San Francisco by George Horn at Columbia. "We had heard such good things about his work. So we flew up there."

Then the photograph was taken by Reid Miles for the jacket. "I was there when they did that but I missed being in the photo for some reason," laughs Fraboni. "It is the basement, if you can dig that, of the YMCA in Hollywood. After the cover photo was taken, Dylan, David Blue, and myself went swimming in the pool there." [9]

The June 25, 1975 release of Columbia's 24-song double-LP set *The Basement Tapes* met with rave reviews from the critics. It topped the *Village Voice* 'Pazz & Jop Poll' for 1975, beating out *Born To Run, Blood On The Tracks*, and Patti Smith's debut *Horses*. In *The New York Times,* John Rockwell called it "the greatest album in the history of popular American music." [10]

*Creem* magazine ran a regular feature, 'Consumer's Guide' by Robert Christgau, and he gave the record a very rare A+. The late, great Paul

Nelson wrote a marvelous short-story-cum-essay about *The Basement Tapes* for *Rolling Stone*, dealing with his subject like a B-movie detective and claiming the set was the equivalent to *Highway 61 Revisited*.

In short, the album was a critical success. It entered the U.S. *Billboard* Top 40 album chart early in August and peaked at Number 7.

None of those fine reviews pointed out the overdubs or the new recordings, which would be rather obvious to any Dylan fanatic who owned *Great White Wonder* or its bastard offshoots such as *Troubled Troubadour*. It stands to reason that Christgau, Nelson, Rockwell, and the rest would own *Great White Wonder* or one of its underground siblings. They were all record fanatics and record collectors. And they were all Dylan fans. That none of them spotted the overdubs on some of Dylan's actual Big Pink basement recordings and none of them spotted the new recordings doesn't say much for their ears – and perhaps makes a statement about the quality of their turntables.

The most obvious question today is, will The Basement Tapes ever be upgraded? In this world of CD boxed sets it seems such an obvious move, particularly in light of the popularity of Dylan's own *Bootleg Series*.

Rob Fraboni: "As far as I know there are no plans to upgrade or re-issue an expanded Basement Tapes set. I want to talk to Bob's people about that." [11]

Joel Bernstein: "I have never copied any of my Basement Tapes transfers as my feeling is that tape, those songs, should come out officially. A *Dylan Bootleg Series Basement Tapes* set. It should happen. It is something which has been discussed." [12]

Robbie Robertson: "I never think about it. I am working on a new project. Always. This is a long time ago. I can't think about that kind of stuff! [laughter] I am not an archivist the way Garth is. I can remember it warmly but I can't, you know, I can't incorporate it into my new things just now." [13]

Columbia's *The Basement Tapes* set remains a remarkable release, even if, as Fraboni puts it, "someone in The Band wanted a chance for them to shine a little, and Bob is always looking forward and not that concerned about the past." [14] Meaning the official release is not what it seems.

But that is life in the world of Bob Dylan, where both art and commerce are as mysterious as a Tarot card face down on a gypsy's table. Never was that more so than with the Basement Tapes.

# MILLION DOLLAR BASH

## 16. And Life Is Brief

*Some views, within and without*

## BILLY BRAGG

"My first inkling of the Basement Tapes was an EP I bought by Coulson Dean McGuinness Flint. I was already into Dylan's music but I didn't really know anything about the Basement Tapes or where they were found. This is when 'Jean Genie' was a hit and 'Angel' by Rod Stewart was a hit. I fell for the Coulson Dean McGuinness Flint version of 'Lay Down Your Weary Tune.' I noticed 'Tiny Montgomery' was on it as well, but when you looked at the Dylan LPs neither 'Lay Down Your Weary Tune' nor 'Tiny Montgomery' were found.

"'Tiny Montgomery' was such a weird, wild song. I used to wonder who he was and why Dylan wrote about him. When the *Basement Tapes* two-LP set came out a few years later, I clocked that poor Tiny was just something Dylan had made up. But I didn't know that the Band stuff on the two-LP set was probably added on later – it all sounded good to me then. Still does.

"Listening back to the Basement Tapes now, it seems to be the beginning of what is called Americana or alt.country. The thing is, that music was around before, but it had no name. And country & western was already getting so polished by the time The Hawks were backing Dylan in the Big Pink basement. The Basement Tapes are a lot of things to a lot of people but they are not overly polished. The warm, folksy feel was a spark that a lot or most of country & western had lost by then, and yet Dylan and the Band guys captured it, they caught that lightning in a bottle, where you have an identifiably conscious creativity occurring alongside a spontaneous or seemingly spontaneous kind of jam session. I mean, these are some pretty loose yet undeniably creative recording sessions, right?

"And the thing about alt.country which makes it 'alt' is that it is not polished. It is not overly rehearsed or slick. Neither are the Basement Tapes. So I think there is a good reason to state that this is where alt. country or Americana starts. Remember too that the Basement Tapes hold a certain value, a certain cultural weight, which is timeless – and the best alt.country or Americana does that as well. Also, it's interesting that Dylan's Basement Tapes flirt with the songs he learned when he visited England in the early 1960s to be in that BBC TV play [*The Madhouse On Castle Street*]. He ended up hanging out with Martin Carthy, visiting Ewan MacColl clubs, playing The Troubadour in London, and all that. It was there he heard 'Nottamun Town,' 'Lord Franklin,' and so forth and they converted him into his early classics.

"Look at things like 'The Banks Of The Royal Canal' and 'Bonnie Ship The Diamond' being on the Basement Tapes. He's reacquainting himself with his original musical inspirations. This is, after all, the man who when asked by Archibald MacLeish who his heroes were answered: 'Robin Hood and George The Dragon Slayer.' Wow! The guy whose music is so steeped in Americana and whose music is such a gift to Americana said that? It's fascinating to ponder – like so much of Dylan's work itself." [1]

## STEVE EARLE

"I now live on the very street that Bob Dylan is walking down on the cover of *Freewheelin'*. After the last few years [in Nashville] I needed to open my door, walk out, and be able to see a mixed-race same-sex couple walking down the streets holding hands. It just makes me feel safer at this point in my life.

"My take on the Basement Tapes is that, for whatever reason, motorcycle accident or not, Dylan withdrew for a while, and he learned very early on about mailbox money [royalty checks]. He was sitting around trying to figure out what he was gonna do next.

"I had heard virtually all of the Basement Tapes by the time the official release came out, and I knew people who had second-generation copies of the original acetates that went out. There are not that many degrees of separation between, for example, Townes Van Zandt and Bob Dylan, when you get down to it. Mutual friends; people in the business they all knew.

"So Dylan is in a reclusive stage and works with The Band as a collective with everybody chipping in. It's great. It's kind of moving, emotionally, the way everybody did what it took to get the song done. I only wish it had, in the long run, worked out a little better for some of the guys. That's kind of sad and you think about that when you hear their songs, their contributions to the stuff recorded in Woodstock in that Summer of Love.

"What was hugely influential was when you go and listen to the Basement Tapes and think about a guy like McGuinn getting acetates of it. A lot of the way we now look at archiving music, at recording music, at music having a certain feel, as due to this one particular place it was recorded, a basement of all things – a lot of that comes from Woodstock '67.

"Dylan stopping folk music, stopping the electric music of the next few years, and doing something different in Woodstock is something I explain by remembering how he is a songwriter first of all. Songs are either broadsides and current events or they are about girls. Or boys if you like boys. There are only so many big topics to write songs about. Dylan elevated pop songwriting, that music which was commercially available to the public, to the level of literature, and no one had ever or had consistently ever done that before.

"Dylan stopped doing one thing he was doing and artistically went into another sound, but the public, who had already had a hard time following his moves, didn't get to hear this new artistic period for a while. But McGuinn did, Brian Auger did, Manfred Mann did, all sorts of people in the business did, and the Basement Tapes kept Dylan going on all fronts and kept his music out there. But it didn't keep Dylan the person out there, as he knew it was time to stay at home and see those kids of his."[2]

## NICK LOWE

"The Band, oh man, The Band. It's funny: you never hear them on the radio any more, and people are forgetting about The Band, which is quite incredible. Because every time I do hear them again – and I was and still am a great fan, I used to listen to them obsessively until I heard every single nuance and note – when I hear a song of theirs today unexpectedly on the radio, it is quite surprising and I always get this jolt. Every time this happens I am always reminded it truly doesn't get any better.

"My mob, Brinsley Schwarz, we loved them. We were crazy about them back when The Band were firing on all cylinders. They came round to our house to practice, to the Brinsleys house which we shared to save money as it was cheaper to live and work that way. This was when they came over in the 1970s to play Wembley with Crosby Stills Nash & Young, a big show there, and The Band did not have anywhere to rehearse.

"Our admiration of them went deep. The very chords they used became iconic. We were at that age where that kind of thing is rather important. [laughter] The Band had such a soulful rhythm section in Rick Danko and Levon Helm. No one knows how to play soulfully any more. Many people can play earnest. Earnest is everywhere. But soulfulness is lost. And earnestness is what people today mistake for soulfulness. That soulfulness is gone, and if you have ears to hear then you can look to people like The Band, or Dylan of course, as your teachers. Certainly you can look to Danko and Helm as the height of soulfulness in playing – and in singing, too. You can also look to where The Band got it from, to where they got this soulfulness from.

"Each guy had a distinctly soulful voice in The Band. We in the Brinsleys did our best to imitate it but it sounded shit. [more laughter] You bet we had a go, but it sounded so bad singing through our noses trying to imitate those great church harmonies that Levon and Rick Danko and Richard Manuel had. We had a go, yes, as did plenty of others who tried to copy The Band, especially at our level back then, when we were rather third or fourth division. All of my contemporaries, as I remember, were trying to copy Band licks.

"As regards the Basement Tapes and some other examples, I feel The Band were one of the few acts who could easily follow it if Dylan went to a 17th bar on a 16-bar song or improvised something else like that. That was their meat and drink. The Band could do that, they were born to do that, to follow a singer wherever he goes. Be it an outside singer or one of their own singers.

"The Band come from an era that's gone and ain't coming back. I think at the time there was The Beatles, some of the West Coast folk-rock bands, and The Band – they all didn't have an obvious frontman. Even, for example, The Kinks had Ray Davies out front to some extent. But The Beatles and The Band are examples of proper bands: each band member was a character in his own right and made an incredible contribution to the whole. That's why they were interesting.

"But even The Band were apart from The Beatles or the Stones or whoever because of their soulful timelessness, the soulful thing they had in their music. It is so wonderful that they got together with Bob Dylan, that those two units ever found each other, because it was so fitting. Bob Dylan, a Jewish bloke from a northern state, a bunch of farm blokes from Canada, and Levon from 2,000 miles away in the South, a white black man. It is absolutely righteous as hell. There is North America, right there! Certainly as far as white popular music can be portrayed. Was there ever anything better or more representative of North America?" [3]

## PETER YARROW

"One of the things about the Basement Tapes which was startling and important was that the value of what they were had a lot to do with their authenticity and sheer starkness. That allowed you to feel the energy of what was being produced. That was seen as valuable, which has been kind of an element in art where the seemingly careless, the gesture, the tracking of real human gut responses is very powerful, as opposed to very polite chamber music by Mozart. Remember this was an era in which nobody had really gone around neglecting precision and well conceived presentation in order to exemplify the creative act. So the Basement Tapes are quite a valid moment in time." [4]

## JOHN HAMMOND, JR.

"These were talented guys on a roll on many levels in 1967, and I was a witness to their unbelievable success. Big Pink was just a weird, nondescript house which three of the guys stayed in and used as a home, as a studio, and as everything else. They were hanging out.

"All the guys except Levon were Canadian, and I had played so many gigs in places like Toronto I was very comfortable around them all. I had known them for years. You could see them growing as Bob was helping them and they were helping him.

"When I first heard the Basement Tapes it was '68 or so, and I didn't know it was Bob with The Band behind him. I didn't know they could do that: I was very surprised and amazed. Same with *Music From Big Pink*. I knew Bob as a changing artist but I didn't immediately recognize this change on the Basement Tapes.

"It was shocking in a way – The Hawks had become The Band and created this evocative, compelling sound which was so immediate, so captivating." [5]

## AL KOOPER

"When I first heard the Basement Tapes, I thought primarily they were demos and made as demos for that purpose. I liked some of the songs and I didn't like some of the other songs so much. I didn't think it was *Sgt. Pepper*.

"If you think about it, if they were songs Dylan regarded as good songs, then he would have recorded them more formally. Even a guy as prolific as Dylan, as changing as Dylan, he would have recorded them. There are worse songs that he has recorded.

"Those Basement Tapes songs were recorded for other people, for that purpose. I got a copy for no other reason than to hear them. I asked for a copy and I gratefully received one a bit later on. This was late 1967. When I was a staff producer at CBS in 1968, I didn't have any of my artists record these songs as I didn't have any artists working with me who these particular songs were the right material for." [6]

## JOHN SIMON

"The guys played the tapes for me way back before they were any big deal at all. I listened to those Basement Tapes just like I would listen to any other tapes or songs brought to me by another band. You know: 'Here's a song we've been working on, what do you think?' I'm asked that and we take it from there.

"The Basement Tapes are rough. They are rough. And they are cherished because they have Bob Dylan on 'em." [7]

## JOE BOYD

"I think the Basement Tapes represent a logical continuity from *Blonde On Blonde*, especially considering the musicians he was living with and in close proximity to in Woodstock.

"The only thing in that saga which strikes me as having the perversity of Dylan trying to hide or change masks, and to get away from the kind of acclaim he had learned to shun following his motorcycle accident, is in his not recording with The Band.

"Maybe something in him realized this stuff, this particular music, was too powerful.

"If he had made a beautifully produced record of all that stuff – 'Quinn The Eskimo,' 'This Wheel's On Fire,' 'I Shall Be Released' – produced by Tom Wilson or Bob Johnston and cut in New York with The Band, a record getting a great mix and a great sound, put out in late 1967 or whenever – it would have been an earthquake. And then he'd *never* have gotten the fans off his roof in Woodstock." [8]

## ROBBIE ROBERTSON

"The Basement Tapes were incredibly different from what we did with Ronnie Hawkins and from what we did with Bob Dylan. When The Band became this character, this kind of sound and music, it had nothing to do with what we had done with either of those two. This was not done on purpose. It is just what came out." [9]

## BOB DYLAN'S OFFICE

"Sid, my friend – Bob just doesn't want to talk about it. Sorry to disappoint." [10]

An entry here with just a surname and a short title is an author's name and book title and refers to books listed in full in the detailed 'Books, Sleevenotes Etc' listing at the end of this book.

**Introduction**
[1] Speaking about 'Stack A Lee,' *World Gone Wrong* booklet
[2] Heylin *Recording Sessions*

**Chapter 1 (pp 16-25)**
**Beginning Of The Beginning**

[1] Author's interview January 14, 2007
[2] Author's interview March 23, 2007

**Chapter 2 (pp 28-41)**
**Backbeat**

[1] *Melody Maker* July 20, 1978
[2] Author's interview August 29, 2006
[3] Author's interview December 13, 2006

**Chapter 3 (pp 44-57)**
**Rolling Down The Road**

[1] Author's interview January 28, 2007
[2] Author's interview January 14, 2007
[3] Author's interview September 29, 2006
[4] *The Telegraph* mid 1990s
[5] Author's corresponence 2006
[6] Sounes *Down The Highway*
[7] Author's interview January 14, 2007
[8] *ISIS* March 2001
[9] Williams *Performing Artist: Early Years*
[10] Shelton *No Direction Home*
[11] *Esquire* July 1987
[12] Helm *This Wheel's On Fire*
[13] Author's interview August 29, 2006
[14] Heylin *Behind The Shades Take Two*
[15] *Time* August 12, 1966
[16] Hoskyns *Across The Great Divide*
[17] *New Musical Express* November 4, 1966
[18] Fong-Torres *Knockin' On Dylan's Door*

**Chapter 4 (pp 58-77)**
**You Are What You Eat The Document**

[1] Hoskyns *Across The Great Divide*
[2] Author's interview August 29, 2006
[3] Author's interview December 10, 2006
[4] Author's interview August 29, 2006
[5] Author's interview December 10, 2006
[6] Author's interview March 23, 2007
[7] Author's interview August 29, 2006
[8] Author's interview October 17, 2006
[9] *Rolling Stone* December 10, 1981
[10] *Rolling Stone* December 4, 1973
[11] *Scram!* February 2003
[12] *You Are What You Eat* booklet notes
[13] *You Are What You Eat* booklet notes
[14] Dylan *Chronicles*
[15] Dylan *Chronicles*
[16] Author's interview March 28, 2007

[17] *Dallas Morning News*, November 18, 1978

**Chapter 5 (pp780-101)**
**The Summer Of Family Love**

[1] Author's interview August 29, 2006
[2] Hoskyns *Across The Great Divide*
[3] Hoskyns *Across The Great Divide*
[4] Interview with Barney Hoskyns 1989
[5] Author's interview August 29, 2006
[6] Author's interview August 29, 2006
[7] Helm *This Wheel's On Fire*
[8] Author's interview November 19, 2006
[9] Author's interview January 11, 2007
[10] Author's interview October 5, 2005
[11] Hawkins *To Kingdom Come* Booklet
[12] Author's interview November 19, 2006
[13] Author's interview November 19, 2006
[14] Author's interview January 11, 2007
[15] Helm *This Wheel's On Fire*
[16] BBC TV *Classic Albums: The Band* 1997
[17] Author's interview November 19, 2006
[18] Author's interview November 19, 2006
[19] Author's interview November 19, 2006
[20] Author's interview November 13, 2006
[21] Author's interview January 11, 2007
[22] Marcus *Invisible Republic*

**Chapter 6 (pp 104-117)**
**Clouds So Swift**

[1] Helm This Wheel's On Fire
[2] *Cheetah* May 1967
[3] Hoskyns *Across The Great Divide*
[4] *Disc*, May 29th, 1971
[5] *Mojo* June 2007
[6] Heylin *Behind The Shades Take Two*
[7] Bowman *Band Musical History* booklet
[8] Helm *This Wheel's On Fire*
[9] Helm *This Wheel's On Fire*
[10] Hoskyns *Across The Great Divide*
[11] Author's interview August 29, 2006
[12] Author's interview August 29, 2006
[13] *Rolling Stone* November 29, 1969

**Chapter 7 (pp 120-135)**
**Now You Must Provide Some Answers**

[1] *Rolling Stone* November 29, 1969

**Chapter 8 (pp 138-147)**
**Lost Time Is Not Found Again**

[1] Author's interview February 16, 2007
[2] Author's interview March 23, 2007
[3] Author's interview November 9, 2006
[4] Interview with Barney Hoskyns 1989
[5] Author's interview February 16, 2007
[6] Author's interview November 9, 2006
[7] Author's interview February 16, 2007
[8] Author's interview February 16, 2007
[9] Author's interview August 29, 2006
[10] Author's interview November 9, 2006

## Chapter 9 (pp 150-155)
## Building Big Ships And Boats

[1] Sounes *Down The Highway*
[2] Sounes *Down The Highway*
[3] Author's interview August 29, 2006
[4] Author's interview August 29, 2006
[5] Author's interview Ocotober 25, 2005
[6] *To Kingdom Come* booklet
[7] Author's interview October 25, 2005
[8] *Mojo* June 2007

## Chapter 10 (pp 158-221)
## Tiny Montgomery Says Hello

[1] Hoskyns *Across The Great Divide*
[2] Interview with Barney Hoskyns 1989
[3] *Cleveland Plain Dealer* September 1967
[4] *Atlanta Journal* September 1967
[5] Williams *Performing Artist: Early Years*
[6] Author's interview March 2, 2007
[7] Author's interview October 17, 2006
[8] Author's interview November 9, 2006
[9] Escott *Live At Vanderbilt* booklet
[10] *Mojo* December 2003
[11] Interview with Barney Hoskyns 1989
[12] Hoskyns *Across The Great Divide*
[13] Helm *This Wheel's On Fire*
[14] Author's interview October 17, 2006
[15] Author's interview August 29, 2006
[16] Bowman, *Band Musical History* booklet
[17] Author's interview August 29, 2006
[18] Bowman, *Band Musical History* booklet
[19] *Biograph* booklet
[20] Author's interview August 29, 2006
[21] *Band To Rock & Roll Hall Of Fame* TV special
[22] Helm *This Wheel's On Fire*

## Chapter 11 (pp 224-233)
## Another Best Friend, Somehow

[1] Hoskyns *Across The Great Divide*
[2] Author's interview October 17, 2006
[3] Author's interview October 17, 2006
[4] *Rolling Stone* November 29, 1969
[5] *Melody Maker* July 13, 1968
[6] *Band To Rock & Roll Hall Of Fame* TV special

## Chapter 12 (pp 236-241)
## Giving Back All Of What You Owe

[1] Helm *This Wheel's On Fire*
[2] Author's interview August 29, 2006

## Chapter 13 (pp 244-265)
## Go Down, Miss Moses

[1] *Band To Rock & Roll Hall Of Fame* TV special
[2] Interview with Barney Hoskyns 1989
[3] Author's interview October 17, 2006
[4] Author's interview October 25, 2006
[5] Interview with Barney Hoskyns 1989
[6] Hoskyns *Across The Great Divide*

[7] Author's interview March 2, 2007
[8] Dylan *Songs Of Jimmie Rodgers* booklet
[9] Author's interview August 29, 2006

## Chapter 14 (pp 268-285)
## That Million Dollar Bash

[1] Author's interview March 23, 2007
[2] Rogan *Byrds: Timeless Flight*
[3] Author's interview September 14, 2006
[4] Author's interview September 16, 2006
[5] Author's interview October 31, 2006
[6] Author's interview October 26, 2006
[7] *Dylan Speaks* DVD
[8] Author's interview October 31, 2006
[9] Author's interview October 26, 2006
[10] Author's interview October 31, 2006
[11] Author's interview July 11, 2006
[12] Author's interview August 29, 2006
[13] Author's interview November 9, 2006
[14] Author's interview July 11, 2006

## Chapter 15 (pp 288-305)
## Deep In Number And Heavy In Toil

[1] *Mojo* December 2003
[2] Bowman, *Band Musical History* booklet
[3] *Mojo* December 2003
[4] Author's interview November 9, 2006
[5] Author's interview August 29, 2006
[6] Bowman *Cahoots* reissue booklet
[7] Author's interview November 9, 2006
[8] Marcus *Basement Tapes* LP notes
[9] Author's interview November 9, 2006
[10] *New York Times* July 4, 1975
[11] Author's interview November 9, 2006
[12] Author's interview February 16, 2007
[13] Author's interview August 29, 2006
[14] Author's interview November 9, 2006

## Chapter 16 (pp 308-315)
## And Life Is Brief

[1] Author's interview November 29, 2006
[2] Author's interview February 27, 2007
[3] Author's interview February 21, 2007
[4] Author's interview March 23, 2007
[5] Author's interview January 11, 2007
[6] Author's interview December 13, 2006
[7] Author's interview October 17, 2006
[8] Author's interview July 11, 2006
[9] Band *Kingdom Come* booklet
[10] Jeff Rosen email to author,
     February 13, 2007

**Million Dollar Bash**
**The Covers**

Here is a selected discography of cover versions of Basement Tapes songs composed or co-composed by Dylan. Under each song title, the covers are listed alphabetically by artist. Following the artist, we give the title (a title *in italics* if the cover is included on the album of that name, with the abbreviation v/a indicating a various-artists collection; or a title 'in quotes' if the cover is on a single), the year of release, and a label.

### CLOTHES LINE SAGA (ANSWER TO ODE)

Suzzy Roche, Maggie Roche
*A Nod To Bob: An Artists' Tribute to Bob Dylan On His 60th Birthday*
2001
Red House

### DON'T YA TELL HENRY

Coulson Dean McGuiness Flint
*Lo And Behold*
1972
DJM

Michel Montecrossa
*Sings Bob Dylan & Himself: Hurricane*
2004
Mira Sound Germany

### CRASH ON THE LEVEE (DOWN IN THE FLOOD)

Ritchie Blackmore
*Take It: Sessions '63–'68*
1998
Cleopatra

Blood Sweat & Tears
*New Blood*
1972
Columbia

Boz
*25 Very Rare Masters From The Sixties*
1997
Line

Rod Clements
*One Track Mind*
2001
Resurgent

Sandy Denny
*The North Star Grassman And The Ravens*
1971
Island

Fairport Convention
*Live Convention*
1974
Island

Howard Fishman
*Basement Tapes*
2007
Monkey Farm

Flatt & Scruggs
*Changin' Times Featuring Foggy Mountain Breakdown*
1967
Columbia

Jimmy LaFave
*Trail*
1999
Bohemia Beat

Michel Montecrossa
*Michel Montecrossa's Michel & Bob Dylan Fest*
2003
Mira Sound

Christine Ohlman
*Hard Way*
1995
Deluge

Pierce Pettis
*State Of Grace*
2001
Compass

Chris Smither
*Don't It Drag On*
1972
Poppy

Roger Tillison
*Roger Tillison's Album*
1971
Atco

### GET YOUR ROCKS OFF

Aviator
*Turbulence*
1980
Harvest

Coulson Dean McGuiness Flint
*Lo And Behold*
1972
DJM

Manfred Mann's Earth Band
*Messin'*
1973
Vertigo

Pat Thomas
*Fresh*
1995
Strange Ways

### GOIN' TO ACAPULCO

Bonnie 'Prince' Billy
'Lay & Love'
2007
Drag City

The Crust Brothers
*Marquee Mark*
1998
Telemomo

### I'M NOT THERE (1956)

Howard Fishman
*Basement Tapes*
2007
Monkey Farm

### I SHALL BE RELEASED

Acquaraggia
*Acquaraggia Sing Dylan*
2004
self-released

After Glo
'I Shall Be Released'
1971
Tree

Alabama 3
*I Shall Be Released EP*
1993
Strictly 4 Groovers

The Alberts
*Stones, Cottages & Curious People*
1999
Newport

Anne Attenborrow
*'I Shall Be Released'*
1971
Polydor

Hughes Aufray
*Aufray Trans Dylan* (as 'Nous Serons Libres')
1995
Arcade

Joan Baez
*Any Day Now*
1969
Vanguard

Bakra Bata
*Blessings In Disguise*
1994
Blakra Bata

The Band
*Music From Big Pink*
1968
Capitol

John Bartus
*Love From The Florida Keys*
2004
Radio Active Productions

Mike Batt Orchestra
*Portrait Of Bob Dylan*
1971
Silverline

The Beverly Sisters
*Universal Soldiers*
1999
Dressed To Kill

Black Stalin
*Rebellion*
1993
Ice

Black Velvet
*Love City*
1969
Okeh

Ritchie Blackmore
*Rock Profile, Vol. 1*
1989
Connoisseur

The Blackjacks
*'I Shall Be Released'*
1969
Columbia

Helena Blehárová
*'I Shall Be Released'*
(as 'Sedmy Pád')
1970
label unknown

Bluebird
*'I Shall Be Released'*
1968
Jerden

Blues & Soda
*Happy Birthday Mr. Dylan*
1991
Blues & Soda

Blues Busters
*Top Of The Pops*
1981
Vista Sounds

James Blundell
*I Shall Be Released – The Best Of James Blundell*
2001
EMI

Bollox & Johnny Busby
*Bob Dylan Revisited*
1992
APiTO

The Box Tops
*Dimensions*
1969
Mala

Boz
*'I Shall Be Released'*
1968
Columbia

Brothers & Sisters Of L.A.
*Dylan's Gospel*
1969
CBS

The Brothers Soul
*'I Shall Be Released'*
1969
Okeh

Jeff Buckley
*Live At Sin-E (Legacy Edition)*
2003
Columbia

Bullfrog Jones
*Ancient Footprints*
2000
self-released

The California Poppy Pickers
*Honky Tonk Women / Blue Eyed Soul*
1969
Alshire

Hamilton Camp
*Welcome To Hamilton Camp*
1969
Warner Bros.

Chasers
*Out Of Control*
1986
Mr. Kite

Chatham County Line
*Chatham County Line*
2003
Bonfire

Clammbon
*Lover Album*
2006
Warner Bros. Japan

Joe Cocker
*With A Little Help From My Friends*
1969
A&M

Bill Collins
*Tribute To Bob Dylan*
1978
Audiomasters

The Coven
'I Shall Be Released'
1968
SGC

Dejan Cukic
*Divlji Med: Pesme Boba Dilana*
(as 'Bicu Slobodan')
2000
Atelje

Elvis DaCosta
*Need Your Love So Bad*
1998
Setanta

Damon & Naomi
*Terrastock: Ptolemaic
Providence Perambulation*
1997
Ptolemaic Terrascope

DanskBob
*Dylansk: 12 Bob Dylan Sange Pa
Dansk (as 'Jeg Vil Bli' Forløst')*
2005
Mixed Media Records

Dark Eyes Electric Band
*Concierto En El Nombre De Bob*
1998
self-released

Francesco de Gregori
*Mix* (as 'Cime Il Giorno')
2003
Sony

Freek de Jonge with Frank
Grasso Big Band
*Een Gebaar* (as 'Eens Zal Het
Licht Hier Schijnen') (v/a)
1983
Ariola

Johnny Dollar
*Quit While You're Ahead*
2002
Ripete

Danny Donnelly
*Passion Tree*
1996
Be Nice Records

Die DoubleDylans
*Ich Und Ein Anderer* (as
'Exmatrikuliert')
2004
Fame

Dylanesque
*Basement Fakes*
2001
self-released

Eldkvam
*Absolut Marie Dimberg (v/a)*
1997
EMI

Marc Ellington
*Marc Ellington*
1969
Philips

Rabbi Abraham Feinberg
*I Was So Much Older Then*
1970
Vanguard

Julie Felix
*Starry Eyed And Laughing*
2002
Track

Dudu Fisher
*Standing Where You Are*
2006
JMG

Howard Fishman
*The Basement Tapes*
2007
Monkey Farm

Flamingo
'Divoka Ruse' (as 'Balada O
Poutnikovi')
1968
Supraphon

The Flying Burrito Brothers
*Farther Along: The Best Of
The Flying Burrito Brothers*
1988
A&M

Four U
*Breakfast*
1999
label unknown

The Free
*The Funky Tree*
1969
Philips

Friends
*Friends*
1971
Oblivion

John Gage & Bruce Krohmer
*Your Way & Mine*
1999
Johnette Productions

Jerry Garcia Band
*Jerry Garcia Band*
1991
Arista

Jonas Gardell
*Dylan På Svenska* (as 'Jag Ska
Bli Fri') (v/a)
2000
Sankt Paul

Kyle Garrahan
'Shame'
1970
Janus

Golden Gate Quartet
*Nobody Knows*
1987
Ibach

Skip Grabow
*Not Just The Blues*
1998
label unknown

The Grand Poo-Bah
Beaner Band
*It Must Be A Breakdown*
1976
Rising Star

The Hanway Band
*Perform The Hits Of Bob Dylan*
2002
Going For A Song

Sting & The Secret Police
*The Secret Policeman's Other
Ball: The Music*
1981
Rhino

Martin Harley
*Martin Harley*
2006

David Hay
*The Bob Dylan Song Book*
2002
Klone

Bill Haymes
*I Shall Be Released*
1970
Resist

Warren Haynes
*Warren Haynes Presents:*
*Benefit Concert Vol. 2*
2000
Evil Teen

Hedge & Donna
*All The Friendly Colors*
1969
Capitol

The Heptones
'I Shall Be Released'
1969
Studio One

P-O Hilli
*Reborn*
2002
Meirecords

The Hollies
*Hollies Sing Dylan*
1969
Parlophone

Ho'omau
*Paradise*
1998
Ord

Hobsons
*Säg Får Jag Lov* (as 'Jag Ser
Ett Ljus')
1976
label unknown

Hooch Gang
*Chimes Of Freedom – Hooch*
*Gang Plays Bob Dylan*
1996
Posthof Records

Frans Hopen
'I Shall Be Released' (as 'Jeg
Vil Vaere Fri')
1969
RCA

Shane Howard
*Time Will Tell*
1993
BMG

Tim Howe
*Mission*
2000
Orchard

Keith Hudson
*Flesh Of My Skin, Blood*
*Of My Blood*
1974
Atra

Chrissie Hynde
*Bob Dylan 30th Anniversary*
*Concert Celebration* (v/a)
1993
Columbia

Peter Isaacson
*Sings The Song Of Dylan,*
*Donovan, Lightfoot, Hardin,*
*And Others*
1971
Altair

Ishan People
*Roots*
1976
GRT

Martyna Jakubowicz
*Tylko Dylan* ('Znów Bede
Wolny)
2005
Song/BMG Poland

Dinnyés József & Band
Of Memory
*Ezt Nem Fújta El A Szél* (as
'Hogy Szabad Legyek')
1992
Hungarotoon-Gong

Daryl Johnson
*Music For A Better Planet*
1999
self-released

Jack Johnson
*Endless Highway: The Music*
*Of The Band* (v/a)
2007
Sony

Heidi Joy
*I'll Take A Melody*
2003
AIKO

Barb Jungr
*Love Me Tender*
2005
Linn

Nis P. Jørgensen
*Toneservice*
1979
label unknown

Petr Kalandra
*Live & Studio 1964–1995*
1998
Sony Music/Bonton

Moussa Kanouté
*Dance Of The Kora*
1996
Rhino

Steve Kekana
*Makhombo*
1992
Celluloid

Kersten & Göran
*Sympathy* (as 'Jag Ser Ett Ljus')
1969
Sonet

Killing Time
*Mystery Line*
1992
Red Eye

Kevn Kinney
*The Flower & The Knife*
2000
Capricorn

Jimmy D Lane
*Long Gone*
1997
Analogue Originals

Long Ryders
*Metallic BO*
1989
Long Ryders Fan Club

Mafia & Fluxy
*Lover's Revival Hits*
1996
Lagoon

Mahotella Queens
*Women Of The World*
1993
Shanachie

Richard Manuel
*Whispering Pines: Live At*
*The Getaway 1985*
2002
Other People's Music

Marjoe
*Bad But Not Evil*
1972
Chelsea

Marmalade
*There's A Lot Of It About*
1969
CBS

Renée Martel
*Mon Roman d'Amour*
1971
Spectrum

Judy Mayhan
*Moments*
1970
Atlantic

Rod McKuen
*Alone*
1974
Warner Bros.

Bette Midler
*Bette Midler*
1973
Atlantic 7270

The Mighty Diamonds
*Blowin In The Wind: A Reggae
Tribute To Bob Dylan* (v/a)
2002
Madacy

Jacob Miller
*Jacob 'Killer' Miller*
1978
RAS

Barb Mitchell
*Low Down Blues*
2003
Barb Mitchell

Michel Montecrossa
*Jet Pilot*
2000
Orchard
Moonshine
*Bootleg*
1977
EMI

The Morgan Brothers
*Mixing It Up Good*
1974
Appleton

Moths
*Heron's Daughter*
1994
Kissing Spell

Judy Mowatt
*Rock Me*
1993
Pow Wow

Mike Mullins
*Pickin' On Dylan*
1999
CMH

Rick Nelson
*Rick Nelson In Concert
(The Troubadour 1969)*
1970
Decca

Aaron Neville
*Devotion*
2000
Chordant

Pearls Before Swine
*These Things Too*
1969
Reprise

Peter Paul & Mary
*Late Again*
1968
Warner Bros.

Lynne Pike
*'I Think I Just Lost Out'*
1970
Phread

Elvis Presley
*Walk A Mile In My Shoes:
The Essential 70s Masters*
1995
RCA

P.J. Proby
*Believe It Or Not*
1968
Liberty

Project Mercury
*Down To Earth*
2005
self-released

Psalms
*Up Front*
1992
RAS

Punch
*Punch*
1971
A&M

The Random Sample
*The Random Sample*
1969
Anodyne

Rebirth
*Into The Light*
1970
RCR

The Rivals
*'I Shall Be Released'*
1972
CBS

Danny Roberts
*Los Exitos De Bob Dylan*
1978
Nevada

Tom Robinson Band
*Power In The Darkness*
1978
Razor & Tie

Roots Odyssey
*Moving Forward*
1998
Ord

Bob Rowe
*When October Goes …*
2006
September

Todd Rubenstein
*The String Quartet Tribute
To Bob Dylan*
2003
Vitamin

Erich Russek
*What Are You Afraid Of?*
2004
Yama Llama

Telly Savalas
*The Two Sides Of Telly Savalas*
1972
MCA

Freddie Scott
*I Shall Be Released*
1970
Probe/ABC

Earl Scruggs
*Rockin' 'cross The Country*
1973
CBS

Terrance Simien
*There's Room For Us*
1993
Black Top

Nina Simone
*To Love Somebody*
1969
RCA

The Slackers/Pulley
*The Slackers/Pulley*
2003
Do Tell

Small Circle Of Friends
*'I Shall Be Released'*
1971
Bonny

Smokehouse Band
*Smokehouse Band*
1981
self-released

The Staccatos
*He Was A Friend Of Mine*
1969
NEM

Steel Train
*Listen To Bob Dylan: A Tribute
Album* (v/a)
2003
Drive Thru

The Tremeloes
*'I Shall Be Released'*
1968
CBS

'Big Mama' Thornton
*Stronger Than Dirt*
1969
Mercury

The Tongues
*The Tongues*
1969
Zodiac

Happy Traum
*Bright Morning Stars*
1979
Greenhays

Dave Travis
*Tribute To Bob Dylan*
1971
Deacon

Walter Trout & The Free
Radicals
*Live Trout: Recorded At The
Tampa Blues Fest March 2000*
2000
Ruf

2 Of Us
*From Zimmermann To
Genghis Khan*
2001
Ruwin

Dan Tyack
*Unsanctified Gospel Revival*
2004
Tyacktunes

The Uniques
*Showcase Volume 1*
1978
Third World

Sal Valentino
*Positively 12th And K: A Bob
Dylan Tribute*
2003
Dig Music

Rob Van Dyke
*Rob Van Dyke Plays Bob Dylan*
1971
CBS

The Violinaires
*At His Command*
1969
Checker

Paul Weller
*Out Of The Sinking EP*
1996
Go! Discs

David West & CMH Studio
Players
*Pickin' On Dylan – A Tribute*
1999
CMH

Marion Williams
*The New Message*
1971
Atlantic

Delroy Wilson
*I'm In A Dancing Mood*
2002
Proper Pairs

Wes Wingate & Julie McGeorge
*Million Dollar Bash: Missouri
Salutes Bob Dylan*
2006
Home Tone

The Youngbloods
*High On A Ridgetop*
1972
Warner Bros.

## LO AND BEHOLD!

Coulson Dean McGuiness Flint
*Lo And Behold*
1972
DJM

The Crust Brothers
*Marquee Mark*
1998
Telemomo

Marjoe
Bad But Not Evil
1972
Columbia

## MILLION DOLLAR BASH

The Crust Brothers
*Marquee Mark*
1998
Telemomo

Carmaig DeForest
*Death Groove Love Party*
1993
Knitting Factory Work

Fairport Convention
*Unhalfbricking*
1969
Island

Jonathan King
*'Million Dollar Bash'*
1970
Decca

The Music Asylum
*Commit Thyself*
1970
United Artists

Tim Rice & Friends
*That's My Story*
2006
Sunbeam

Stone Country
*The Songs Of Bob Dylan, Vol. 2: May Your Song Always Be Sung*
2001
BMG International

**NOTHING WAS DELIVERED**

The Byrds
*Sweetheart Of The Rodeo*
1968
Columbia

Buddy Emmons
*Steel Guitar*
1975
Flying Fish

Howard Fishman
*Basement Tapes*
2007
Monkey Farm

The Original Marauders
*Now Your Mouth Cries Wolf*
1977
Pied Piper

**ODDS AND ENDS**

Coulson Dean McGuiness Flint
*Lo And Behold*
1972
DJM

The Weather Prophets
*Temperance Hotel*
1989
Creation

**OPEN THE DOOR, HOMER**

Coulson Dean McGuiness Flint
*Lo And Behold*
1972
DJM

Marc Ellington
*A Question Of Roads*
1972
Philips

Howard Fishman
*Basement Tapes*
2007
Monkey Farm

Fairport Convention
*Red And Gold* (as 'Open The Door, Richard')
1989
Rough Trade

The Floor
'You Ain't Goin' Nowhere'
1968
Philips

Robyn Hitchcock
*The Kershaw Sessions*
1994
Strange Fruit

Thunderclap Newman
*Hollywood Dream*
1970
Track Record

Titus Groan
'Open The Door, Homer' EP
1970
Dawn

Trials & Tribulations
*Trials & Tribulations*
1970
Vanguard

John Walker
'I'll Be Your Baby Tonight'
1968
Philips

**PLEASE MRS. HENRY**

Cheap Trick
*Sex, America, Cheap Trick*
1996
Sony

The Crust Brothers
*Marquee Mark*
1998
Telemomo

Manfred Mann's Earth Band
*Manfred Mann's Earth Band*
1972
Philips

Chris Spedding
*Backwoods Progression*
1970
Harvest

Trials & Tribulations
*Trials & Tribulations*
1970
Vanguard

**QUINN THE ESKIMO (THE MIGHTY QUINN)**

Agneta & The String Brass
*Bonnie & Clyde*
1971
Discos RVV

Angela
*Sex Is Moving*
1990
label unknown

Brewer & Shipley
*Archive Alive*
1999
Archive

Brothers & Sisters Of L.A.
*Dylan's Gospel*
1969
CBS

Smokey John Bull
*Smokey John Bull*
1968
Avco Embassy

The Bunnies Of London
*Caught Live At The Playboy Club*
1969
Decca

Solomon Burke
*Proud Mary: The Bell Sessions*
2000
Sundazed

Carmen
*Carmen!*
1969
Epic

Cats & Boots
*Déja Vu*
2005
Edel

The Chicks
*A Long Time Comin'*
1969
Polydor

Claude & Gino
B-side of Lyn Taitt & The Jets
'Mr. Dooby'
1969
Merritone

Dave Coleman Und Das
Orchster Mark Wirtz
'Alaska Quinn'
1967
EMI/Columbia

Daco
'The Mighty Quinn'
1986
Time Records

Diego de Cossio Y Los
Barrocks
*Diego de Cossio Y Los Barrocks*
1968
Orfeon

Peter Drake
*Peter Drake*
1999
First Generation

Ducks Deluxe
*Last Night Of A Pub Rock Band*
1981
Blue Moon

The Family Frog
'Mighty Quinn'
1968
White Whale

Fuzzface
'Mighty Quinn (Quinn The
Eskimo)'
1968
Dorset

Jerry Garcia
*Ladder To The Stars: Garcia
Plays Dylan*
2005
Rhino

Gotthard
*G*
1996
Ariola

Grateful Dead
*Dick's Picks Vol. 17*
2000
Grateful Dead

Joe Harnell
'Mighty Quinn'
1968
Columbia

Dennis Heller
*Dylan In My Soul*
2003
self-released

Merit Hemmingson
*Merit Hemmingson Plays*
1969
RCA Camden

Dan Hill
*Sounds Electronic 5*
1968
RPM

The Hollies
*Hollies Sing Dylan*
1969
Parlophone

Hooch Gang
*Chimes Of Freedom – Hooch
Gang Plays Bob Dylan*
1996
Posthof Records

I Dik Dik
'L'esquimese'
1968
Dischi Ricordi SRL

Ian & Sylvia
*Nashville*
1968
Vanguard

Moe Koffman
*Turned On*
1968
Jubilee

Lalo
*Lalo* (as 'Quin, El Esquimal')
1968
RCA

James Last
*Non Stop Dancing 68*
1968
Polydor

Ramsey Lewis
*Maiden Voyage*
1968
Chess

Little Angels
'Mighty Quinn'
1993
Polydor

Julie London
*Yummy, Yummy, Yummy*
1969
Liberty

Los Belmonts
*15 Exitos: Cuando Calienta El
Sol* (as 'El Esquimal')
1969
Orfeon

Los Chijuas
*Los Chijuas* (as 'El Esquimal')
1968
Musart

Los Duros
*Caras Nuevas #1* (as 'El
Esquimal')
1969
Istmo

Lulu
*It's Lulu*
1970
Epic

Manfred Mann
*Mighty Garvey!*
1968
Fontana

Meisberg & Waters
*Love's An Easy Song*
1977
Casablanca

Mellow Fruitfulness
*Music For Meditation*
1968
Columbia

Michael Montecrossa
*Born In Time*
2000
Orchard

Hugo Montenegro
*Dawn Of Dylan*
1970
GWP

New Salem Witch Hunters
'Mighty Quinn'
1986
St. Valentine

1910 Fruitgum Company
*1, 2, 3 Red Light*
1968
Buddah

No Comments
*Untitled EP* (v/a)
1968
Juke Box

Ingemar Olsson
*I Alla Fall* (as 'Kom Om Du
Vill')
1973
Polydor

Os Carbonos
*As 12 Mais Da Juventude Vol 3*
1969
AMC

Michel Pagliaro
*Premiere Éopque* (as 'JoJo Le
Clown')
1970
Spectrum

T. Parker
*Power Dance '96*
1996
Dance Street

Peter Pan Pop Singers &
Orchestra
*The Unicorn*
1968
Peter Pan

Phish
*Hampton Comes Alive*
1999
Elektra

Gary Puckett & The Union
Gap
*Young Girl*
1968
Columbia

Sheryl Lee Ralph
*The Mighty Quinn (Original
Soundtrack)*
1989
A&M

The Renegades
*'L'Amore È Blu'*
1968
Columbia

Danny Roberts
*Los Exitos De Bob Dylan*
1978
Nevada

Rob Van Dyke
*Rob Van Dyke Plays Bob Dylan*
1970
CBS

The Ventures
*Flights Of Fancy*
1968
Liberty

Ken Woodman
*The Kenny Woodman Sound*
1969
Vibration

**SANTA FE**

Howard Fishman
*The Basement Tapes*
2007
Monkey Farm

**SIGN ON THE CROSS**

Coulson Dean McGuiness Flint
*Lo And Behold*
1972
DJM

**TINY MONTGOMERY**

Coulson Dean McGuiness Flint
*Lo And Behold*
1972
DJM

Michel Montecrossa
*Sings Bob Dylan & Himself:
Hurricane*
2004
Mira Sound Germany

**THIS WHEEL'S ON FIRE**

The Band
*Music From Big Pink*
1968
Capitol

Mike Batt Orchestra
*Portrait Of Bob Dylan*
1971
DJM Silverline

The Byrds
*Dr Byrds & Mr Hyde*
1969
Columbia

Hamilton Camp
*'This Wheel's On Fire'*
1968
Warner Bros.

The Cuckoos
*Outlaw Blues - A Tribute
To Bob Dylan* (v/a)
1992
Imaginary

Rick Danko
*Times Like These*
2000
Breeze Hill Records

Julie Driscoll with Brian Auger
and the Trinity
*'This Wheel's On Fire'*
1968
Marmalade

Julie Felix
*This World Goes Round &
Round*
1968
Fontana 5473

Howard Fishman
*The Basement Tapes*
2007
Monkey Farm

Flake
*'This Wheel's On Fire'*
1970
Festival

The Fontana Concert Orchestra
*Portrait Of Bob Dylan*
1968
Fontana LPS 16257

The Golden Earring
*Lovesweat*
1995
Columbia 481122-2

Guster
*Endless Highway: The Music
Of The Band* (v/a)
2007
Sony

The Hi-Revving Tongues
*The Tongues*
1970
Zodiac

The Hollies
*Hollies Sing Dylan*
1969
Parlophone

Hot Off The Press
*Hot Off The Press*
1978
American Heritage Music

Ian & Sylvia
*Nashville*
1968
Vanguard

Paul Jones
*Come Into My Music Box*
1969
Columbia

London Sound & Art Orchestra
*The Music Of Bob Dylan*
1993
Mega-Sound

Nature
*Earthmover*
1974
Sonet

Brenda Patterson
*Keep On Keepin' On*
1970
Epic

Second Floor
*Plays Dylan*
2001
Buma/Stemra

Siouxsie & The Banshees
'This Wheel's On Fire'
1987
Polydor

Stone Country
'This Wheel's On Fire'
1968
RCA

Suns Of Shiva ft. Angie Gold
'This Wheel's On Fire'
1995
Klone

Ian Thomas
*Long Long Way*
1974
Janus

Leslie West
*Mountain*
1969
Windfall

**TEARS OF RAGE**

Joan Baez
*Any Day Now*
1968
Vanguard

The Band
*Music From Big Pink*
1968
Columbia

Gene Clark
*White Light*
1971
A&M

Country Fever
'Tears Of Rage'
1969
Bell

Barbara Dickson
*Don't Think Twice It's All Right*
1992
Columbia

Dish
*Boneyard Beach*
1995
Interscope

Marc Ellington
*Marc Ellington*
1969
Philips

Howard Fishman
*The Basement Tapes*
2007
Monkey Farm

Jerry Garcia Band
*How Sweet It Is*
1997
Arista

Ian & Sylvia
*Full Circle*
1968
Vanguard

Albert Lee
*Black Claw & Country Fever*
1999
Line

Richard Manuel
*Whispering Pines: Live At The Getaway 1985*
2002
Other People's Music

Bob Margolin
*In North Carolina*
2006
Steady Rollin'

**TOO MUCH OF NOTHING**

Felix Caberera
*Pressure Cooker*
2001
Fountainbleau

Country Fever
'Too Much Of Nothing'
1969
Bell

Five Day Rain
*Five Day Rain*
1969
self-released

Fotheringay
*Fotheringay*
1970
Island

Merit Hemmingson
*Merit Hemmingson Plays*
1969
RCA Camden

Albert Lee
*Black Claw & Country Fever*
1999
Line

The New Seekers
*The New Seekers*
1970
Elektra

Peter Paul & Mary
*Late Again*
1968
Warner Bros.

The Sounds Of Our Times
*Play Love Is Blue*
1967
Capitol

Spooky Tooth
*It's All About*
1968
Edsel

We Folk
*Get Together*
1969
Gordon Associates

**YEA! HEAVY AND A
BOTTLE OF BREAD**

Bassholes
'Interzone'
1996
Seldom Scene

Howard Fishman
*The Basement Tapes*
2007
Monkey Farm

Marc Riley & The Creepers
*Peel Sessions EP*
1987
In Tape
Taylor Bacon

*Million Dollar Bash: Missouri
Salutes Bob Dylan*
2006
Home Tone

**YOU AIN'T GOIN'
NOWHERE**

Joan Baez
*Any Day Now*
1968
Vanguard

The Bluegrass Alliance
*Newgrass*
1970
American Heritage Music
Corporation

The Byrds
*Sweetheart Of The Rodeo*
1968
Columbia

The Calico String Band
*Unearthed*
1976
Red Rag

Phil Carmen
*Bob Dylan's Dream*
1996
Hypertension

David Christian
*Windows & Doors*
1973
Nutmeg

The Coal Porters
*The Chris Hillman Tribute
Concerts*
2001
Prima

Shawn Colvin
*Bob Dylan: The 30th
Anniversary Concert
Celebration* (v/a)
1993
Columbia

Counting Crows
*Hard Candy* (Import/Extra
Tracks Edition)
2003
Universal

Cracker
*Garage D'Or*
2000
Virgin

Deep Timbre
*Deep Timb're*
1972
Westwood

Rick Dill
*Unfinished Business*
2000
CliMax

Dumptruck
*Lemmings Travel To The Sea*
2001
Devil In The Woods

Marc Ellington
*Restoration*
1973
Philips

Fairport Convention
*Festival*
2003
Talking Elephant

Feel Like You
*The Times They Are A-Changin'
… Volume 1*
1990
Sister Ruby

Feelsaitig
*Bruno: Mega Live Now!*
2000
Bruno

The Floor
'You Ain't Goin' Nowhere'
1968
Philips

Flying Burrito Brothers
*Live From Amsterdam 1985*
1987
Relix

Larry Groce
*Junkfood Junkie*
1976
Warner Bros

Hamilton County
Bluegrass Band
*Kersbrook Cottage*
1972
Columbia

Bill & Bonnie Hearne
*Watching Life Through
A Windshield*
2000
Back Porch

Dennis Heller
*Dylan In My Soul*
2003
self-released

Marsha Hunt
*Woman Child*
1971
Track

Karlsson
'En Morgon Gick –
En Morgon Korn'
1970
Music Network

David Lannan
*Street Singer*
1970
San Francisco

Lesley Miller
'You Ain't Goin' Nowhere'
1969
MGM

Michel Montecrossa
*Michel Montecrossa's Michel &
Bob Dylan Fest 2003*
2003
Mira Sound

Mountain Line
*10,000 Horsepower*
1975
Transatlantic

Maria Muldaur
*Heart Of Mine: Love Songs Of Bob
Dylan*
2006
Telarc

The Nitty Gritty Dirt Band
*Will The Circle Be Unbroken
Vol. 2*
1989
Universal

Odessa
'You Ain't Goin' Nowhere'
1970
Chart

Gene Parsons
*In Concert: I Hope They Let Us In*
2001
StringBender

Perth County Conspiracy
*Alive*
1971
Columbia

The Rave-Ups
*Town And Country*
1985
Demon

Danny Roberts
*Los Exitos De Bob Dylan*
1978
Nevada

Sands Of Time
*Sands Of Time*
1970
self-released

Earl Scruggs
*Live At Kansas State*
1972
Columbia

Philip Shackleton
*Sylkie*
1981
Musik Kiste

Silkworm
*New School / Old School*
1997
Matador

Solid Air
*Tailgates & Substitutes*
1999
Globe

The Spotnicks
*Something Like Country*
1971
Polydor

The Tadpoles
*Whirlaway*
1999
Camera Obscura

Texas Instruments
*Sun Tunnels*
1988
Dr. Dream

Dave Travis
*Tribute To Bob Dylan*
1971
Deacon

2 Of Us
*From Zimmermann To
Genghis Khan*
2001
Ruwin

Unit 4 Plus 2
'You Ain't Goin' Nowhere'
1968
Fontana

Village Green
*Our Generation*
1978
Triskel

Doc Watson & Frosty Morn
*Round The Table Again*
2002
Sugar Hill

Wheatones
*Backporch Song*
1972
Fleetwood

## AUTHOR'S THANKS

Author Sid Griffin would like to thank those without whom he would still be musician Sid Griffin. The first tip of the hat has to go to all my interview subjects, for without their stories and insight, without each of them sharing their time with me, this book would not exist. I hope they all feel I did them and their myriad contributions justice. Thanks to: Joel Bernstein; Joe Boyd; Billy Bragg; Steve Earle; Ramblin' Jack Elliott; Barry Feinstein; Rob Fraboni; John Hammond Jr.; Ronnie Hawkins; Chris Hillman; Billy James; Al Kooper; Nick Lowe; Manfred Mann; Roger McGuinn; Tom McGuinness; Robbie Robertson; John Samways; John Simon; and Peter Yarrow.

A warm hello and a very sincere thank you goes out to those who helped me in my research: the great Clinton Heylin; Bill Wasserzieher; my old Long Ryder bandmate Tom Stevens; Derek Barker at ISIS; Cheryl Pawelski; Stratton Owen Hammon; my friends at *Mojo* magazine here in London such as John Harris and Phil Alexander; Barney Hoskyns; Bill Inglot; Stephen Paul of Stephen Paul Audio; and everyone at Jawbone. I know now I have completely disproved the old teacher's saying "there are no dumb questions" as I have certainly asked my share of them.

A special thanks to: Greg Sowders of Warner-Chappell; Jared Levine; Dan Perloff at Concord Music Group; and Art Fein for extending needed help all the way from my native country's left coast. From its opposite side I enjoyed a healthy and humorous email conversation with a tolerant Jeff Rosen and I owe him for that. Thanks to Allie Fox of Foxy Music and Andy Richardson of the Adastra agency for bearing with musician Sid Griffin during this more-than-two-year project.

The following musicians must be acknowledged, especially Peter Case who told me: "Man, you oughta be writing books – it is only a matter of time." He was right – and even before his prediction I owed Pete greatly for his inspiring music. I was and remain a Peter Case fan. Bob Neuwirth and Tom Paley were not only there back in the early days of His Bobness but they have always been cordial with me, and now is as good a time as any to let these two gentlemen know how much I enjoy their own art. To my beloved Coal Porters and all who have ridden tall in the saddle alongside us, particularly Neil Bob Herd, Paul Sandy, Miss Gemma White, Miss Hana Loftus, and Dr. Rhiannon Owen, I say may God bless and keep you always.

The late John Bauldie at Q magazine was always kind to me during my tenure there and I turned to his writing many times during the course of this work. He is missed.

Finally I must acknowledge my family. My late father was never happy with anything less than a first rate, full-speed-ahead effort. I so hope I haven't let him down here. My mother may not make it to the day where she can read this book upon its publication but I see her warm, conversational style of writing in every page. My sister Eleanor knows very well why I thank her; she's a hard act to follow but little brother does try.

My daughter Esther Mae Griffin is seven and a half years old. She told me she wanted to be the first person anywhere to buy this book. When I told her daddy would give her one for free she said: "Nah, you give that one to your friend Bob Dylan, I'll bet he'd like to read it too." I hope so, Esther Mae, I hope so.

## PUBLISHER'S THANKS

Jawbone would like to thank Stuart Blacklock, Doug Hinman, Tom Jerome, John Morrish, Ian Purser, Dave Simons, Richie Unterberger and Adam Yeldham.

## BOOKS, SLEEVENOTES, ETC

**The Band** *To Kingdom Come* promo CD booklet (Capitol 1989)
**Derek Barker** (ed) *Isis: A Bob Dylan Anthology* (Helter Skelter 2004)
**Derek Barker** (ed) *Isis: A Bob Dylan Anthology Volume Two, Twenty Years Of Isis* (Chrome Dreams 2005)
**Olof Bjorner** *Olof's Files: A Bob Dylan Performance Guide, Volume One, 1958–1969* (Hardinge Simpole 2002)
**Mark Blake** *Dylan: Visions, Portraits, & Back Pages* (DK 2005)
**Rob Bowman** *The Band: A Musical History CD* booklet (Capitol 2005)
**Rob Bowman** *Cahoots* CD reissue booklet (Capitol 2000)
**Rob Bowman** *Music From Big Pink* CD reissue booklet (Capitol 2000)
**Jonathan Cott** (ed) *Dylan On Dylan: The Essential Interviews* (Hodder & Stoughton 2006)
**Glen Dundas** *Tangled: A Recording History Of Bob Dylan* (SMA Services 2004)
**Bob Dylan** *Biograph* CD booklet (Columbia 1985)

● ● ● ● ● ● ● ● ● ● ● ● ● ● ● ● ● ● ● ● ● ● ● ● ● ● ● ● ● ● ● ● ●

**Bob Dylan** *Chronicles Volume One* (Simon & Schuster 2004)
**Bob Dylan** *Dont Look Back/'65 Tour Deluxe Edition* DVD (Docurama 2006)
**Bob Dylan** *No Direction Home* DVD (Paramount 2005)
**Bob Dylan** *A Tribute: The Songs Of Jimmie Rodgers* CD booklet (Egyptian 1997)
**Bob Dylan** *World Gone Wrong* CD booklet (Sony, 1993)
***Dylan Speaks:*** *The Legendary 1965 Press conference In San Francisco* DVD (Eagle Rock 2006)
**Bob Dylan** *Writings & Drawings* (Panther 1974)
**Colin Escott** *Lester Flatt: Live At Vanderbilt* CD booklet (Bear Family 2002)
**Ben Fong-Torres** *Knockin' On Dylan's Door* (Straight Arrow 1974)
**John Gibbens** *The Nightingale's Code: A Poetic Study Of Bob Dylan* (Touched Press 2001)
**Michael J. Gilmour** *Tangled Up In The Bible: Bob Dylan & Scripture* (Continuum 2004)
**Michael Gray** *The Bob Dylan Encyclopedia* (Continuum 2006)
**Levon Helm with Stephen Davis** *This Wheel's On Fire: Levon Helm And The Story Of The Band* (Morrow 1993)
**Clinton Heylin** *Bob Dylan: The Recording Sessions 1960–1994* (St Martin's 1995)
**Clinton Heylin** *Bootleg: The Secret History Of The Other Recording Industry* (St. Martin's 1995)
**Clinton Heylin** *Dylan: Behind The Shades: The Biography – Take Two* (Penguin 2001)
**Clinton Heylin** *A Life In Stolen Moments, Bob Dylan, Day By Day: 1941–1995* (Schirmer 1996)
**Christopher Hjort** *Eric Clapton & The British Blues Boom: The Day-By-Day Story 1965–1970* (Jawbone 2007)
**Barney Hoskyns** *Across The Great Divide: The Band And America* (Viking 1993)
**Rick Danko**, interview with Barney Hoskyns, 1989
**Michael Krogsgaard** *Positively Bob Dylan: A Thirty Year Discography, Concert & Recording Session Guide 1960–1991* (Popular Culture Ink 1991)
**C.P. Lee** *Like The Night: Bob Dylan And The Road To The Manchester Free Trade Hall* (Helter Skelter 1998)
**Greil Marcus** *Bob Dylan & The Band: The Basement Tapes* 2-LP sleevenotes (Columbia 1975)
**Greil Marcus** *Invisible Republic: Bob Dylan's Basement Tapes* (Picador 1997)
**Mike Marqusee** *Wicked Messenger: Bob Dylan And The 1960s* (Seven Stories 2005)
**Andrew Muir** *Troubadour: Early & Late Songs Of Bob Dylan* (Woodstock 2003)
**John Niven** *Music From Big Pink, A Novella* (Continuum 2005)
**Christopher Ricks** *Dylan's Visions Of Sin* (Penguin Books 2003)
***Robbie Robertson:*** *From The Band To The Rock & Roll Hall Of Fame* (TV special, Cherry Lane 1994)
**Johnny Rogan** *The Byrds: Timeless Flight Revisited: The Sequel* (Rogan House 1998)
**Robert Santelli** (text) *The Bob Dylan Scrapbook, 1956-1966* (Simon & Schuster 2005)
**Robert Shelton** *No Direction Home: The Life And Music Of Bob Dylan* (Da Capo 2003)
**Howard Sounes** *Down The Highway: The Life Of Bob Dylan* (Doubleday 2001)
**Oliver Trager** *Keys To The Rain: The Definitive Bob Dylan Encyclopedia* (Billboard 2004)
**Paul Williams** *Bob Dylan, Performing Artist: The Early Years 1960–1973* (Underwood-Miller 1990)
***You Are What You Eat*** soundtrack CD booklet (Sony Japan 1997)

**PICTURE CREDITS**
The pictures in this book came from the following sources, and we are grateful for their help. Location or page number is followed by the name of the source. **Jacket** Dylan in Copenhagen 1966: Jan Persson/Redfern's. **4–5** Dylan in Paris 1966 and The Hawks early shots: Michael Ochs Archives/Getty Images. **8–9** Band on Ed Sullivan 1969, Dylan Isle Of Wight 1969, Dylan Columbia Studio Nashville 1969: Michael Ochs Archives/Getty Images. **13** Ampex tape recorder, Stuart Blacklock at vintagerecorders.co.uk.

**FEEDBACK**
Comments? Complaints? Updates? Email us – thebasement@jawbonepress.com – or write – Million Dollar Bash, Jawbone Press, 2A Union Court, 20-22 Union Road, London SW4 6JP, England.

"Music is what we do." Robbie Robertson.